Peace Philosophy in Action

Peace Philosophy in Action

Edited by
Candice C. Carter
and
Ravindra Kumar

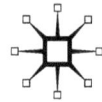

PEACE PHILOSOPHY IN ACTION
Copyright © Candice C. Carter and Ravindra Kumar, 2010.

All rights reserved.

First published in 2010 by
PALGRAVE MACMILLAN®
in the United States—a division of St. Martin's Press LLC,
175 Fifth Avenue, New York, NY 10010.

Where this book is distributed in the UK, Europe and the rest of the world, this is by Palgrave Macmillan, a division of Macmillan Publishers Limited, registered in England, company number 785998, of Houndmills, Basingstoke, Hampshire RG21 6XS.

Palgrave Macmillan is the global academic imprint of the above companies and has companies and representatives throughout the world.

Palgrave® and Macmillan® are registered trademarks in the United States, the United Kingdom, Europe and other countries.

ISBN: 978–0–230–62240–1

Library of Congress Cataloging-in-Publication Data
    Peace philosophy in action / edited by Candice C. Carter and Ravindra Kumar.
      p. cm.
    Includes bibliographical references and index.
    ISBN 978–0–230–62240–1 (alk. paper)
    1. Peace-building—History. 2. Peace-building—Philosophy.
  I. Carter, Candice C., 1953– II. Kumar, Ravindra, 1959–

JZ5538.P3738 2010
303.6′601—dc22   2010007921

A catalogue record of the book is available from the British Library.

Design by Newgen Imaging Systems (P) Ltd., Chennai, India.

First edition: September 2010

10 9 8 7 6 5 4 3 2 1

Transferred to Digital Printing in 2014

CONTENTS

List of Figure and Tables   vii
Acknowledgments   ix

Introduction   1
Ravindra Kumar

Part 1   Political Applications

One   Peace Philosophy of Gandhi: Reality, Evolution, and Application in the First Decade of the Twenty-First Century   7
Ravindra Kumar

Two   War Renunciation and Abolishment by Japan   21
Kazuyo Yamane

Three   Retooling Peace Philosophy: A Critical Look at Israel's Separation Strategy   43
Kristofer J. Petersen-Overton, Johannes D. Schmidt, and Jacques Hersh

Part 2   Curricular Applications

Four   History Curriculum with Multiple Narratives   79
Esther Yogev

Five   Pluralism and Transformative Social Studies "Us and Them": Challenges for the Indian Classroom   105
Teesta Setalvad

Six	Peace Education in Elementary Teacher Education of Tamilnadu *Savarimuthu Vincent De Paul*	141

Part 3   Program Applications

Seven	Restorative Practices for Reconstruction *Candice C. Carter*	163
Eight	Cosmopolitanism as a Philosophical Foundation of Post-Yugoslav Peace Studies in Higher Education *Andria K. Wisler*	185
Nine	Children Are Made to Love: Liberation Education in India *Michael R. Hubert*	205
Conclusion *Candice C. Carter*		213
Contributors		217
Index		221

FIGURE AND TABLES

Figure

7.1 Passing a Talking Stick   167

Tables

6.1 Typical Content of Peace Education   142
6.2 Peace Strategies   144
6.3 Issues Included in the Curriculum   149
6.4 Participants in Training   155
7.1 The Support-Group Method   169
9.1 Children's Community Activities   209
9.2 Advancing Liberation Education   210
10.1 Philosophical Applications for Peace   214

ACKNOWLEDGMENTS

We appreciate many people who supported the production of this book. We gratefully honor everyone whose shared insights about and initiatives for peace inspired and advanced its development.

Introduction

RAVINDRA KUMAR

Through the ages peace has been a vital subject in theory and practice. It has also been one of the chief aims of all religious communities; therefore, the guardians of religious communities and social reformers have maintained visions of it. The importance of peace remains evident for its affect on human life and human development. In its meaning and purpose, peace is neither a state of perpetuation nor the status quo. It has nothing to do with inactiveness. Yet compulsion has no place in it. Those who try to equate peace with inactiveness and compulsion or who take it to be a static condition are not correct. In doing so, they evidence their lack of understanding and wisdom.

Rather, peace is an active, dynamic force. Committing to it as a goal offers an individual or a group the strength to respond to any and all types of conflict. Furthermore, ideas of peace generate enthusiasm and illuminate the path for humanity's progress. Not only this, despite being the basic source and center of peace, communicating ideas for it bring a human being out of the domain of individualism and inspires action for the welfare of others.

Through learned practices and new activities, people move forward on the pathway to peace. Commitment to the purpose of achieving peace sustains the needed actions, especially when we are facing challenges. With commitment is knowledge that includes the ideological basis of peace development: the foundational principles. Comprehension and articulation of those principles is the basis for furthering peace steps, for example, from individual to community, community to society, society to nation, and nation to other nations. From ancient times to the present age, this process has been continuing. It will remain continuous and perhaps expand an outcome of peace education scholars. Among them are renowned activists and peace educators. In both theory and practice, they have been constantly and significantly contributing to the development of a sustainable "culture of peace." Through their ideas, writings, and actions, they are giving new dimensions to the philosophy of peace, while at the same time making it useful and practical. Moreover, they are in one way or the other demonstrating that a peace philosophy without practicability is imperfect and incomplete; its beauty and worth remains in how it is applied to actively connect people to its process.

This book includes description and analysis of how a peace philosophy has been applied in political spheres, in the area of education, and in different programs in response to prevailing circumstances. These accomplishments have implications for current and future peace actions.

The first part of this book reveals the relevance and adaptability of a philosophy of nonviolence in the responses to structural conflicts. The contributors describe the challenges facing nations, for example, Japan's efforts to maintain political nonviolence and Israel's strategies to eliminate violence. Initially, the book evidences the relevance and adaptability of a philosophy of nonviolence in Asia as well as in other world regions.

The second part of the book includes curricular developments in response to interethnic strife, inappropriate educational practices, and the lack of teacher preparedness for providing peace-oriented instruction. The contributors describe transformative social studies that have taken place in the context of the Palestine-Israel conflict and throughout India's conflict-ridden state of Tamilnadu. The theoretical bases of the curriculum development that these chapters describe has been useful in other regions characterized by structural violence.

In the third part of the book, the contributors reveal the philosophical foundations of peace-oriented programs. From both informal and formal changes in education to legal innovations, it is evident that humans have the capacity to create institutions that can respond to conflict without furthering harm. Analysis of the cases presented in this section provides insights for development and refinement of programs that have a peace philosophy at their core.

Each chapter of this book is not only inspirational but also useful in aiding those who are, or will be, working for the establishment of peace. I am thankful to Kazuyo Yamane, Jacques Hersh, Johannes D. Schmidt, Kristofer J. Petersen-Overton, Esther Yogev, Teesta Setalvad,

S. Vincent De Paul, Candice C. Carter, Andria K. Wisler, and Michel R. Hubert for their invaluable contributions to this work. I am particularly grateful to Candice C. Carter for her great efforts and for the great intellect that she brought to the creation of this book. This expression of my gratitude will not complete unless I convey my sincere thanks to the Palgrave Macmillan team for undertaking its publication.

I am confident that all those who think and work for peace will benefit from the use of this publication, while all those who grapple with conflict and violence will see the value of philosophy in formulating the optimal responses to the challenges they face.

PART 1
───────
Political Applications

Political responses to structural conflicts result from a mixture of beliefs and values. Shading the perception of widespread conflict are beliefs derived from prior experience and available information. Values are the lens through which we view conflict. The information we receive from schools, spiritual advisors, the media, and politicians typically influences our thinking about how to respond to problems within and between groups. An oppositional stance, ready to respond to conflict with competition and aggression, has been normalized in many of these information sources. In the context of structural conflict, these norms often evidence the acceptance, thus the apparent valuing, of harm. Such situations demonstrate a need to turn back to the philosophical foundations of humanity that support mutual well-being.

The valuing of optimal mutuality and peace has throughout human history justified the resolution of conflicts without the use of violence. Awareness of the many places, time periods and ways in which politicians, nongovernmental organizations, and civilians responded to political conflicts without damage or destruction counters the norms of harm that are unintelligent and unnecessary. Along with knowledge, a belief in the power of change through cooperation and assertiveness versus competition and aggression needs to be developed during information dissemination and in government institutions. The real competition is within the mind, it is in the struggle to maintain a commitment to peace when there is pressure to respond to conflict with violence or within a climate of its apparent normalization.

Introduction to Part I

This part of the book reviews political peace actions that have been taken and explores opportunities for current ones. Understanding the ideology that underlay those past and present situations contributes to the knowledge base that is needed for constructive transformation of structural conflicts. The actions evidence the continual awareness of peace as a method, as well as a goal, during problem solving.

CHAPTER ONE

Peace Philosophy of Gandhi: Reality, Evolution, and Application in the First Decade of the Twenty-First Century

RAVINDRA KUMAR

This chapter describes Gandhi's technique of nonviolent resistance, *Satyagraha*, which he used in South Africa and India to transform structural conflicts. It then reviews the evolution of his ideas beyond his lifetime, particularly the ways in which Gandhi's philosophy of peacemaking matured, expanding beyond the political sphere into the social and economic ones. After describing contextually responsive applications of Gandhi's philosophy, the chapter identifies the fundamental points to be considered in the current and future use of nonviolence as a path to peace.

Mohandas Karamchand Gandhi (1869–1948), popularly known all over the world as Mahatma Gandhi, was a great man of contemporary history. His philosophy, practices attracted the attention of millions of people during his lifetime. And after his death, he continued to be a source of inspiration for thousands of people in India, in other countries who were seeking peace. Inspired by the accomplishments of Mahatma Gandhi, people all over the globe struggled for freedom, many of them united in successful pursuits of justice. At least fifty struggles carried out in different parts of the globe between 1948, 1998 evidence the influence of Gandhi's ideas and strategies. Among them were the civil rights movement in the United States, which included freedom rides and initiatives led by Martin Luther King Jr. (1929–1968) that were aimed at ending segregation and all forms of discrimination against African Americans—in public places as well as the racial criteria used by employers in hiring practices. A student-led civilian insurrection resulted in Pinellas's fall in Colombia (1957). There were also the peasants' struggles in Pacora Valley in Panama and Peru (1962); the major nonviolent action in Hue, Danang, Vietnam (1966); student demonstrations in Germany, Italy, Poland, and Yugoslavia (1968); protests involving workers, students, and priests in Spain (1968–1969); the Epifanio de Los Santos Avenue Revolution in the Philippines (1986); the Zapatist Movement for National Liberation in Mexico (1996); the students' nonviolent protests to pressure the Clinton administration to adopt codes that would guarantee living wages for workers manufacturing products in North Carolina, USA (1997–1998); and the people's struggles for the restoration of democracy in many countries in eastern Europe during the last decades of the twentieth century. Moreover, interest in and curiosity about the Gandhian philosophy have grown. During the past decade (1998–2008), the way in which people at all levels of society and from walks of life who, inspired by Gandhi's philosophy, have begun to actively work to establish justice and secure freedom shows the continued adaptability and relevance of Gandhi's ideas.

This chapter reveals how Gandhi, encouraged by the notion of *ahimsa* (nonviolence) developed *Satyagraha*, his technique of nonviolent resistance, first in South Africa, with the purpose of getting repealed acts and laws that discriminated against the country's Indian immigrants, and then in his homeland of India. It explores these questions: How did his techniques succeed in achieving India's freedom from British colonial rule? How was it that after Mahatma Gandhi died, his philosophy matured, acquiring social and economic dimensions? And how did his ideas prove their relevance for people around the world, particularly during the past decade, in getting rid of atrocities and exploitation and in pursuit of justice at different levels?

Philosophy of Gandhi: Reality and Evolution

Fully imbued with morality and ethics, Gandhi's philosophy incorporates the views of nonviolence that he developed in response to contextual conditions. He was born into a Gujarati Vaishnava family that was committed to the *Sanatana Dharma* old rule. Under this rule, nonviolence was considered as the *Parmodharmah*. It meant to make nonviolence the basis of activities was one's prime duty. Gandhi's mother, Putalibai (1822–1891), also had sympathy for India's most ancient religion, Jainism. In Jainism, the belief in nonviolence occupies the supreme place and embraces every type of violence, small or large, committed by a human being against any living thing, whether knowingly or unknowingly. Consequently, Gandhi's reverential belief in nonviolence started in his home, particularly from instruction by his mother. During his secondary and post-secondary education, he found that, in spite of the disparity in its quantity, a belief in nonviolence was common to all religious communities, as he expressed in his statement, "Non-violence is common to all religions." (*Young India*, October 20, 1920).

This discovery undoubtedly deepened Gandhi's faith in nonviolence. His life experiences led Gandhi to the conclusion that nonviolence is the law of life, an essential condition of existence, of progress, and of goal achievement. It can be said with certainty that, unlike many other philosophies of the world, Gandhi's is not the outcome of theoretical argumentation; rather, it is based upon true life experiences. In other words, it is guided by the *Sanatana Dharma*.

Those who are familiar with life and works of Gandhi know that after his coincidental arrival in South Africa in 1893, he, as an Indian, was subjected to some bitter experiences of racial discrimination, inequality, injustice, and exploitation as an immigrant. The Colonial Government of South Africa carried out acts of racial discrimination toward Asians in general and Indians in particular. Gandhi's reactions to these experiences were the catalyst for the formation of his ideas. Gandhi stayed in South Africa from 1893 to 1914. During his twenty-one years there, he successfully launched actions to abolish The Indian Franchise Bill, the Black Act, the Immigration Act, the Pound Three Tax Act, and other unjust pieces of legislation. In his nonviolent actions, known as *Satyagrahas*, he demonstrated an effective philosophy, which after its applications according to the demands of prevailing circumstances in India, proved to be relevant and welfaristic.

Through one dozen *Satyagrahas* carried out between 1918 and 1942 under the guidance and leadership of Gandhi and some of his prominent comrades, particularly in Gujarat and the United Provinces, an unprecedented wave of social, political, and economic awakening has taken place in India. It was this massive awakening that ended colonialism and the centuries-old practice of slavery in India.

Gandhi carried out his nonviolent actions in three stages: the Non-Cooperation Movement (1920); the Civil Disobedience Movement, which started with the breaking of the Salt Law at Dandi (1930); and the Quit India Movement (1942). Through these, his compatriots became conscious of their right to freedom from political oppression. Later, his actions became exemplars for people around the world. They also revealed the adaptability and relevance of his philosophy. Many pages of Indian and world history maintain the account of nonviolent actions predicated on the ideas of Gandhi. The following example of one philosophical application will be illustrative.

The application of Gandhian philosophy through the Bhoodan Movement in the 1960s was astonishing in a country like India that had much cultural diversity. The Bhoodan Movement gave a new dimension to Gandhi's philosophy. Simultaneously, it confirmed his philosophy to be one of peace. The Bhoodan Movement had two chief aims: One was to accord social justice; the other was to provide equal economic opportunity in India. The nation achieved its political independence from the colonial rule in the year 1947. Nevertheless, many of its citizens, particularly those living in India's more than seven hundred thousand villages, continued to suffer socially and economically. They were landless in India, a country where agriculture was, and still is, the backbone of the society and economy. In spite of becoming politically free, a large number of people now looked for opportunities that could propel them toward economic self-reliance. It was a predictable reaction. If the Indian people were not accorded equal opportunities in social and economic arenas, peace would remain only a dream. Recognizing this fact, Mahatma Gandhi wrote, on January 29, 1948, a day before his assassination, "India has still to attain social...and economic independence in terms of its seven hundred thousand villages as distinguished from its cities and towns." (Gandhi, *India of My Dreams* 1960, p. 290.)

"Peace" is not just a word; it is an active force, an outcome of practice. Gandhi's philosophy holds that peace is dynamic (Kumar 2007, p. 193). Characterized by this dynamism, the Bhoodan Movement added dimensions to the application of Gandhi's philosophy in social and economic spheres and that, too, according to the demand of time and space. It became a commendable nonviolent action without participation by Mahatma Gandhi, successfully carried out after Gandhi passed away. It without doubt paved the way for subsequent applications of Gandhian philosophy.

In India, the Bhoodan Movement also became an ideal because it opened the door for application of an important aspect of Mahatma Gandhi's philosophy known as *Sarvodaya* (the welfare of all). Based upon Sanatana, and Indian notion that "All...belongs to Gopal (God)", the *Sarvodaya* is a doctrine that Gandhi developed in 1905 after he read *Unto This Last,* a book by John Ruskin (1819–1900) published in 1862. Gandhi translated Ruskin's book into Gujarati and published it with the title *Sarvodaya*.. The book is a basic work of Christian socialism. In it John Ruskin quotes Jesus in the parable of the laborers in the vineyard, "I will give unto this last, even as unto thee." (Gandhi 1955, p. 4; Gandhi December 1, 1926.)

Like John Ruskin, Gandhi was an ardent supporter of equality for all. He was of the opinion that nobody in a society should be exploited. Everyone should be accorded equal opportunity to rise in the social field. "Unto this last" was Ruskin's ideal, essence of which can be expressed in following three points:

1. The good of the individual is contained in the good of all.
2. A lawyer's work has the same value as the barber's: Both have the same right to earn their livelihood by working.
3. The life of the laborer—the tiller of the soil and the handicraftsman— is the life worth living. (Gandhi 1927, p. 223)

After adopting those three points in his life, Gandhi incorporated them in the doctrine of *Sarvodaya*. He had made up his mind to apply this doctrine on a wider scale after India gained its political freedom from colonial rule. But, unfortunately, only after a few months of the dawn of India's independence, he was assassinated on January 30, 1948. However, although he never got the opportunity to spread his doctrine on a wider scale, he left it as a legacy for his compatriots and, particularly, for his successors.

It was Vinoba Bhave (1895–1982), one of Ghandi's disciples and a member of the Acharya caste, who carried forward his *Sarvodaya* mission through the Bhoodan Movement.

The Bhoodan Movement began in April 1951 in the village of Pochampalli,—the first village in the Telangana region of the present-day state of Andhra Pradesh. Why? Even before the dawn of Indian in 1947, there were serious clashes in the region between the wealthy landowners, who occupied most of the land, and the landless, who despite being the vast majority of population, were poor and backward. This unjust distribution of land had led many of the landless to become violent; some were influenced by the Communists. Many landlords had to flee from the region for their safety. Controlling the violent attacks on the landlords became a serious challenge for the authorities. Vinoba Bhave was well acquainted with the problems in

Telangana. He was of the firm opinion that this serious and complicated problem could be solved by goodwill, which of course, is the nucleus in Gandhi's philosophy, and to attain goodwill, Bhave wrote, "Removal of unjust distribution of land in a peaceful way is (absolutely) necessary." (Narayan 1970, p. 189.)

Therefore, it was decided to launch the Bhoodan action from Pochampalli, and Vinoba Bhave started his journey to that village. On April 15, 1951, he reached the Central Jail in Hyderabad, where as a goodwill gesture, he met with the Communists who had been imprisoned there because of their involvement in antisocial activities and for provoking violence in the Telangana region.

Soon after reaching Pochampalli on April 18, 1951, Vinoba Bhave started an open dialogue with the village's landless Harijans (the lowest caste in India), which continued in an atmosphere of goodwill and in the presence of the landlords. During those discussons, the Harijans told Vinoba Bhave, "If they [the landless] get only eighty acres of land, they will cultivate it and eke out their living." (Tandon 1992, p. 52.) The Acharya Vinoba Bhave considered this proposition, and after some time, turned to the landowners present and asked if any of them would give away the land as a gift (Bhoodan) for the purpose! A *zamindar* (landlord) named C. Ramachandra Reddy immediately offered a donation of one hundred acres of land instead of eighty acres. It was astonishing for the Acharya. He considered it as a "divine revelation." He also saw in such generous and voluntary donation of land the possibility of resolving the centuries-old problem of landlessness experienced by India's millions of agricultural laborers.

From Pochampalli, the great work of the voluntary donation of land, the Bhoodan, started successfully. The Acharya stayed in the Telangana region for about a month and a half and collected donations of 1,201 acres of land. Before leaving the region, he put together a committee of locals to distribute the land among the landless. This was the first step of the Bhoodan Movement, an application of Gandhi's philosophy in the social and economic spheres of India.

The second phase of the Movement started in 1952 during the Acharya's long journey on foot with his companions from *Pawnar Ashram* (abode) to Delhi, which lasted for nearly two months. After requesting gifts of land from landlords, they reached Delhi. During this journey, Vinoba Bhave extended the Bhoodan program and started asking rich people for donations of *Sadhanadan*—means of cultivation such as wells, bullocks and other inputs. He also started asking for *Shramdan* (gifts of labor or voluntary work) and *Gramdan* in which over 80 percent or the villagers surrendered their ownership of land in the village to a committee responsible for equitable its distribution among them. This expansion of the program was highly successful. From Delhi, the Bhoodan leader and his co-workers traveled to the province of Uttar Pradesh and then to Bihar. In both these provinces, besides *Sadhanadan*, *Shramdan* and *Gramdan*, they also acquired 295,028 and 2,200,000 acres of acres of gifted land, respectively.. Later, under Vinoba Bhave's leadership, they reached the state of Orissa via West Bengal, and there they received donations of 812 villages. Similarly, in Tamilnadu, they received donations of 175 villages. Kerala, Karnataka, Maharashtra, Jammu and Kashmir as well as other provinces also followed Tamilnadu in making donations. Under Vinoba's leadership, the great work, which was based on Gandhian principles, helped to pave the way to a peaceful and bright future for millions of landless, yet hard-working, Indians.

Vinoba Bhave wanted fifty millions acres of land, approximately one-sixth of all the agricultural land in India, to be gifted to the landless so that a new society based on nonviolence could be formed in which all people could advance toward a peaceful life. In Vinoba's own words, "We seek to reconstruct society on a new basis. That is the purpose behind the Bhoodan work…What we want to establish are new values—to make morality the guiding principle of social life and to make economics, which enjoys undue importance at present…The Bhoodan Movement is for us an instrument for achieving a nonviolent and peaceful change of values as per the demand of time." (Tandon, 1992, p. 58.)

The Bhoodan Movement paved the way for similar peaceful actions around the world. A complete account of those actions would require volumes. Here, it is enough to say that until today, the relevance and significance of Gandhi's philosophy has been continually evident.

It is worthwhile to review some of those actions.

Application of Gandhian Philosophy: 1998–2008

After the evolution of Gandhi's philosophy in political, social, and economic spheres under Gandhi's guidance himself, and later mainly through the Bhoodan program, the process of its application has been continued throughout the world. In this regard the role of some people, who came on the forefront to lead nonviolent actions during the recent decade, has been extraordinary and noteworthy.

In this regard, the nonviolent struggle of Aung San Suu Kyi against the ruling Junta-military dictators in Burma-Myanmar since 1988 is one of the living examples before us. Aung San Suu Kyi launched an agitation for the restoration of democracy in 1988 when military rulers of Burma who denying it deprived the people of their rights. They started suppressing people forcefully. Resultantly, Suu Kyi was arrested in 1990 under the "State Protection Act-1975." This Act grants the government the power to imprison persons for up to five years without a trial. From the jail, she continued inspiring people to nonviolently fight against injustice. She followed the course of several others Gandhian techniques including hunger-strike or fasting.

Since May 30, 2003 Aung San Suu Kyi is completely under house arrest. Although she has no direct contact with her compatriots; no visitor is allowed to her except government-appointed physicians and one or two more people. She remains a ray of hope for thousands of Burmese who occasionally come forward to nonviolently challenge the ruling Junta. Through their actions, they attract the attention of all those who are concerned about human equality, freedom and justice (Joshi, 2009). Aung San Suu Kyi, without caring for her individual sufferings, and making sacrifices for compatriots and humanity, has shown selflessness for the last twenty years (1988–2008). Undoubtedly, she is a source of inspiration for many in the world who sustain their work for peace.

Another person, Sharmila Chanu from the Province of Manipur, India, is demanding an amendment to the 1972 Armed Forces Special Powers Act, known as the AFSPA. She has been involved in this struggle since November 2000 and she has emerged as one of the leading activists engaged in applying Gandhian philosophy. The AFSPA Act accords the armed forces, down to the rank of a noncommissioned officer, the power to kill as well as shoot and to enter, search and arrest without warrant any person about whom reasonable suspicion exists that an offence was, or will be, committed in the northeastern provinces of India. When many ordinary people were killed by the armed forces under the provisions of the AFSPA, Sharmila Chanu went on an indefinite fast for demanding repeal of that act. Hence, she took the course of Gandhian *Satyagraha*. With the charge of making an effort to commit suicide, Chanu was arrested under section 309 of the Indian Penal Code. Chanu remains under detention. In response to her protest, she has been experiencing forced injections (Dobhal, 2006). However, she is firm on her way and still fasting in her nonviolent struggle. Her determination and actions have attracted attention of many of those who are concerned for human values and who desire transformation through nonviolent methods.

Both these persons-Aung Sang Suu Kyi and Sharmila Chanu-have not yet recorded victory through their nonviolent actions. However, the manner they have come forward by applying Gandhian philosophy to counter injustice and atrocities are mentionable. Hopefully, both of them will achieve success beyond their service as role models for nonviolent activism. Gandhi's philosophy conveys the message of becoming adherent to truth and with truth to march forward without apprehension. As both of them have been following this message and they have been in action for years, there is possibility of their ultimate success in one way or the other.

Two other people-Ela Bhatt and Vandana Shiva, through their respective organizations, namely the Self Employed Women's Association (SEWA), and the Navdanya, are carrying out noteworthy constructive activities in the social field of India for the last thirty years (Shiva, 1991 & 1992).

The SEWA, a nongovernment organization of Ahmedabad, Gujarat, is functioning for the uplift of women. Micro finance management through the SEWA Bank, which provides loans to women and allows them to set up bank accounts in their names only, are the central activities of this organization. Moreover, cooperative activity, such as the collection of milk, is also carried out by this organization. As its furthering step, the SEWA has during the last decade expended its activities in the form of solution to the labour problem. Resultantly, today a strong community of three hundred thousands women works tirelessly and with enthusiasm in its supervision to develop their self-reliance. This important work of the SEWA can be the source of inspiration for those desired to go forward in this direction.

Promotion of biodiversity conservation, organic farming, and seed saving are the main activities being carried out by the Navdanya, which is a leading voluntary organization for the last thirty years. Mahatma Gandhi gave priority to constructive works in his programs for reconstruction of society. In it the protection of natural resources occupied prominent place. Hence, this organization is engaged in carrying out these activities, which function for the awakening among the rural masses, particularly for the progress of farming community of India.

In brief, works being done by the SEWA and the Navdanya-as constructive actions are methods of social change. They can be considered experiments with Gandhi's philosophy according to the demand of time. These applications can be adaptable models for nongovernment organizations in other regions of the world where women are struggling for economic well-being and where rural conditions play a pivotal role in development.

In other regions of the world, people have also applied Gandhi's ideas in the prevailing circumstances. For example, Julia Butterfly Hill, an American activist and environmentalist, has used nonviolent action to bring about justice for Nature. She is best known for living on a six-hundred-year-old and one-hundred-eighty-foot tall California redwood tree for seven hundred thirty eight days, between December 1997 and December 1999. As known to many, Julia lived barefoot on the tree, known as LUNA, to prevent a lumber company from cutting it down. Julia's work can be compared with many other leading environmentalists who have worked individually, as well collectively, to preserve natural resources.

The applications of Gandhi's philosophy comprise a long list. It includes many people of various backgrounds and different levels of engagement through their respective organizations and institutions. It is apparent that thousands of people are trying to carry out their activities pertaining to human welfare more or less on the basis of Gandhian philosophy. They, by adopting refined nonviolent methods, which can be applicable in a prevailing circumstance or as per the demand of time, are advancing cultures of peace. In India alone, there are one hundred Gandhian organizations and institutions. The Banwasi Sewa Ashram (U.P.), the Gandhi Peace Foundation (New Delhi), the Gandhi Peace Foundation Trust and the Andhra Mahila Sabha (Andhra Pradesh), the G. R. Institute of Non-Violence (Kerala), the Institute of Gandhian Studies, Wardha (Maharashtra), the Mahatma Gandhi Center, Coimbatore (Tamilnadu), the M. C. Mehta Environmental Foundation (New Delhi), the Rashtriyashala, Rajkot (Gujarat), the Sampurna Kranti Vidyalaya (Gujarat), the Sarvodaya International Trust, Bangalore (Karnataka), the Saurashtra Rachnatmak Samiti, Rajkot (Gujarat), etc., which accepting the inevitability of the *Law of Change*, and without compromising with the principle of *Ahimsa*-the fundamental basis of Gandhi's philosophy, are carrying out their activities. In this regard, important works being done by the Anandawana Ashram for treatment and rehabilitation of leprosy patients, the disabled and other people from marginalized sections of society in the remote and economically less-privileged district of Chandrapur in Maharashtra and also for environmental awareness and wildlife preservation, the Gram Sewa Samaj, established in 1957 at Vedachhi (Gujarat) and which runs a number of *Ashramshalas*-Gandhian Education Institutes, and in which 4,945 girls and boys from tribal areas are studying currently, the Vedachhi Pradesh Sewa Samiti, formed in 1952 at Vadod (Gujarat), and which for the last one decade is working for spreading education in tribal areas, health in the rural areas and awakening among peasantry, particularly for preserving water, the Sarvodaya Parivar, founded in 1968–1969 in Gujarat, which for the last seven years is carrying out noteworthy activities relating to village development like roads-construction, water-management and distribution, the Gandhi Vidyapeeth Vedachhi, established in 1967 at Vedachhi (Gujarat), which since 1990 is preparing social workers committed to Gandhian ideas and the Sarvodaya Mandal, formed fifty years ago in Mumbai, which besides educating people, promotes Gandhian ideals all over India., are worth mentioning. All the activities of these organizations and institutions for the tribal people, farmers, laborers and the rural populations, and of which this writer himself is a witness, encouraged people to re-evaluate the adaptability and relevance of Gandhi's philosophy and use of his ideas.

Gandhi's philosophy, as mentioned in the beginning, is not the outcome of theoretical argumentation. Rather Sanatana Dharma guides it. By staying within the domain of nonviolence, it is dedicated to the welfare of all general and particular. It can be called the philosophy of the common people. Yet, this philosophy has a direct appeal for everyone involved with resolution of difficult conflicts. Therefore, there can always be a possibility of its application. But, those who wish success through this philosophy need to follow certain things, which are essential conditions for the success with Gandhi's philosophy. What are those conditions? Before clarifying it, it is appropriate to describe here nonviolent actions, which have been recently carried out in the name of Gandhigiri.

Inspired by some of the illustrations of the feature film, *Lage Raho Munnabhai*, released in October 2006, people have tried to set examples of peacemaking through their nonviolent actions in response to conflicts they were experiencing. Particularly, people have come forward to resist injustice in the name of Gandhigiri. They have done so nonviolently, and on most of the occasions they have experienced success. The term Gandhigiri was used for the first time by Sardar Vallabhbhai Patel (1875–1950) during the first phase of the Civil Disobedience Movement (1930–1931). The Sardar used this with some unusual intention or in a joking manner as he used to do with the Mahatma. But recognizing Gandhigiri as a kind of *Satyagraha* some people declared it to be an effective method of Gandhi's philosophy in changed circumstances of the Twenty-First Century. They have explained Gandhigiri in the following manner: 'Gandhi' is Gandhi, the Mahatma, and 'giri' is the way. It is, according to the users of this concept, the way to end forcibly inflicted injustice. Therefore, it is a kind of *Satyagraha*. It has been an application of Gandhi's philosophy, often with positively transformative outcomes.

Examples of using Gandhigiri in this decade evidence its applicability in the pursuit of transformation. During the month of October 2006, actions by doctors and students embarrassed the Union Health Minister of India, for not making strong response to the issue of the Dengue Fever, which claimed twenty six deaths in Delhi alone. During that very month, writers proposed reforms to the educational system by using Gandhigiri as a concept in Karur. Carpenters practiced it to make sure unreliable clients paid for service they received. Low-income farmers in drought-ridden areas of Maharashtra used it to make officers of the provincial government ashamed to sanction loans to them. In all of these cases, people used peaceful methods including offering of flowers, lightening candles and demonstrating without violence. During 2007, old people taking the course of Gandhigiri protested at the Akota Provident Office after they tired of obstacles to their acquisition of provident-fund money from that office. In Hyderabad, a section of doctors adopted Gandhigiri against atrocities of a member of the provincial legislative assembly, first by forming a human chain and later by offering petrol to spray it and set them on fire.

These applications ranged further. Not only in Allahabad, Chandigarh, Delhi, Patna, Pune and Vishakhapatnam, practices of Gandhigiri were reported from London, United Kingdom and Washington, DC, United States. People adopted this method in their own unjust arrests and that of others involving their acquaintances. They chose this way in responding to conflicts associated with job security, sanitation, and water-supply management. In almost all activities that were associated with the concept of Gandhigiri justice-seekers and protestors were nonviolent during their actions. It can be considered a matter of great satisfaction. Along with this, they have, more or less, tried to apply this method after assessing the prevailing circumstances. The contextual analysis and personal satisfaction that characterized those experiences have been components of successful engagement with Gandhigiri. In spite of not agreeing with those who take Gandhigiri to be synonymous of *Satyagraha*, as egoism can be seen in the word Gandhigiri, which has no place in Gandhi's philosophy, it is nevertheless satisfying to people like me that in the actions taken through this method, people in experiencing or witnessing difficult conflict have been trying to make a commitment to and applying nonviolence.

Conclusion

Before ending this discussion, is it is appropriate to suggest factors associated with successful applications of Gandhi's peace philosophy. Mindfulness of these factors may be aids in future practice with this philosophy. In spite of its core of nonviolence, Gandhi's philosophy is not static. Rather, it is dynamic. Its central concept of nonviolence is a subject of refinement in contextually responsive applications. Therefore, those who desire success with Gandhi's philosophy must go forward only after bringing it into harmony with the prevailing circumstances. This is the first condition of its success. Contrary to Utilitarianism, which includes the idea of the greatest happiness of the greatest number, Gandhi's philosophy is dedicated to *Sarvodaya*—the welfare of all. Therefore, if appliers of Gandhi's philosophy bear this fact in mind at the time of their actions, there is a greater possibility of their success. In addition, they should not become apprehensive of an immediate result. They must become ready for long-term nonviolent struggle for solving problem because an action being carried out on the strength of nonviolence can take a long time. In addition, if directive principles set by the Mahatma himself, and later from time-to-time by other great Gandhians, are followed at the launch and during the course of action, there remain all possibilities of eventual success. Such actions will illustrate the relevance, importance, and adaptability of Gandhi's peace philosophy while they advance peace.

References

Aiyar, P. S. (1942). *Stateless Indians in South Africa*. Allahabad: K. R. Mehta.
Andrews, C. F. (1929). *Mahatma Gandhi's ideas*. London: George Allen.
Arillo, C. (1986). *Breakaway: The inside story of the Four Day Revolution in the Philippines*. Manila: CTA and Associates.
Bhave, V. (1973). *Vinoba on Gandhi*. Wardha: Sarva Sewa Sangha.
Evangelista, S. (1994). *Non-violence: A text*. Manila: Ateneo de Manila University.
Fisher, L. (1994). *Gandhi: His life and message for the world*. New York: Penguin.
Gandhi, M. K. (1919–1931). *Young India Weekly* (Republished in 13 Volumes in 1984). Ahmedabad: Navajivan.
——— (1927). *An autobiography or the story of my experiments with truth* Ahmedabad: Navajivan.

Gandhi, M. K. (1938). *December 3 and 24, 1939: May 13, 20, September 30, and October 7). Harijan Weekly* (Volumes 6 & 7). Ahmedabad: Harijan Sewak Sangh.

——— (1955). *Sarvodaya*. Ahmedabad: Navajivan.

——— (1960). *India of my dreams*. Ahmedabad: Navajivan.

Holmes, R. L. (1990). *Non-violence in theory and practice*. Belmont, CA: Wadsworth.

Joshi, V. (November 14, 2009). Obama tells Myanmar junta to free Suu Kyi. *Associated Press*. Retrieved November 14, 2009, at http://news.yahoo.com/s/ap/20091115/ap_on_re_as/as_asean_us_myanmar.

Kripalani, J. B. (1970). *Gandhi: His life and thought*. New Delhi: Publications Division, Ministry of Information & Broadcasting, Government of India.

Kumar, R. (2002). *Theory and practice of Gandhian non-violence*. New Delhi: Mittal.

——— (2003). *Non-violence and its philosophy*. Meerut: Dynamic.

——— (2007). *Towards peace*. New Delhi: Gyan.

——— (2008). *Gandhian thought: New world*, new dimensions. New Delhi: Kalpaz.

Narayan, S. (1970). *Vinoba: His life and work*. Bombay: Popular.

Patel, B. J. (1990). *Mahatma Gandhi: A source of inspiration* (Sardar Literature Series-4) Ahmedabad: Sardar Patel National Memorial.

Ruskin. J. (1901). *Unto this last: Four essays on the first principles of political economy*. New York: Crowell.

Shiva, V. (1991). *Ecology and the politics of survival: Conflicts over natural resources in India*. Newbury Park, CA: Sage.

——— (1992). *The violence of the* Green Revolution*: Ecological degradation and political conflict in Punjab*. New Delhi: Zed.

Tandon, V. N. (1992). *Acharya Vinoba Bhave*. New Delhi: Publications Division, Ministry of Information & Broadcasting, Government of India.

Tendulkar, D. G. (1951–1954). *Mahatma: Life of Mohandas Karamchand Gandhi* (8 Volumes). Bombay: V. K. Jhaveri & D. G. Tendulkar.

Tolstoy, L. (1959). *The law of violence and the law of love*. London: Unicorn.

CHAPTER TWO

War Renunciation and Abolishment by Japan

KAZUYO YAMANE

Humans did not learn enough from World War II, as is evidenced by their engagement in subsequent wars in Korea, Vietnam, Afghanistan, Iraq, and many other armed conflicts all over the globe. Perpetual wars illustrate the ongoing normalization of violence as a political response to conflict. This chapter reviews an initiative to transform political conflicts without resorting to war. Japan's history of international violence renders it an important case in the study of applied peace philosophy. Japan invaded other Asian countries in World War II, resulting in the deaths of an estimated 20 million people. Adding to that tragedy were the deaths of approximately 3.1 million Japanese, including over 200,000 people who were killed by atomic bombs in Hiroshima and Nagasaki (Makino, 2008). Many people have been killed in Iraq, Afghanistan, and other places because force has been used to solve problems instead of sustained dialogue and negotiation. However, it is encouraging that a manual *Conflict Transformation by Peaceful Means*[1] has been used for training ambassadors, members of the United Nations, nongovernmental organizations (NGOs), professors, students, and even disputants in conflict (Galtung & Jacobsen, 2000). The manual emphasizes empathy, nonviolence, and creativity for conflict transformation as dialogue guidelines. While Gandhi's nonviolence is well-known and respected throughout the world, Japan's nonviolent ideas, especially those that supported the development of Article 9 of the Japanese Constitution, are less known.

The Japanese Constitution was proclaimed on November 3, 1946 and was enforced on May 3, 1947. Article 9, which stipulates the renunciation of war and military force is especially important. It declares that, "Japanese people forever renounce war as a sovereign right of the nation and the threat or use of force as means of settling international disputes." However, there have been initiatives in the United States and Japan attempting to revise Article 9 since the end of World War II because it became an obstacle for them to rearm Japan. Akihiko Kimijima analyzed the situation: "The issue of revising Article 9 of Japan's Constitution has been a matter of contention in Japan consistently during the post war years, and the issue has been placed before us again as a major point of political contention." (Kimijima, 2009). If Article 9 is revised, Japan's Self-Defense Forces (JSDF) will have an increased military role in Japan and abroad, while the military burden of the United States will be reduced. This means that the retention or abolition of Article 9 is a political matter not only for Japan but also for the world. It would be worth learning lessons from Article 9 if it is used to transform conflicts nonviolently and to abolish war internationally.

In this chapter, the philosophical foundation and history of nonviolence in Japan are discussed, focusing on the historical background of Article 9 of the Japanese constitution as well as other such constitutions that exist in the world. Included in the picture of political conflict are challenges to state nonbelligerence in Japan and other nations. Responses to those challenges, especially the efforts and initiatives being carried out in Japan and elsewhere that reference nonviolent and peaceful responses to global conflicts, will also be discussed. Finally, there is a discussion of what the field of conflict transformation can learn from these efforts.

Philosophical Foundation and History: Nonviolence

The desire to preserve human life is displayed using written texts at an exhibition about respect for life from various civilizations at the International Red Cross and Red Crescent Museum, as follows: "Thou shalt love thy neighbor as thyself," Moses (Mayou, 2000, p. 10) and "Do not impose on others what you yourself do not desire" by Confucius (551–479 BC) (Mayou, 2000, p. 11) Emperor Aśoka (third century BC) said, "The conquest of an independent country means murder, death or captivity for the people who live in it, a thought that should deeply affect anyone who is a friend of the gods and weigh heavily upon his conscience." (Mayou, 2000, p. 12). In eighth century, Saint Matthew said, "I was hungry and you gave Me food; I was thirsty and you gave Me drink: I was a stranger and you took Me in: I was naked and you clothed Me: I was sick and you visited Me: I was in prison and you came to Me." (Mayou, 2000, p. 13). These words show that mankind has always been concerned with the preservation of human life. This idea denies the violence and war that destroys human life.

As for Japan, it should be noted that the nonviolent idea in Buddhism, that "we should not kill life," is written in Dhammapada's *The Buddha's Path of Virtue*, a sacred book of Buddhism. It is possible to think that Article 9 expresses the same idea in the sense that it says that violence should not be used toward living things. Actually, there is the book, *Article 9 is Buddha's Wish* (*Kenpo 9 jowa Hotokeno Negai*) by Takamaro Shigaraki, a well-known Buddhist and a scholar of religion (edited by Buddhists' Article 9 Association and published by Akashi Publication in 2006). The book shows that Buddha's wish for peace was like that desire expressed in Article 9. According to the Agency for Cultural Affairs in Japan, there were approximately 89 million followers of Buddhism in Japan as of December, 2007, which is about 70 percent of the Japanese population. It is interesting that Buddhists strongly support Article 9 and even founded Buddhists' groups of the Article 9 Association, which will be explained later.

It should also be noted that pacifists such as Senji Yamamoto (1889–1929) in Japan have respected nonviolence. Yamamoto was a biologist as well as a social reformer who was elected as a member of the Diet which is similar to U.S. Congress, representing a political party called the Party for Workers and Farmers which insisted on drastic disarmament in 1928. He protested against Order Maintenance Law issued in 1925 that oppressed human rights, such as freedom of speech. As a result, he was killed by a nationalist in 1929 because "He made efforts to disseminate ideas of world order based on nonviolence" in 1928. (Morita, p. 49). It seems that Yamamoto had been influenced by humanitarians and Christian socialists when, starting in 1906 at the age of eighteen, he went to Canada to study horticulture for five years. There have been many other pacifists who worked toward nonviolence, though few have received the same recognition as Yamamoto in Japan. This is likely because they are not studied in school, and their achievements are rarely reported in the media. However, it is encouraging that the work of some of them is exhibited in private peace museums such as the Kyoto Museum for World Peace at Ritsumeikan University.

A commitment to pacifism in resolving structural conflicts can be seen in the philosophy of organizations such as the Fellowship for Reconciliation (FOR). According to FOR's website, its vision is for "a world of justice, peace, and freedom...a revolutionary vision of a beloved community where differences are respected, conflicts are addressed non-violently, oppressive structures are dismantled, and traditions that foster compassion, solidarity, and reconciliation." Its mission is "to replace violence, war, racism and economic injustice with nonviolence, peace and justice." FOR describes itself as "an interfaith organization committed to active nonviolence as a transforming way of life and as a means of radical change" (FOR, 2009). It educates, trains, builds coalitions, and engages in nonviolent and compassionate actions locally, nationally, and globally. Since 1915, the FOR has carried on programs and educational projects concerned with domestic and international peace and justice, nonviolent alternatives to conflict, and the rights of conscience such as calling on U.S. Congress to initiate an independent investigation into American soldiers' torture of Iraqi civilians in Iraq as part of the call to resist the war in Iraq. The FOR promotes nonviolence and has members from many religious and ethnic traditions. It is a part of the International Fellowship of Reconciliation, which has affiliates in over 40 countries. For example, British Quakers are involved in a current conflict situation in Israel and Palestine. Beryl Milner, a British Quaker, explained the group's role in a lecture at Japan's Kochi University on July 24, 2008.

> We ask ordinary people to go to Israel/Palestine for about 12 weeks as volunteers. We train them and we pay their travel and living expenses. They are called 'accompaniers'—and that is what they do. They stand alongside.
> They stand alongside the few courageous Israeli men and women in the Israeli peace movement who believe that Israeli aggression should stop. They stand alongside ordinary Palestinian people. They go around with them in their daily lives. They watch at the checkpoints and observe any acts that may violate the human rights of the Palestinians. Their presence reminds the Israeli soldier at the checkpoint that the world is watching him. They help with the harvest. They play with the children—all quite ordinary activities, but very important ones.

It is encouraging to know about such nonviolent ideas and concrete actions for peace.

Today ordinary people can express their ideas against war on a website that presents the "Manifesto Against Conscription and the

Military System" to all those interested. The Manifesto was made to contribute to the abolition of military conscription, the military system and the military—in favor of complete disarmament and of a global culture of nonviolence. This Web site shows "Anti-Conscription Manifesto 1926" signed by Albert Einstein; M. K. Gandhi; Japanese pacifist Toyohiko Kagawa (1888–1960); Romain Rolland; Bertrand Russell; Rabindranath Tagore; and many others. This manifesto called for the League of Nations to outlaw compulsory military service as a first step to total disarmament. The Manifesto Against Conscription and the Military System expresses its key ideas as follows:

> Barrack life, military drill, blind obedience to commands, however unjust and foolish they may be, and deliberate training for slaughter undermine respect for the individual, for democracy and human life.

Actually, many Japanese men were forced by their emperor during World War II to obey orders, give up their lives, and fight against Japan's "enemy." It was almost impossible for them to protest against the war. There were, however, some antiwar activists: They were tortured to death by the special police. The Manifesto also points out that conscription perpetuates violence.

> Moreover, by conscription the militarist spirit of aggressiveness is implanted in the whole male population at the most impressionable age. By training for war, men come to consider war as unavoidable and even desirable.

The belief in nonviolence is clearly expressed in the manifesto. It is encouraging that such an initiative exists.

Peace Brigades International is an international grassroots NGO that has promoted nonviolence and protected human rights since 1981. It sends volunteers from all over the world into areas of conflict as protective accompaniers to human rights defenders who are threatened by political violence. There is also Nonviolent Peaceforce, an unarmed, nonpartisan peacekeeping force composed of trained civilians from around the world. In partnership with local groups, Nonviolent Peaceforce members base their work on proven nonviolent strategies to protect human rights, deter violence, and help local peacemakers carry out their work. For example, Nonviolent Peaceforce has been working in Sri Lanka, after the end of the civil war declared in May 2009.

This is because there is still much to do to meet the needs of human rights defenders, journalists, community activists and vulnerable communities facing increasing threats and attacks from armed groups and individuals seeking to impose their own ideology and culture on this multi-ethnic and diverse island. The organization has a branch in Japan, and efforts are being made to spread its ideas. For example, Professor Akihiko Kimijima and Mr. Yutaka Ohata, who are representatives of Japan's branch, gave a lecture on activities in Sri Lanka to citizens in Kochi City in Kochi Prefecture on October 21, 2009.

Some organizations are motivated by religious faith, such as Christianity and Buddhism. Those without a religious affiliationsee nonviolence as a tactic that can have a significant impact in affecting personal, community, and structural changes for peace. Regardless of religious differences, they wish for peace without using violence.

Historical Background of Article 9

What does Article 9 of the Japanese Constitution actually say about nonviolence? There are two provisions.

(1) Aspiring sincerely to an international peace based on justice and order, the Japanese people forever renounce war as a sovereign right of the nation and the threat or use of force as means of settling international disputes.
(2) In order to accomplish the aim of the preceding paragraph, land, sea, and air forces, as well as other war potential, will never be maintained. The right of belligerency of the state will not be recognized.

The source of Article 9 is disputed among scholars. According to Professor Teruhisa Horio, it was former Prime Minister Kijūrō Shidehara who suggested Article 9 to Allied Supreme Commander Douglas MacArthur (Horio, 2008, pp. 14, 15). It should be noted that Shidehara had signed the Pact of Paris of 1928, also called the Kellogg-Briand Pact, when he was the Ministry of Foreign Affairs and had promoted peaceful diplomacy. Article 1 of the pact says, "The High Contracting Parties solemnly declare in the names of their respective peoples that they condemn recourse to war for the solution of international controversies, and renounce it as an instrument of national policy in their relations with one another" (Niihara, 2000). Therefore, it is likely that Shidehara supported the renunciation of war as an instrument of national policy in writing Article 9 of the Japanese Constitution. Professor Hiroyoshi Makino points out that MacArthur and Shidehara agreed on the renunciation of war and of the use of military force at a meeting on January 24, 1946. Why did they make such an unprecedented agreement? The Japanese government wanted to maintain the emperor system by any means because the Japanese people had been taught to believe that the emperor was a living God and that they had fought for the emperor in World War II. However, the maintenance of the emperor system would not be supported at a Far Eastern Commission that consisted of representatives of the eleven countries that would decide policies of the occupation of Japan. Some Allied leaders regarded the emperor as the primary reason for Japan's aggression and thought that he should be tried as a war criminal. Therefore, "[t]hey thought that it would be indispensable for Japan to make clear the abolition of war without recognizing military force and the right of belligerency of the state" (Makino, 2008).

The Constitution, including Article 9, was drafted by the members of Government Section under the Supreme Commander of the Allied Powers General Headquarters (GHQ) who had analyzed the draft Constitution written by some progressive Japanese intellectuals. For example, Yasuzo Suzuki, a constitutional historian and a central figure in the Constitutional Research Association, published the Outline for a Draft Constitution in which the people's sovereignty and equality under law was emphasized. Suzuki studied the democratic draft constitutions that had been proposed by the people's rights movement groups in the 1880sand he adopted some of those items. The people's rights movement (1874 to about 1890) had been much "inspired by the Great Charter and the constitution of France, Belgium, Prussia, the Netherlands, the United States and so forth" and Emori Ueki (1857–1892) had drafted constitution in Kochi which is the birthplace of the democratic movement in Japan (Kumon, 2007). Suzuki submitted his draft to the Japanese government and the GHQ, but the Japanese government ignored it. However, GHQ's Government Section examined it carefully and concluded that the articles it contained were generally very democratic. Article 9 was discussed and endorsed by the Diet of Japan on November 3, 1946. The new Japanese Constitution, especially Article 9, was widely welcomed by Japanese people.

Two other national constitutions contain similar articles. One is Italian constitution and the other is the constitution of Costa Rica.

Article 11 [Repudiation of War] of the Constitution of Italy (adopted on December 22, 1947 and effective as of January 1, 1948) says,

> Italy repudiates war as an instrument offending the liberty of the peoples and as a means for settling international disputes; it agrees to limitations of sovereignty where they are necessary to allow for a legal system of peace and justice between nations, provided the principle of reciprocity is guaranteed; it promotes and encourages international organizations furthering such ends. (Morita, 2004)

Article 12 of Constitution of Costa Rica (adopted and effective in November 1949) says,

> The Army as a permanent institution is abolished. There shall be the necessary police forces for surveillance and the preservation of the public order.
> Military forces may only be organized under a continental agreement or for the national defense; in either case, they shall always be subordinate to the civil power: they may not deliberate or make statements or representations individually or collectively. (Morita, 2004)

Articles 11 and 12 of the Italian and Costa Rican constitutions, respectively, should be disseminated along with Article 9 of the Japanese Constitution in order to abolish war in the world . If such an article could be included in the Israeli constitution and abided by, by the Israeli government, the attacks in Gaza would likely end.

Challenges to State Nonbelligerence in Japan and Other Nations

The ideals expressed in Article 9 are excellent, but they do not reflect the reality in Japan. Though it was stipulated that military force would never be maintained, a strong National Police Reserve of 75,000 men was created by General Douglas MacArthur, Supreme Commander of the Allied Powersin 1950. The People's Republic of China was established in 1947, and "the United States expected Japan to take a more active military role in the struggle against communism during the Cold War" (Hayes, 2001). In 1950, when the Korean War broke out, U.S. military forces stationed in Japan were sent to Korea to fight on the front lines. The National Police Reserve that was created by MacArthur's order for the purpose of maintaining order in Japan became the Japan Self-Defense Forces (JSDF) in 1954, in violation of Article 9 that not only forbade the use of force as a means of settling international disputes but also forbade Japan from maintaining an army, navy, or air force. The JSDF did not become just a police force in Japan because the United States wanted to rearm Japan against communism in the Cold War.apanese laws justifying the JSDF deployment overseas have been enacted as follows. In 1992, the National Diet of Japan passed the United Nations Peacekeeping Operations Cooperation Bill allowing the JSDF to be sent abroad. One of the conditions of the bill was that use of weapons would be limited to the minimum necessary to protect life or JSDF personnel. Japan dispatched the JSDF to Cambodia for the first time in 1992. The JSDF personnel monitored the cease-fire, repaired infrastructure, and supplied food and medical care as part of the United Nations Transitional Authority in Cambodia. Japan kept sending the JSDF personnel abroad, for example, they went to the Persian Gulf in 1991, the Golan Heights in 1996, Afghanistan and the Indian Ocean in 2001, East Timor in 2002, Iraq and Mozambique in 2003, Rwanda in 2004, Indonesia in 2005, and Nepal in 2007, and so forth.

It was 1978 when the Guidelines for U.S.-Japan Defense Cooperation were agreed on, ensuring that Japan and the United States would cooperate in military operations. In 1997, the Guidelines were revised to increase Japan's role in the event of crisis in the Asian region. After the attacks on September 11, 2001, the Japanese Diet passed the Anti-Terrorism Special Measures Law in October, 2001. This law allows the JSDF to engage in cooperation and support activities, such as fuel supply, transportation, and assistance to suffering people such as supplying water. The law further stipulates that these operations can take place on the high seas and in foreign territories where there is no combat. In 2001, Japan provided noncombat support for the UN-sanctioned coalition against the Taliban in Afghanistan. In 2003, the Japanese Diet passed the Law Concerning Special Measures for Humanitarian and Reconstruction Assistance in Iraq, which stipulates that the mission of the JSDF is limited to humanitarian and reconstruction assistance and that it will not become involved in any combat action.

As a result, Japan sent the JSDF personnel to Iraq to provide medical treatment, supply water, and reconstruct public facilities, along with another group of JSDF personnel who were sent to the Persian Gulf to transport vehicles and other equipment in 2004. In 2006, Japan passed a bill to consolidate the JSDF operations, marking the first organizational change to the JSDF since its founding in 1954. The law made it easier to send the JSDF abroad, and it became easier for the JSDF to get involved in wars waged by United States. In 2007, then Prime Minister Shinzo Abe upgraded the Japan Defense Agency, making it a cabinet-level ministry called the Ministry of Defense. In December, 2008 Prime Minister Taro Aso passed a new Anti-Terrorism Special Measures Law providing a continual supply of oil to the U.S. military and others in the Indian Ocean. In light of the increased oil prices and the hardship for many people that has resulted, the free supply of oil in the Indian Ocean was criticized by Japanese tax payers. The supply of oil ended in January 2010 under the new government ruled by Democratic Party. (This is because the new Anti-Terrorism Special Measures Law was effective until January 15th, 2010.)

What are the defense expenditures in Japan? Japan's military expenditure was USD $46.3 billion in 2008 according to the Stockholm International Peace Research Institute (SIPRI) military-expenditure database. What does this mean compared to the rest of the world? Japan was ranked 7th in the world in total military expenditures, behind the United States, China, France, UK, Russia and Germany according to the SIPRI.[2] The Liberal Democratic Party has been trying to change Article 9 in order to resolve the disconnect between the Article 9 and the reality, and to be able to send the JSDF overseas more freely in the future.

However, Japanese citizens still approve of Article 9, according to an April 17–18, 2010 opinion poll on the Japanese Constitution that was taken by Asahi Shinbun (Newspaper). The number of people supporting Article 9 was 67% while 24% of people supported the revision of Article 9 according to Asahi Newspaper dated May 2nd, 2010.

There is a different poll that shows that people support Article 9. eople's opinions were solicited on the streets in 80 cities, towns, and villages and in 27 prefectures from April 19 to May 9, 2009, by NGOs for peace. According to its Web site (Retain Article 9 or Change It?, 2009), 13,420 of 16,568 people (81 percent) answered that they would protect Article 9, while 1,582 (10 percent) answered that they agreed on changing Article 9. Nine percent (1,548) answered that they didn't know.

Responses to Challenges to State Nonbelligerence: Lawsuit against Sending Japan's Self-Defense Forces to Iraq

There has been a huge gap between the ideas of Article 9 and the reality, but citizens have been working hard to change the reality.

On July 26, 2003, following the March 20, 2003 attack on Iraq by the United States and Britain, Japan enacted a special law to allow the JSDF to provide humanitarian support for Iraqi reconstruction. An Air Self-Defense Forces (ASDF) unit composed of C-130 transport aircrafts and about 200 ASDF personnel were sent to Iraq and Kuwait on December 26, 2003. Initially, the unit's transport mission was limited to southern Iraq, but the ASDF flights were subsequently expanded into Baghdad and Arbil in northern Iraq. A ground SDF unit was sent to Samawah in southern Iraq on January 16, 2004, but it was withdrawn on July 17, 2006.

The special law bans the JSDF from using force or the threat of force and requires it to carry out its missions in noncombat zones. Therefore, sending the JSDF to Iraq on December 26, 2003 to support the multinational forces' combat activities was a violation of Article 9. Twelve hundred sixty-two people filed a lawsuit at Nagoya District Court on February 23, 2004, and the number of plaintiffs later increased to 3,268. The plaintiffs demanded that the Japanese government stop dispatching the JSDF to Iraq and the surrounding areas, that it recognize that doing so is unconstitutional, and that it compensate the plaintiffs for causing psychological pain among them. Similar lawsuits were filed in eleven district courts. The plaintiffs lost these cases. However, the Nagoya High Court ruled on April 17, 2008 that the ASDF's mission in Iraq included activities that violated the war-renouncing Constitution. The high court ruling said that Baghdad should be considered a combat zone because of the killings and subversive activities taking place there. The ruling also said that the ASDF's transport mission did not in itself constitute use of force but that, since transportation is so important to combat activities in modern warfare, the ASDF's activities constituted rear logistic support that was indispensable to the multinational forces' combat activities. It concluded that the ASDF's transport mission violated the Special Law's prohibition of the use of force and combat activities in a combat zone, and Section 1 of Article 9 of the Constitution.

Although the government responded that the ruling would not bind its actions because the constitutional issue had not been addressed in the main part of the ruling, the Nagoya High Court's ruling was nonetheless significant because, for the first time in 35 years, the court had dealt fairly with the question of whether the JSDF and its activities are constitutional or not. In fact, the high court turned down the plaintiffs' request that the mission be ended, which means that the state won. Nonetheless, the high court's decision concerning the constitutionality of the ASDF's Iraqi mission concluded the trial because the state, which won the ruling, cannot appeal to the Supreme Court, and the plaintiffs decided not to appeal to the Supreme Court.

Professor Takeshi Kobayashi of Aichi University called the judgment historic because it was the first time that a court had ruled that dispatching the JSDF to Iraq violated Article 9. The Naganuma lawsuit in Hokkaido in 1973 resulted in a decision that the JSDF is unconstitutional. In 1969, the government planned to make a military base for the ASDF in the town of Naganuma , Yubari-gun, Hokkaido. However, citizens, protesting that the JSDFs are unconstitutional, filed a lawsuit against the government. There was also a plan to expand U.S. military base in the town of Sunagawa , Kita Tama-gun, Tokyo. Seven citizens who protested against the plan were prosecuted for entering the base on July 8, 1957. In the 1959 Sunagawa case in Tokyo, it was judged that the U.S.-Japan Security Treaty is unconstitutional. However, these judgments, which were made at the district court level, were rejected by the upper courts. Therefore, the judgment at the Nagoya High Court was indeed historic, as Professor Kobayashi said.

It was reported in the *Japan Times Weekly* on April 20, 2008, that "The [Nagoya] ruling serves as a reminder that when Japan dispatches SDF units overseas, it should be done in strict adherence to the war-renouncing Article 9. It also strengthens the case that the government must disclose detailed information about the ASDF's activities in Iraq so that the Diet and people can scrutinize them." The fact that the government did not disclose detailed information on the JSDF's activities in Iraq implies that they were not acting on behalf of the people of Iraq. After Japan's general election on August 30, 2009, the ruling party was changed from the Liberal Democratic Party to the Democratic Party. It was disclosed that "the ASDF transported a total of 28,000 people in Iraq and 70% of them were armed U.S. soldiers" ("Airlift in Iraq," editorial in *Kochi Shinbun* (Newspaper), October 7, 2009). This means that the ASDF's activities were without a doubt unconstitutional. Mr. Yoshinori Ikezumi, the representative of "Jieitai Iraq Hahei Sashidome Soshono Kai" (the Association for Lawsuit against Dispatching SDF to Iraq), mentioned that the lawsuit was brought by citizens at a grassroots level. The purpose of the association was to halt the sending of the JSDF to Iraq and to get a court judgment that dispatching the JSDF to Iraq was unconstitutional. The number of plaintiffs reached over 3,000; it was a diverse group: There were differences of age, nationality, religion, and political parties, and so on. Ikezumi talked about how he filed the lawsuit at the conference of Peace Studies Association of Japan on November 22, 2008. He told the audience that no journalist wrote a draft of an article that dispatching the JSDF to Iraq is unconstitutional when the judgment was made at Nagoya High Court, and journalists got into a panic when the historic judgment was made. The journalist had to write an article about the judgment which they had not expected at all.

Although there is a gap between Article 9 and reality, it is encouraging that it is possible to use Article 9 of the Japanese Constitution against militarism in Japan.

Article 9 Association: Its Origin and Activities

On June 10, 2004, an Appeal from the Article 9 Association was issued by nine famous people. Hisashi Inoue (1934–2010) was renowned for his theatrical works and novels and the chairman of the Japan PEN Club, the Japanese branch of International PEN, a world association of writers that promotes literature and defends freedom of expression; Shuichi Kato (1919–2008), a medical doctor, was also well-known for his vigorous critical works and his expertise in cultures of the East and the West; Mutsuko Miki (born in 1917), the wife of the late Takeo Miki, former Prime Minister of Japan, is the president of the Asia-Pacific Ladies Friendship Society and active in international exchange programs; writer Makoto Oda (1932–2007) was active in the anti-Vietnam war movement and sought individual compensation for the victims of the Hyogo earthquake; novelist Kenzaburo Oe (born in 1935), winner of the 1994 Nobel Prize in Literature, has freely and imaginatively portrayed people living in nuclear age; Yasuhiro Okudaira (born in 1929) is a leading jurist and an expert of the study of "freedom of expression" and Professor Emeritus at The University of Tokyo; Hisae Sawachi (born in 1930) unearthed tragic experiences of women in times of war in her books and is also known for her essays; philosopher and critic Shunsuke Tsurumi (born in 1922) developed a flexible system of thought that was grounded in everyday life, and started a monthly magazine, "Science of Thought"; Takeshi Umehara (born in 1925) is a philosopher noted for his work with International Research Center for Japanese Studies based on his research on pre-modern history and literature, and Emeritus Professor of Kyoto City University of Arts.

What these nine inaugural members of the association have in common is that they all experienced World War II. Thus, they knew how horrible the war was, and their wish for peace therefore seems much stronger than that of politicians who lack experiences of war. They explain their reasons for founding the association on its Web site.

> This (change of the Constitution)...threatens to convert Japan from a country that strives to resolve conflicts without military force to a nation that prioritizes military action above all else. We cannot allow that conversion to occur (2004).

This statement evidences the determination of the inaugural members that the Constitution not be changed. Their appeal criticizes the use of force against Iraq and emphasizes the importance of resolving conflicts through diplomacy and dialogue. That citizens have a role in creating peace by protecting Article 9 is made clear.

> Thus, in the interest of a peaceful future for Japan and the world, we would like to appeal to each and every citizen to come together for the protection of the Japanese constitution (2004).

Responding to this appeal for peace, Japanese citizens started the movement to protect Article 9. Many branches of the association have been organized since June, 2004; as of April 22, 2010, there are about 7,507 branches all over Japan. Since the number of cities, towns, and villages in Japan was 1782 as of November 29, 2008 (Web site of the Ministry of Internal Affairs and Communications, 2008), this means that there are on average about four branches of Article 9 Association in each city, town, or village, which may be hard for the Establishment to ignore. The National Exchange Conference of Article 9 Association is held every year, and its members exchange their ideas and activities for peace and Article 9. The 3rd National Exchange Conference of Article 9 Association was held in Tokyo on November 24, 2008, and it was reported that not only ordinary people but also mayors and presidents and executives of companies became active in protecting Article 9.

Booklets on Article 9 have been published in various places. For example, a booklet of *Article 9: Door to Happiness* (Kenpoh 9 Jou: Shiawaseno Tobira, 2008) was published by Kochi Shinbunsha in 2008, and the author's article is included in it. Big signboards that read, "Let's Retain Article 9! No More War!" can be seen in various places in Japan and are a good way of raising the awareness of ordinary people. Posters are also used: A unique one was made in Kochi, where the author lives. A big shape of the number 9 was formed to show the many names of the persons who donated money to make the posters.

The website of the Article 9 Association is available in Japanese, English, French, Korean and Chinese. The website contains a list of lecturers who are willing to give lectures on Article 9 so that anyone who wants to organize a lecture can easily find a speaker. Online news and magazine is also available. On ninth of each month, the members go out into the public to collect signatures for protecting Article 9 and inform people of the situation related to Article 9 all over Japan.

Japanese ideas about nonviolence have been influenced by various people in other countries. One of them is Bertha von Suttner (1843–1914), whose influence on Japan is explained next.

Pacifism in Europe: Bertha von Suttner

The idea of solving problems, not violently, but peacefully was a theme in Bertha von Suttner's antiwar novel *Lay Down Your Arms* (1889). How did she express her ideas in the novel, and how did she live her ideals? How did she influence the Japanese?

Bertha von Suttner was the first woman to be awarded the Nobel Peace Prize. It was she who suggested that Alfred Nobel should establish the Nobel Peace Prize. A writer, journalist, and lecturer, in *Lay Down Your Arms,* she realistically described the horror and misery of war and the importance of peace.

On October 30, 1891, Bertha von Suttner founded the Austrian Peace Association whose membership grew to 2000. Alfred Nobel became a member, donating 2000 francs to the group, which made it possible for von Suttner to carry out her work internationally (Hamann, 2005). In 1899, the first Hague Peace Conference was held in The Hague. Bertha von Suttner attended it as a journalist for the newspaper *Die Wel,* which was published by Theodor Herzl, the founder of the modern Zionism movement. She posited that conflicts should be transformed peacefully using a court of arbitration instead of force. In 1901, the Permanent Court of Arbitration was founded in The Hague as a result of the Hague Peace Conference. The main character in *Lay Down Your Arms,* Martha Althaus, whose first husband was killed in war in Solferino in 1859, criticizes war. Her second husband suffered a war injury before he was subsequently killed as a war spy. The book provided a critical perspective on the tendency to glorify war. It is often said that soldiers fight to defend their motherland, but it is described in her novel that they tend to fight for other reasons, such as protecting their monarch's honor and land. The novel became a bestseller. In 1905, when von

Suttner was awarded the Nobel Peace Prize, it had been translated into 16 languages and was in its 37th printing. Bartholomäus von Caneri, the Austrian philosopher, wrote in 1890 that "never has militarism been shown so drastically how much misery it spreads around itself and how beautiful life can be" (Reutter, 2004, p. 21). In 1914, the book was also reviewed in *The Nation*, a weekly magazine published in New York, which wrote that "(the novel) opened the eyes of millions to the horrors of war" (Hamann, 2005).

Bertha von Suttner criticized European countries that were trying to colonize Asian countries, regarding this as a crime. Together with Henri Dunant, the founder of the International Red Cross, she made an appeal to the public for peace for people of Asia. During the Sino-Japanese War (1894–1895), Japan occupied the Liaodong Peninsula in China, but Russia, France, and Germany made Japan return it to China. Suttner was against Japan's invasion of China and Western colonialism. She kept in touch with Asian peacemakers until she passed away protesting war and acting for peace.

In December, 1903 before the Russo-Japanese War (1904–1905) started, Suttner appealed to the governments of various countries in the world to act as mediator between Japan and Russia. When Japan broke off relations with Russia on February 6, 1904, she was disappointed with the European governments which had made no efforts for peace, and she soon sent a telegram as the president of the Austrian Peace Association to U.S. President Theodore Roosevelt asking him to be a mediator in February 1904. However, Japan had already attacked a Russian vessel without a declaration of war on February 9, 1904, and the telegramwas too late. Suttner had also asked the prime minister of Austria-Hungary to be a mediator between Russia and Japan. (Hamann, 2005). However, she was not listened to, not only at home, but also abroad. She did her best trying to stop the Russo-Japanese war through the International Peace Association, through petition campaigns and holding lectures. Suttner met President Roosevelt on September 17, 1904, and he promised that he would end the Russo-Japanese war by mediation. The war ended on September 5, 1905 as a result of President Roosevelt's mediation, and the Portsmouth Treaty was signed. Suttner admired Roosevelt because he recognized the importance of solving conflicts through negotiation.

According to Suttner's diary, she attended a concert held at the Japanese Embassy on April 4, 1911. How was she introduced in Japan? On January 31, 1910, the Japan Peace Association wrote to her to ask her permission to translate *Lay Down Your Arms* into Japanese. The letter suggested that 2,000 copies be printed and kept at the library of the League of Nations. The first part of the novel was translated into Japanese and published in a magazine called *Heiwa* (*Peace*) (edited and published by Setsuzo Toyama) in February and April 1911. Then a magazine called *Taiyo* (*The Sun*), published a translation of Alfred Fried's article "Heroine of Peace Movement" chronicling her life and work. Alfred Fied (1864–1921) was an Austrian and Jewish pacifist, journalist, co-founder of the German peace movement, and winner (with Tobias Asser) of the Nobel Prize for Peace in 1911. The translation project was abandoned for some reason in 1911, but a new project started by different translators. Several people have been translating the novel into Japanese including the author, but it has been difficult to find a publisher because it will be a thick and expensive book.

It is hoped that Bertha von Suttner's ideas for nonviolence and peace will be known more, not only in Japan, but also in the world.

Responding without Violence to Global Conflict

In Japan, the Representatives Alliance for Enacting a New Constitution, the group that aims to change Article 9, held a General Assembly on March 27, 2007 in which they decided to work hard for a Constitutional amendment against the Article 9. At their March 4, 2008 General Assembly, they also decided to make efforts to establish strongholds in local areas to counter grassroots activities of the Article 9 Association. Conservatives had become unhappy about efforts of the Article 9 Association.

Nevertheless, it has been encouraging to know about nonviolent activities for peace in Japan and other countries. For example, a conference was held by the Movement for the Abolition of War and the International Peace Bureau in March 2008 in London, where this author talked about two Japanese peacemakers. The situation in Japan is serious because a law on the procedure of revising the Japanese Constitution was approved at the plenary session of the House of Councilors on May 14, 2007, and the law will be enforced on May 18, 2010. This means that Article 9 will change and that Japan could start using force in the future as a response to international conflict. This is why the Article 9 Association has remained very active for peace. It is hoped that the Japanese movement for peace will be strengthened by more cooperation with various NGOs, as well as the Movement for the Abolition of War and the International Peace Bureau.

It is also encouraging and interesting to see the Department of Peace initiatives around the world. The Peace Alliance is a nonpartisan citizen-action organization established in 2004 in the United States that represents a growing constituency for peace. Its mission is to empower civic activism for a culture of peace. Its current focus is the campaign for a cabinet-level Department of Peace in the United States. It explains that,, "We must create the possibility for applied peacebuilding to identify and resolve conflict before it erupts into violence" (The Peace Alliance, 2009). This demonstrates a desire in the United States to solve conflicts without violence. In Japan, the first National Conference for the Department of Peace was held in Tokyo in 2005, and the importance of Article 9 was emphasized. The third International Conference for the Department of Peace was held in Japan. It confirmed that Japanese peace promoters, such as Yumi Kikuchi, have been active in bringing about a national Department of Peace so that conflicts can be resolved nonviolently, and eventually transformed (Lederach, 2003).

Peace education plays important roles in teaching nonviolent ways to deal with conflicts. What has been done in peace education to teach about resolution of structural conflicts without resorting to war? In Japan, Article 9 has been an important theme that is tackled and exhibited at peace museums. For example, lectures on Article 9 have been given at Grassroots House, a peace museum in Kochi. The members planted various kinds of saplings at a forest in Kochi and named it, "Forest for Constitution" in 1995. The name symbolizes the Japanese Peaceful Constitution, especially Article 9, as well as a clean environment: These have been the most crucial issues: abolition of war and a clean environment. Children also planted saplings and drew a huge picture based on their experience in the Constitution Forest. It became a traveling exhibit and was sent to International Museum of Peace and Solidarity in Samarkand, the Republic of Uzbekistan, and was seen by many people, including children. In response, the painting of Uzbek's children were also sent to Grassroots House, and it was a good exchange of art works between two countries. This is an example of peace education about nonviolent resolution of conflicts and peacebuilding by peace museums.

Lessons Learned from Article 9

What can the field of conflict transformation learn from Article 9? With the philosophical foundation and long history of nonviolence, it is reasonable to expect that national maintenance of nonbelligerence in global conflict would lead to transforming conflicts without violence and the prevention of future wars. In order to abolish war, it is necessary for international organizations, national organizations, including governments and NGOs to learn from Article 9 and make the most use of it in their own way. It is human beings who start war and therefore, it should be possible for them to abolish war using philosophical concepts and agreements they can make, such as Article 9.

The Liberal Democratic Party and New Komei Party have been trying to change the Japanese Constitution, especially Article 9. There was a political change in 2009: a general election was held on August 30, 2009, for all 480 seats of the House of Representatives of Japan, the lower house of the Diet of Japan. In the election, the opposition Democratic Party of Japan (DPJ) defeated the ruling coalition (Liberal Democratic Party and New Komeito Party). The DPJ leader Yukio-Hatoyama became the Prime Minister of Japan on September 16, 2009. What is the DPJ's attitude toward Article 9? Ichiro Ozawa, the Secretary General of the DPJ, insists on sending the Self Defense Forces abroad as a part of multi-national forces, if such a case would be resolved at the United Nations without changing Article 9. This means that he would ignore Article 9 and people should try to be careful about the future of Article 9. Awarding the Article 9 Association the Nobel Peace Prize could play a great role in making abolition of Article 9 difficult because the Nobel Peace Prize is very influential in Japan and throughout the world. If the Article 9 Association were awarded the prize, it would be unfeasible for the Establishment in Japan to change Article 9 and this would promote peace not only in Japan but also in other countries, especially throughout Asia.

Notes

1. The manual emphasizes the importance of transforming conflict not by violence, but by peaceful means. This is significant because force tends to be used instead of negotiation, such as the war on Iraq.
2. Military expenditure in SIPRI Yearbook. (2009). Retrieved on May 13, 2010 from http://www.sipri.org/yearbook/2009/files/SIPRIYB0905.pdf/.

References

Airlift in Iraq (October 7, 2009). *Kochi Shinbun* (Newspaper).
An appeal from the Article Nine Association (2004). Retrieved on November 19, 2009 at http://www.9-jo.jp/en/appeal_en.html.

Article 9 Association Newsletter No. 125. Retrieved on January 13, 2010 from http://www.9-jo.jp/news_list/index.html.
Article 9: Door to happiness (Kenpoh 9 Jou: Shiawaseno tobira) (2008). Kochi Newspaper Publisher.
Dhammapada. *Buddha's path of virtue* (2002). New York: AMS Press Inc.
Fellowship for Reconciliation. Retrieved on January 13, 2010 from http://www.forusa.org.
Fried, A. (1894). Heroine of peace movement translated into Japanese by Minami Koden. Taiyo (The Sun). Volume 18, Number 11, 94–96.
Galtung, J. & Jacobsen, C. G. (2002). Searching for peace—Second edition. London: Pluto Press.
Hamann, B. (2002). *Bertha von Suttner: A life for peace*. New York: Syracuse University Press.
Hayes, L. D. (2001). *Japan and the security of Asia*. Lanham, MD: Lexington Books.
Horio, T. (2008). Was it MacArthur or Shidehara who proposed Article 9? *Kiron 21*, 14–15.
It is better not to change Article 9: 67%. (May 2, 2010). Asahi Shinbun (newspaper).
Kimijima, A. (2009). Peace in East Asia and the Japanese Constitution: A reexamination 60 years after its making. *Ritsumeikan Journal of International Studies 21*(3), 169–179.
Kumon, G. (2007). *Guide to movement for freedom and human rights in Tosa* (Tosano Jiyuu Minken Undo Nyumon). Kochi: *Kochi Shinbunsha*.
Last Unit of the MSDF Leave for Indian Ocean (Saigono Kaiji Hakenbutaiga shuppatsu: Indoyou Kyuyu Katsudo) (November 9, 2009). Tokushima Shinbun.
Lederach, J. P. (2003). The little book of conflict transformation. Intercourse, PA: Good Books.
Major ruling on SDF's Iraq mission (April 20, 2008). Editorial. *The Japan Times*. Retrieved January 13, 2010 at http://search.japantimes.co.jp/cgi-bin/ed20080420a1.html.
Makino, H. (2008). Thought of Article 9. *Kiron 21*, 60–61.
Manifesto Against Conscription and the Military System (2009). Retrieved January 13, 2010 at http://www.themanifesto.info/manifesto.htm.
Mayou, R. (2000). *International Red Cross and Red Crescent Museum*. Geneva: International Red Cross and Red Crescent.
Ministry of Internal Affairs and Communications. Retrieved January 13, 2010 from http://www.soumu.go.jp/gapei/index.html.
Morita, T. (2004). Philosophy of restriction and renunciation of war in world history and the trend of international laws (Sekaishio tsuranuku sensouno seigen, sensouno houkino rinennto kokusaihouno nagare). In A. Furukawa, Y. Hoshino, & K. Watanabe (Eds.), *Article 9 of Constitution in the world (Sekaino Nakano Kenpo Dai9jou)*, 23–83. Tokyo: Koubunken.
Niihara, S. & Yoshioka, Y. (2000). *20 Seikino Sensouto Heiwa* (War and peace in the 20th century). Tokyo: Shinnihon Shuppansha.
Opponents of the revision of the Constitution are more than supporters of the revision after 15 years (April 9, 2008). *Akahata*.
Retain Article 9 or Change it? Retrieved January 13, 2010 from http://qjyot.exblog.jp/.
Reutter, A. U. & Rüffer, A. (2004). *Peace women*. Translated from the German original by Salomé Hangartner. Italy: Rüffer & Rub.
Shigaraki, T. (2006). *Article 9 is Buddha's Wish* (Kenpo 9 jowa Hotokeno Negai). Tokyo: Akashi Publications.
Stop all forms of support to war (November 29, 2009). *Japan Press Weekly*. Retrieved October 28, 2009 from http://www.japan-press.co.jp/2008/2600/military_1.html.

Suttner, B. (1892). *Lay down your arms: The autobiography of Martha von Tilling.* Authorized translation [of *Die Waffen nieder*]. London: Longmans.

Suttner, B. (1892). Lay down your arms: The autobiography of Martha von Tilling in Heiwa (Peace) April. Translated into Japanese by Mitsuko Mishima. (1911), 9–16. The Constitution of Costa Rica (2009). Costa Rica Law. Retrieved on January 13, 2010 from http://www.costaricalaw.com/legalnet/constitutional_law/constitenglish.html.

The Peace Alliance (2009). Retrieved January 13, 2010 from http://www.thepeacealliance.org/.

CHAPTER THREE

Retooling Peace Philosophy: A Critical Look at Israel's Separation Strategy

KRISTOFER J. PETERSEN-OVERTON,
JOHANNES D. SCHMIDT, AND JACQUES HERSH

"The significance of our disengagement plan is the freezing of the peace process... It supplies the formaldehyde necessary so there is no political process with Palestinians. When you freeze the process, you prevent the establishment of a Palestinian state... Effectively, this whole package called a Palestinian state, with all it entails, has been removed indefinitely from our agenda." (as cited in MacKinnon, 2004).

Dov Weisglass, aid to Ariel Sharon

The Israeli–Palestinian conflict is a source of enduring tension in the Middle East. Its resolution would go a long way in creating a semblance of stability in this volatile region. Pitting occupant against occupied, Israel, as the foremost military power, holds the key to such resolution. Therefore the focus of this analysis will be on Israeli strategic thinking and policy making with regard to the Palestinian question.

In response to a 1994 Palestinian suicide attack in Tel Aviv, Israeli Prime Minister Yitzhak Rabin expressed his opinion that Israel "will have to decide on separation [from the Palestinians] as a philosophy" (as cited in Makovsky, 2004, p. 52). There needed to be "a clear border," as he put it (as cited in Cook, 2006, p. 145). Echoing this sentiment during his own tenure as prime minister, Ehud Barak also called for "disengagement" from the Occupied Palestinian Territories (OPT)—and nearly every Israeli leader since then has supported ethnic separation in one form or another (Cook, 2006). Indeed, during the past decade, Israel has gradually moved away from the imposition of direct military control over the lives of the occupied Palestinian population to the implementation of policies inspired by a philosophy of separation. With the completion of the 2005 unilateral disengagement of Israel's presence in the Gaza Strip, Israel has attempted to secure the safety of its citizens by physically separating them from Palestinian population centers and simultaneously increasing the level of military control—albeit from the periphery. This chapter argues that the philosophy of separation is a logical extension of Zionism's exclusionary ideological history and that its implementation in the Gaza Strip has not reduced the level of violence against Israeli civilians. Instead, it has actually exacerbated Israel's security crisis.

While the process of ethnic separation has taken many forms during Israel's short history, we believe that the 2005 unilateral disengagement from the Gaza Strip and the subsequent military containment of that territory represent a new approach: the justification of separation as the basis for establishing peace. For this reason, our chapter focuses primarily on Israel's policies in the Gaza Strip. Though we do reference the ongoing settler movement and Israel's recent construction of the West Bank barrier (WBB) in the familiar context of separation, it is the situation in Gaza that most clearly demonstrates the dramatic shift in Israel's approach. With this in mind, we have divided the chapter into two sections. The first addresses the ideological emergence of the philosophy of separation by linking it with the historic concept of "transfer" in Zionist thought.[1] Tracing the exclusionary elements of Zionism from before 1948, the beginning of the occupation in 1967, and the Greater Israel project up to the construction of the WBB, we argue that the philosophy of separation is simply the most recent incarnation of a long-held Zionist theme—albeit refocused as a potential path to peace. Our analysis reveals that in an effort to lower the intensity of violence against Israeli citizens while retaining control in Gaza, Israel has shifted the nature of its occupation in Gaza from direct military control and partial integration to indirect control and separation—or as Gordon (2008) succinctly writes, a shift "from colonization to separation" (p. 199). Armed with this background, the second section of the chapter reviews the contemporary implementation of Israel's separation philosophy using the 2005 unilateral disengagement from the Gaza Strip. This section addresses the security implications of Israel's extensive military control in Gaza as permitted under the terms of disengagement. Finding no improvement, but rather an exacerbation of Israel's security crisis, we then address the economic and humanitarian consequences of disengagement for the Gazan population—both of which have been crippled by Israel's disengagement plan. Ultimately, we conclude that Israel's use of the philosophy of separation is counterproductive, especially with regard to its stated goal of peace. As implemented in Gaza, the philosophy of separation undermines basic conditions for peace in the long term by predicating Israeli security interests on disproportionate Palestinian suffering.

Before commencing, we need to be clear about what we mean by the philosophy of separation. By this we refer to the belief in the physical separation of Israelis and Palestinians as a means of curbing violence and promoting peace.[2] While the notion of ethnic separation has been a familiar theme throughout Israel's history, we focus here on Israel's specific implementation of this philosophy as a means of attempting to contain the violence in Gaza and of achieving peace. Given the historical context of the Israeli occupation, the wider Arab-Israeli conflict, and the elusive nature of peace in the Middle East, we believe it is prudent to consider the ramifications of any normative peace philosophy hailed as a solution (or even a path toward a solution). We acknowledge that this book has taken a special interest in decidedly positive examples of theory in action, but because Israel has specifically embraced separation as a philosophy of peace, we hope our contribution will widen the perspective of the discussion in general.

"Transfer" in Zionist Thought

The Ideological Roots of Separation

While the implementation of separation policies is a relatively recent phenomenon in Israel's history, the ideological roots of the philosophy enjoy a much longer history, hailing back to the earliest manifestations of Zionism. In 1994, when Yitzhak Rabin spoke of a "philosophy of separation," he was surely aware of the parallels to an older variation of the concept: "transfer" of the Palestinian population. Because the animus for Israel's very creation sprang from Zionism's desire to establish "a publicly and legally secured home in Palestine for the Jewish people" (Morris, 1988, p. 1),[3] it caused early Zionists great consternation to consider that a large number of people were already living in the region they intended to constitute as the fledgling Jewish state.[4] However much the 'land without a people for a people without a land' stoked the nationalist sentiments of post-WWII European Jewry. It was pure fantasy given the demographics of the time—and early Zionists were well aware of the fact. Thus, from the very roots of Zionist thought, beginning with the influential writings of Moses Hess, Judah Alkalai, and Zvi Hirsch Kalischer,[5] and culminating with the publications of Theodor Herzl, Ahad Ha'am, and Menahem Ussishkin, it was acknowledged that for a Jewish state to emerge in Palestine, the resident Palestinian population would have to become a minority or be removed altogether (Gorni, 1987, pp. 26–39).[6] Fundamental to this belief was the perception that Jews and Palestinians could not live together and that in order to preserve the integrity of both communities they should be separated—if not willingly, then by force. Today's emergence of the philosophy of separation is a logical offshoot of this historical assumption of the Zionist ideology, repackaged as a path to peace. This section reviews the concept of "transfer" in Zionist political thought from before 1948, during the expansion of Jewish settlements after 1967, and up to the construction of the WBB. We perceive the philosophy of separation as the latest in a series of Zionist attempts to separate Palestinians from Israelis, albeit retooled and justified as a peace philosophy.

In order to understand the importance of ethnic separation in the mainstream Zionist worldview, it would be prudent to review four central tenets of the ideology.[7] The first principle of pre-1948 Zionism was the desire to establish a "territorial concentration of the Jewish people in Palestine" (Gorni, 1987, p. 2) based on the firm belief that the Jews are a "distinctive entity possessing attributes associated with the modern concept of nation, as well as attributes associated with religion" (Shimoni, 1995, p. 52). It is worth pointing out that prior to WWII and the Holocaust, the bulk of European Jewry was not receptive to the Zionist discourse, instead seeking salvation in emigration to the United States or through assimilation into European societies.[8] The second principle of Zionism then sought to create a Jewish majority in Palestine. Without a majority of Jews, "Zionism would [have forfeited] its meaning" by allowing Jews to exist as a minority population in a land governed by an alien power (Gorni, 1987, p. 2). Such an outcome was unconscionable when placed against the backdrop of Jewish persecution across much of Europe. Indeed, Zionism was at least partly conceived in response to the vulnerability of European Jewry to anti-Semitism prior to and during the twentieth century. For the early

Zionists, the only possible way of securing a prosperous future for the Jews was to build a Jewish state on Jewish terms in the land of Palestine. The third most common principle of Zionism dealt with Jewish labor and the strongly nationalistic imagery of Jews tilling Jewish land; it was also believed that the practice of employing exclusively Jewish labor would aid Jewish economic independence. The fourth principle, driven by fears of cultural assimilation during the Diaspora, sought to promote a rebirth of Hebrew culture, which occurred later on.[9] The first of these tenets is entirely dependent upon separation through the "transfer" of much of the Arab population; likewise, the third and fourth are more feasible with a Jewish majority.

The establishment of a Jewish majority in Palestine necessitated a single outcome: the Arab majority needed to become a minority—preferably as small a minority as possible.[10] In this way, the notion of "transfer" was married to Zionist thought almost from its inception. Nearly all echelons of the Zionist political sphere shared the desire that Palestinians should somehow be "spirited" across the border—that is, physically separated from the Jews.[11] The idea was by no means relegated to fringe politics; any debate on the matter was reserved for the practicalities of implementation rather than for the morality of the proposition itself. For example, many among the Zionist leadership, including David Ben-Gurion, cited the post-WWI Greco-Turkish population exchange as a positive paradigm for their own vision of a future Jewish state,[12] and later, the more violent Hindu-Muslim population exchange between India and Pakistan was viewed favorably (Schechtman, 1949).[13] From Zionism's earliest days in the late nineteenth century through Israel's 1948 War of Independence, Zionist writers, intellectuals, and political figureheads, though frequently at odds on many other elements of the ideology, spoke with one voice on the question of separating the Palestinians from the Jews. Israel Zangwill, a prominent author and an especially outspoken early Zionist thinker, once stated "it is utter foolishness to allow [Palestine] to be the country of two peoples. This can only cause trouble. The Jews will suffer and so will their neighbors" (as cited in Gorni, 1987, p. 271).[14] The persistence of these beliefs has contributed greatly to the emergence of Israel's contemporary philosophy of separation.

It should be noted that it is not entirely clear how the "transfer" ideology translated into policy during the events of 1948 and the debate over incidental or intentional Palestinian expulsion continues.[15] The classic Zionist narrative, as articulated at the time by Chaim Weizmann, argued that the events of 1948 resulted in a "miraculous clearing of the land," apparently orchestrated by the Palestinian leadership without Jewish pressure (Chaim Weizmann as cited in Masalha, 1992, p. 175). Such a perspective absolves Israel of responsibility and "leave[s] intact [Israel's] untarnished image as the haven of a much persecuted people, a body politic more just, moral and deserving of the West's sympathy and help than the surrounding sea of reactionary, semi-feudal, dictatorial Arab societies" (Morris, 1988, p. 1). Likewise, the Palestinian narrative traditionally attributes all blame for the refugee crisis squarely to Israel. Planned or not, most contemporary Zionist thinkers and historians agree that Israel benefited greatly from the sudden absence of Palestinian Arabs in 1948; indeed, the almost total realization of Zionism's demographic goals ensured Israel's very existence.

Yet even after the flight and removal of 750,000 Palestinians in 1948, Israel's demographic problems were not entirely solved, and numerous measures were hastily undertaken to ensure Israeli hegemony. The idea was to discourage United Nations insistence on a return to the 1947 partition borders by creating fait accompli "facts on the ground." This tactic buttressed the concept of "transfer" by seeking to grant a degree of permanence and legitimacy to the immediate postwar situation. Following the Palestinian exodus, Ezra Danin, a member of the Yishuv's[16] Committee for Abandoned Arab Property, wrote, "if we do not seek to encourage the return of the Arabs...then they must be confronted with *fait accomplis*" (as cited in Morris, 1988, p. 135). Such plans, according to Danin, included the destruction of Arab houses, the expedient resettling of Jews on the evacuated land, and the expropriation of Arab property (Morris, 1988). Danin later formed a self-appointed Transfer Committee with Yosef Weitz, the director of the Jewish National Fund's Land Department. Together they issued a short memorandum, intended for Ben-Gurion's approval, entitled "Retroactive Transfer" (Masalha, 1992; Morris, 1986). The scheme acknowledged that a postwar "Israel must be inhabited largely by Jews, so that there will be in it very few non-Jews" and that "the uprooting of the Arabs should be seen as the solution to the Arab question" (Morris, 2004, p. 313).

Although the temporary Transfer Committee was not permitted to operate officially as a branch of government, Ben-Gurion approved the plan (Morris, 1986; Morris, 2004). The Yishuv proceeded to carry out systematic village destruction followed by prompt Jewish settlement—a strategy complimented by an intense propaganda campaign against Palestinian hopes of return.[17] Jewish forces destroyed hundreds of Palestinian villages between 1948 and 1949, and the Yishuv actively encouraged Jewish settlement, in most cases literally on top of

Palestinian ruins. Such tactics proved extremely useful in discouraging Palestinian hopes of return, but because the retroactive "transfer" policies began in June 1948 (after the majority of Palestinian refugees had already fled or been expelled), the politically opportunistic motives were clear. Despite the unsure status of the refugees and notwithstanding the rights of Israeli Arabs, Israel began to classify much Arab land as "absentee"—a condition under which the Israeli government was able to seize property even if the owner had merely left town for a single day on or after November 29, 1947. This practice (which continued during peacetime until 1950) served to provide housing for the massive influx of Jewish immigrants from Europe that Israel experienced during the late 1940s and further discouraged Palestinian hopes for return by removing thousands more Palestinians from their land (Pappé, 2006). When village destruction eventually became politically untenable, the Yishuv turned to purchasing land from Arab tenants. Despite concern that some of the money paid to Arab farmers might be used to finance the Arab war effort, Moshe Shertok (later Sharrett), a prominent member of the Yishuv and second prime minister of Israel concluded that "[t]he reasons for buying [Arab land] outweigh [the reasons against]" (as cited in Morris, 1986, p. 543).[18] This perspective underscores the importance placed on removing the native Palestinian population, even considering the possible security risks that entailed. For Israel to exist, the Palestinian population could not have been allowed to remain in situ, and as scores of historical documentation has since revealed, the Yishuv encouraged the flight or directly forced 750,000 Palestinians (more than 80 percent of the population at the time) from their homeland in 1948 and destroyed 531 Palestinian villages.[19] The only retrospective regret of this outcome was that Jewish forces had not managed to remove all of the Palestinian population.[20]

From Colonization to Separation

During the Six-Day War of 1967, Israel quickly seized control of Gaza and the West Bank (including East Jerusalem) and expelled an additional 100,000 to 260,000 Palestinians (Chomsky, 1999; Morris, 1999; Kimmerling, 2003; Mearsheimer & Walt, 2007). With the beginning of the occupation and the colonial-settler movement, demography reemerged at the fore of Israeli politics virtually overnight (Masalha, 2000).[21] For Israel to have simply absorbed the newly occupied Palestinian population as citizens was out of the question, as it would have diminished Israel's Jewish majority. Many were concerned about Yasser Arafat's ill-conceived boast of a "biological time bomb" and feared the high Palestinian birthrate as a threat to Israel's Jewish nature. The preoccupation with demography underscores Zionism's desire to separate Jews from Palestinians and, as Masalha (2000) has observed, simply "reinforc[es] the notion that an integralist Jewish state was and remains Zionism's aim" (p. 200). Thus, when Israel summarily declared the 1949 armistice borders to be invalid and assumed control of the territories, Israeli citizenship was denied to West Bank and Gaza residents (Smith, 2004). Within months of the Six-Day War, Israeli citizens began to settle in the West Bank, Gaza and even the captured Golan Heights "to 'create facts' to establish a Jewish presence that would become inalienable, thereby negating future calls for a compromise" (Smith, 2004, p. 295). This pattern of settlement has been ongoing ever since, a project linked with the uncertain awareness that Israel may one day be obliged to relinquish control over the land it conquered in 1967. However, the sheer longevity of the occupation has secured a significant foothold for many of the settlements, rendering an Israeli withdrawal all the more difficult and severely undermining Palestinian hope of regaining lost territory.[22] The colonial-settler vision of a Greater Israel is especially important to consider when tracing the historical emergence of the philosophy of separation. At a minimum, it should be clear that "the vision of 'greater Israel' as Zionism's ultimate objective did not end with the 1948 war" (Morris, 1993, p. 11).

Since 1967, the Jewish settlements in Gaza and the West Bank have cut to the very heart of Zionist thought; land expropriation, colonization, and the imposition of strict military law in the OPT paved the way for Israel's adoption of the contemporary philosophy of separation. Despite the settlers' comparatively small numbers, they possess immense political clout and serve as civilian proxies of Israel's occupation; as *The Economist* has reported, "[Jewish] settlers have subverted government decisions and co-opted local army commanders over the past 40 years, contriving to align the state's security interests with their own plan to populate the occupied territories" ("A Survey of Israel," 2008).[23] In direct contravention of international law, which forbids the settlement of occupied territory, the Israeli Interior Ministry officially recognizes and supports the settlements, granting settlers numerous incentives, including military protection, lucrative tax breaks, and housing subsidies.[24] Furthermore, to exercise control in the OPT, Israel has imposed separate legal regimes, which are applied according to ethnic and religious background. Because Palestinians in the OPT (excluding East Jerusalem) are ineligible for Israeli citizenship and are barred from marrying Israeli citizens, Israel has created a veritable separation cum discrimination regime replete with "Israeli-only" bypass roads and other segregated public utilities.[25] According to the Israeli human rights organization B'Tselem (n.d.):

> Israel forbids Palestinians to enter and use these lands [occupied by settlers], and uses the settlements to justify numerous violations of Palestinian rights, such as the right to housing, to gain a living, and freedom of movement... The great effort Israel has expended in the settlement enterprise—financially, legally, and bureaucratically—has turned the settlements into civilian enclaves within an area under military rule and has given the settlers a preferred status. To perpetuate this unlawful situation, Israel has continuously violated the Palestinians' human rights. ("Land Expropriation and Settlements")

Such a categorical distinction between the occupied Palestinian population and Israeli settlers has led some to draw comparisons with South African apartheid, a parallel that has become increasingly justified as the Palestinian population in Israel and the OPT edge closer to exceeding Israel's Jewish population.[26] Meanwhile, the Israeli government has vowed never to relinquish the largest of its settlement blocs including Ma'ale Adumim, Ariel and Gush Etzion—much of which has been built on private Palestinian land seized through tendentious or outright manipulative use of the law (Erlanger, 2007; "Legitimization of Land Theft," 2007; Peace Now, 2006). For example, the Israeli government justifies the demolition of Palestinian homes as punishment for building without a permit, yet "Israeli officials enforce the rules in a discriminatory manner, strictly denying construction permits for Palestinian homes while allowing the construction of Israeli settlements to proceed" (World Refugee Survey, 2003, p. 159). In this vein, Gordon (2008) points out that Israel has frequently gone to great lengths to give its actions the appearance of legality, resorting to the use of Ottoman and British Mandatory laws as well as obscure regulations from the Jordanian and Egyptian legal regimes to confiscate Palestinian land. Through land expropriation, colonization, and the imposition of discriminatory laws, Israel's embrace of the Greater Israel project has served to normalize the ethnic hierarchy between Israelis and Palestinians and to clearly separate the two.

In 1987, the ephemeral nature of this situation became clear as tensions boiled over and Israel witnessed the angry emergence of a

Palestinian generation born and raised under Israeli dominance. The violence of the first intifada ended with the initiation of a formal peace process—yet even then, Israel's settlements continued to expand. Upon leaving office in 1992, Yitzhak Shamir explained that his purpose "was to drag out the talks on Palestinian self-rule for 10 years while attempting to settle hundreds of thousands of Jews in the occupied territories" (as cited in Hoffman, 1992). In this way, the peace process "gave the appearance of accommodation while working to ensure Israeli retention of the territories" (Smith, 2004, p. 419). The second (al-Aqsa) intifada was much the same, though it was far bloodier. The economic and humanitarian conditions in the occupied territories had declined sharply and the uprising itself was directed not only at Israel but also at the corrupt Palestinian leadership. Nevertheless, Ariel Sharon was ideologically sympathetic to the Greater Israel vision; under his watch, the settlements rapidly expanded in defiance of international and even American disapproval (Goldberg, 2001).[27] This kind of expansion continued during the construction of the WBB and under the post-disengagement containment of Ehud Olmert. Moreover, despite the much-touted American demands for a total settlement freeze, Benjamin Netanyahu's government has so far not agreed to any meaningful halt to settlement activity and has defiantly approved the construction of hundreds more units (McCarthy, 2009).[28] At a minimum, it can be said that Israel's incessant policy of establishing "facts on the ground" has been exceedingly effective at discouraging the return of Palestinian refugees and continuing the process of depopulating Palestinian territory—in effect, the forced separation of Palestinians from Israelis.

A Codified Philosophy

Neve Gordon (2008) has convincingly argued that the prosecution of Israel's occupation gradually changed course during the first intifada from a straightforward, colonial-style exploitative relationship (what he calls the colonization principle) to a more apathetic system of control in which the occupying power loses nearly all consideration for the lives and welfare of the occupied population and focuses solely on exploitation (what he calls the separation principle). Whereas Israel formerly viewed the fate of the occupied population as tied to its own and took measures to improve the Palestinian economy, after the first intifada and especially after the Oslo period, with the creation of the Palestinian Authority, it no longer took any interest in their destiny. Thus, if the colonization principle "reflect[ed] the logic of the occupation," then the separation principle "offer[ed] a solution to the occupation," at least in theory (Gordon, 2008, p. 200). This belief is clearly enshrined in the various Oslo agreements signed over the years, which succeeded in transferring responsibility for the occupied population's welfare to newly formed Palestinian institutions while retaining control over the territory and continuing to colonize the West Bank. Increasingly, the methods of fervid settlement and land expropriation directed themselves toward isolation and intentional separation from the occupied population so as to limit virtually all contact with the occupied Palestinian population. Israel's entire perception and prosecution of the occupation shifted to the philosophy of separation—the idea Israel should not only separate itself from the occupied population for reasons of security, but for the noble cause of peace in the face of unmitigated terror.

This new way of conceptualizing Israel's occupation led to significant changes in its application of separation, which reached new heights in the aftermath of the first and second (al-Aqsa) intifada. This shift paved the way for the construction of barriers around both Gaza and, more recently, the West Bank.[29] As we have already discussed, Yitzhak Rabin declared the need for a "philosophy of separation" and presided over the construction of the Gaza barrier before his assassination in 1995. Similarly, Ariel Sharon pushed ahead with the construction of the West WBB in the midst of the second (al-Aqsa) intifada. Between the two barriers, however, there is a significant difference: the WBB is built on the Palestinian side of the Green Line and effectively annexes large swathes of Palestinian land in its attempt to include as many Jewish settlements as possible on the Israeli side of the barrier.[30] Widely viewed as a "land-grab," the International Court of Justice (ICJ) unanimously condemned the border in a 2004 advisory opinion demanding that Israel immediately cease construction and dismantle the sections of the barrier that had already been completed (ICJ, 2004). The proportionality of the WBB's justification to Palestinian human rights was found to heavily favor Israel at the peril of Palestinian self-determination, economic growth, and hopes for future peace. Moreover, the final advisory opinion noted that the route of the barrier, with all its topographical peculiarities, "gives expression in *loco* to the illegal measures taken by Israel with regard to Jerusalem and the settlements, as deplored by the Security Council" (ICJ, 2004, par. 122). Security arguments notwithstanding, the barrier effectively represents the physical reinforcement of Israel's illegal annexation of East Jerusalem and an additional 10 percent of the West Bank that now lies on the western, Israeli side of the WBB

(Usher, 2005). The approximately 49,000 Palestinians on this land, caught between the WBB and the Green Line (the so-called 'seam-line'), have either been forcibly removed or have been granted only temporary permission to remain on the land. Israel has not expressed any intention to assimilate these people into the Israeli population and it would seem that "through settlement expansion, restrictions on entry into Israel, and isolation from PA services, the likelihood is that these enclaves will wither away" (Usher, 2005, p. 35). Expressing his displeasure with the situation at the time, U.S. President George W. Bush commented that "I think the [WBB] is a problem, and I discussed this with Ariel Sharon. It is very difficult to develop confidence between the Palestinians and Israel with a wall snaking through the West Bank" (White House, 2003). However, Bush did not press the issue further and acquiesced to Sharon's determination to go ahead with the barrier's construction. Under the new leadership of Barack Obama's administration, the United States has taken a more rhetorically assertive approach toward the settlements but has so far declined to take a position on the WBB.[31] Meanwhile, the settlements continued to expand in defiance of international law, Israel's obligations under the U.S.-sponsored Roadmap to Peace, and the Obama Administration's protestations.[32]

Some Preliminary Observations

As the historical background evinces, there was an early understanding within Zionism that the Palestinians needed to be physically separated from Jews, and this understanding has been applied repeatedly throughout Israeli history. Indeed, just as "transfer" was widely hailed as a solution to the "Arab question" and led to the expulsion of 750,000 Palestinians in 1948 Jewish colonization was used to create "facts on the ground" after 1967 and to further depopulate vast swathes of Palestinian land. Today, after the first and second (al-Aqsa) intifada, demographic and security concerns have led Israeli policymakers to erect physical barriers separating Palestinians from Israelis, isolating and depopulating the land still further. Yet, while both the WBB and the disengagement plan were unilateral decisions on Israel's behalf, and while the WBB physically embodies the concept of separation in a very incisive way, it was not carried out under the pretence of peace; rather, the WBB was justified merely as temporary method of protecting the security of Israeli citizens from Palestinian attacks, both in the major West Bank settlements and in Israel proper. As the ICJ ruled, however, the path of the barrier clearly takes demographic issues into consideration to the extent that it surrounds entire Palestinian villages and separates Palestinian population centers from one another.[33] A specific version of this tactic has been directed today at the Gaza Strip, albeit repackaged as a philosophy of peace. It is this application of separation that we have identified specifically as the philosophy of separation, the application of which we explore in the next section.

The Philosophy of Separation Imposed

Israel's Disengagement from the Gaza Strip

In April 2004, apparently frustrated by what he termed the lack of a "partner of the other side with whom to conduct genuine dialog," Israeli Prime Minister Ariel Sharon presented the Knesset with a highly contentious plan to disengage Israel's permanent presence from the Gaza Strip (Israel Ministry of Foreign Affairs, 2005, p. 36). In implementing the plan, Sharon hoped to bring about a situation in which "no permanent Israeli civilian or military presence" would remain in the evacuated areas and consequently there would "be no basis for the claim that the Gaza Strip is occupied territory" (Sharon, 2004). Yet, because Israel had never officially recognized its status as occupant in the Gaza Strip,[34] this phrasing was removed from the final version, leaving the definitive draft stating: "completion of the plan will serve to dispel the claims regarding Israel's responsibility for the Palestinians in the Gaza Strip" (Office of the Prime Minister, 2004, add. A1). Insofar as Israel's historic policies of separation are concerned, the plan was significant in that it was depicted as a bold, unilateral move toward peace with the Palestinians and was duly framed in the context of Israel's security. Separation from the Palestinians via disengagement, according to Israeli officials, would "[ensure] the future of Israel"; it was "good for Israel's security" (Israeli Ministry of Foreign Affairs, 2004) and constituted "the threshold of a new era" (Silvan Shalom, as cited in Israel Ministry of Foreign affairs, 2005, p. 18). Expressed most explicitly, Ariel Sharon stated that "[t]he purpose of the Disengagement Plan is to reduce terror as much as possible, and grant Israeli citizens the maximum level of security... [It] will help reduce friction between [Israel] and the Palestinians" (as cited in Israel Ministry of Foreign affairs, 2005, p. 25).

After much debate, the Knesset eventually approved the disengagement plan, and in August 2005, eviction notices were served to the 9,000 Jewish settlers in Gaza (Wilson, 2005). The Israel Defense Forces (IDF) oversaw the settlers' dramatic evacuation over the next few days, and after a small ceremony on September 12, 2005, the last remaining Israeli soldiers exited Gaza. Later that day, Major-General Dan Harel signed a declaration nullifying the 1967 decree that had established Israeli military rule in the territory ("Israel Completes Gaza Withdrawal," 2005). Because of Sharon's focus on jump-starting the moribund peace process, it would be prudent to analyze the consequences of Israel's disengagement from the Gaza Strip in terms of its immediate security implications. According to Sharon, "only security will lead to peace—and in that sequence" (as cited in Israel Ministry of Foreign affairs, 2005, p. 18). Thus, with the requisite security provided by Israel's disengagement, unilateral action was "the only way [of attaining] the vision of two states living side-by-side in peace and tranquility" (as cited in Israel Ministry of Foreign affairs, 2005, p. 15). Indeed, Israel's implementation of the disengagement plan was a watershed moment in the history of the occupation. While Israel has implemented other policies in line with ethnic separation, the disengagement plan is the first instance of such policies being explicitly justified on the basis of establishing peace. We have called this concept the philosophy of separation and in embracing this outlook, Israel has attempted to achieve peace by military containment and by imposing draconian restrictions over Gaza's inhabitants.

The first part of this section offers a critical analysis of disengagement according to its expressed purpose: to ensure Israel's security and move toward achieving peace with the Palestinians. Developing our argument that Israel's philosophy of separation via disengagement has hindered prospects for peace, we also look at the economic and humanitarian consequences of disengagement—which constitute further means of exclusion and control. In both respects the results contradict Israel's purported goal of peace. Moreover, while disengagement has not diminished Israel's military dominance in Gaza, Israel's general security situation has actually worsened, roughly commensurate with the plummeting humanitarian conditions in Gaza. As a manifestation of the philosophy of separation, Israel's disengagement and the ongoing military containment of Gaza have been characterized by harsh restrictions that have failed to achieve the goals for which they were ostensibly imposed and have instead fostered the emergence of an abject and hostile population in Gaza. In short, the security benefits for Israel under the philosophy of separation have been negligible or counterproductive at the cost of wreaking humanitarian chaos in Gaza. Ultimately, acknowledging Israel's historical record of exclusion as outlined in the previous section, we believe the disengagement and subsequent isolation of Gaza under the philosophy of separation represents the latest incarnation of Zionism's long-standing process of isolation and ethnic separation.

Military Control

Under the philosophy of separation, Israel has attempted to remove itself physically from the Gaza Strip while ensuring peripheral military dominance. The text of the disengagement plan asserts that "Israel reserves its fundamental right to self-defense, both preventive and reactive," that "Israel will guard and monitor the external land perimeter of the Gaza Strip, will continue to maintain exclusive authority in Gaza air space, and will continue to exercise security activity in the sea off the coast of the Gaza Strip" (Office of the Prime Minister, 2004, add. A3). In this way, Israeli ships fire on fisherman sailing too far from Gaza's coastline, Israeli aircraft patrol Gaza's airspace, and the IDF has bulldozed a 500-meter buffer zone along the heavily fortified border. Despite Israel's retention of military control in the postdisengagement period, however, there is no evidence to suggest that a more peaceful situation has resulted. Instead, it seems that Israeli civilians living near the Gaza Strip are now significantly more at risk of Palestinian attacks than before disengagement, while since disengagement, Palestinians have endured the bloodiest Israeli attacks in the history of the conflict. The alleged security benefits of disengagement for the Israelis are negligible at best—not to mention the terrible consequences for Gaza's civilian population—and this raises serious questions regarding the credibility of Israel's philosophy of separation.

Israel's current military dominance in Gaza relies primarily on maximizing peripheral control; this includes the continuation of air assaults and occasional military incursions into Gazan territory. With regard to air control, the Gazan skies are teeming with exclusively Israeli combat and intelligence-gathering aircraft, as permitted under the terms of the Oslo agreements and the disengagement plan.[35] As Major General Amos Yadlin has conceded, "Our vision of air control zeroes in on the notion of control. We're looking at how you control a city or a territory from the air when it's no longer legitimate to hold or occupy that territory on the ground" (as cited in Scobbie, 2006, p. 18). Indeed, Israel has proven itself quite capable of launching periodic large-scale military operations in Gaza, and such attacks have intensified since disengagement. In response to the cross-border abduction of an Israeli soldier by Palestinian militants in June 2006, Israel launched Operation Summer

Rains, reoccupying significant portions of Gazan territory and bombarding the region with aerial assaults (Fisher & Erlanger, 2006). In late December 2008, Israel pushed the carnage of the conflict to entirely new levels with Operation Cast Lead, a 22-day air assault and ground invasion, which together resulted in the deaths of between 1,200–1,400 Palestinians—the bloodiest Israeli attack in the history of Israel's occupation. While Israel's postdisengagement attacks have not always caused such extreme destruction, they have become a more frequent occurrence since withdrawal. According to the Palestinian human rights organization Al-Haq "both air and artillery shelling increased throughout the year after the withdrawal" (Al-Haq, 2006). During these attacks, international human rights organizations reported daily shellings, ground incursions, and air operations in densely populated residential areas. In Operation Cast Lead, Israel resorted to using weapons never previously wielded against the Gazan population, including white phosphorus and mortar shells.[36] The aerial use of white phosphorus against densely residential neighborhoods was especially criticized by human rights organizations, the "indiscriminate or disproportionate" use of which, alleges Human Rights Watch, "indicates the commission of war crimes" (Human Rights Watch, 2009, p. 65). In addition to its ability to launch overwhelming military power in Gaza, Israel has also used its control of the territory's airspace for the purpose of harassment; the practice of intentionally causing powerful sonic booms by flying low-altitude sorties over Gazan neighborhoods continued periodically for one year after disengagement. According to erstwhile Israeli Prime Minister Ehud Olmert, "thousands of residents in southern Israel live in fear and discomfort, so I gave instructions that nobody will sleep at night in the meantime in Gaza" (B'Tselem, n.d., "Sonic Booms in the Skies Over Gaza").

In addition to such dramatically expressed forms of control and containment, Israel has also continued with its controversial policy of targeted killing. Sustained by legal approval in Israeli courts, the policy has been used against suspected Palestinian militants, and many bystanders have been killed in the process.[37] The Israeli branch of Physicians for Human Rights has described these acts as "the deliberate and conscious killing of civilians" (Physicians for Human Rights, 2006, p. 12.) Moreover, Israel's containment of Gaza has involved establishing a virtual "death zone" on the Gazan side of the border—an area of approximately 500 meters inside the Strip's perimeter cleared by Israeli bulldozers. Since disengagement, over a dozen unarmed Palestinians have been killed in the vicinity of this area, none of whom had been participating in hostilities at the time. Consequently, according to B'Tselem, they were victims of "'indiscriminate firing,' which is liable to constitute a war crime" (B'Tselem, n.d., "Hostilities in the Gaza Strip..."). On Gaza's Mediterranean coastline, Israeli control is just as aggressive and is in some ways more restrictive; Palestinian fisherman must receive permission from Israel to use the sea, and if permission is granted, they are limited to a distance of only three nautical miles. Israeli sea vessels patrol the waters and occasionally open fire on Palestinian fisherman to enforce the coastal restrictions. Israel's absolute military control in Gaza is aimed at one purpose, and that is the protection of Israeli civilians according to the philosophy of separation. Yet, despite the draconian restrictions and notwithstanding the devastating offensives that have been portrayed as justified retaliations for Palestinian attacks, Israel has been unable to stymie the most obvious threat emanating from the Gaza Strip: rocket fire.

Palestinian militants have fired rockets into Israel since 2001, and activity that has described by an Israeli research center as a "response to Israel's military superiority" (Intelligence and Terrorism Information Center, 2007, p. 4). Launched indiscriminately over the border, approximately 45 percent of these rockets land in the vicinity of the Israeli town of Sderot, causing psychological trauma and occasional casualties.[38] The frequency of such attacks increased throughout the duration of the second (al-Aqsa) intifada, but until 2006, Palestinian groups lacked the capacity to launch more than fifty rockets a month. Since the implementation of disengagement plan, however, there has been a 500 percent increase in rocket attacks from the Gaza Strip (Israel Ministry of Foreign Affairs, 2006; Gold, 2008). Moreover, there is evidence that militant groups have gained greater access to high-tech weaponry for use against Israel. In January 2008, a Katyusha rocket launched from Gaza struck the northern edge of the Israeli city of Ashkelon, demonstrating a much greater ability on behalf of Palestinian militants to strike Israeli population centers (Katz, Toameh, & Keinon, 2008; McCarthy, 2008). The increase in the rockets' range and capacity for destruction has only emerged since Israel's disengagement, and although we do not infer a direct correlation, this information certainly suggests that Israel's military containment of Gaza under the philosophy of separation is contradictory. As one Israeli official put it, "Ashkelon has turned into a theater of terror [and] there are indications that Beersheba will be at risk of rocket strikes" (as cited in Keinon & Katz, 2008). With respect to its military policies, the disengagement plan was preoccupied with control—containing the Gazan threat was meant to secure peace for

Israel and thereby advance the overall cause of peace. From a security standpoint, this has failed abysmally, but we should also consider the dire economic consequences that have resulted from the philosophy of separation.

Economic Control

The philosophy of separation in Gaza has been characterized not only by physical separation and isolation but also by economic devastation brought on by the imposition of severe restrictions on the flow of goods and people—most notably Israel's so-called closure policies. According to Harvard economist Sara Roy (1987), "[t]he lack of economic development inside the Gaza Strip has been a result of specific Israeli policies which have aimed to restrict and have, in effect, undermined the ability of the Gazan economy to create the necessary infrastructure required for sustained economic growth" (p. 83). Presciently, this assessment was published in 1987—prior to the two Palestinian uprisings, long before the grim economic deterioration of the post-Oslo period and the ongoing blockade. Since the implementation of the disengagement plan and the subsequent unabated use of closure policies, Gaza has plummeted to depths of poverty and despair that were unthinkable when Roy conducted her landmark study. The World Bank has described the Gazan economic crisis as "among the worst in modern history" (World Bank, 2004, p. i; Roy, 2006) and life there is now described as "intolerable, appalling and tragic" (as cited in Reuters, 2006). While Gaza's economic deterioration should not have been an unavoidable consequence of disengagement, the restrictive measures imposed since that time are an extension of Israel's policy of containment in Gaza, that is, the philosophy of separation.

As Israel was preparing to evacuate forces from the Gaza Strip in 2005, the World Bank issued a report predicting that the postdisengagement economic benefits for Gaza would be "very limited" without a change in Israel's control over border regimes. The mild adjustments derived from increased freedom of movement within Gaza and the return of land formerly occupied by Israeli settlers, the Bank reported, "would not deliver significant economic benefits" to the Palestinians (World Bank, 2004, pp. 4–5). In comparison, the disengagement plan itself promised a "better security, political, economic and demographic situation" in declaring Israel's support for "the improvement of the economy and welfare of the Palestinian residents" (Office of the Prime Minister, 2004, add. A1). Paradoxically, the plan also states "the economic arrangements currently in operation between the State of Israel and the Palestinians shall remain in force" (Office of the Prime Minister, 2004, add. A1). These arrangements include "the entry and exit of goods," "the monetary regime," "tax and customs envelope arrangements," and "the entry of workers into Israel" (Office of the Prime Minister, 2004, add. B10). Indeed, the only alteration of policy enshrined in the plan was the gradual cessation of employment for Gazan workers inside Israel. There is nothing at all to indicate a serious interest in pursuing Gazan economic recovery on Israel's behalf.[39] To any objective viewer, it would seem that Israel had lost all interest in the lives and welfare of the people it had so long subjugated; separation was to be not only physical, but economic as well.

While Israel did little to boost economic recovery, it should be noted that serious *international* efforts were undertaken to ensure Gaza's prosperity during the immediate postdisengagement period. The World Bank, leading a team of international economists, met with Palestinian and Israeli officials in 2004 to discuss the potential "modernization" of military checkpoints to better accommodate trade activity. U.S. Secretary of State Condoleezza Rice appointed a Middle East Quartet Special Envoy for Gaza Disengagement and, to help him initiate Palestinian economic growth, world leaders pledged an annual $3 billion budget at the 2005 G-8 summit in Scotland. International businesses began to take interest in Gaza's market potential—especially investment in land recently evacuated by Israeli settlers. Any possibility of economic recovery on Gaza's behalf, according to the World Bank, was ultimately contingent upon two crucial factors: (1) the easing of Israeli closure policies by implementing technologically advanced border trade strategies and (2) unobstructed access to international markets (World Bank, 2004). Neither of these factors was discussed in the disengagement plan, and neither was implemented; rather, there is evidence to suggest that Israel actively worked against these factors.

Israel has maintained strict control over all border regimes in place prior to the disengagement.[40] The Rafah crossing on the Gazan/Egyptian border remains sealed, a U.S.-backed plan to ease restrictions on movement—especially between Gaza and the West Bank—went unimplemented, and Israel instead constructed a second barrier around Gaza (McGirk, 2005). In March 2006, adding to the depth of the economic crisis, Israel began to withhold tax revenues from the Palestinian Authority in protest of the recently elected Hamas government and halted much of the bilateral aid, grants, and loans provided by the IMF, World Bank, and other international institutions.[41] Moreover, numerous economic development projects have withered on the vine. Israeli bulldozers and Palestinian looters destroyed the remaining sections of the Erez Industrial Estate, which had previously earmarked for renovation, and Israel's prolonged closure policies caused the much-touted Palestinian greenhouse project to end in failure.[42] In June 2005, just months prior to Israel's unilateral disengagement from the Gaza Strip, there were thirty-nine hundred factories operating in Gaza, employing thirty-five thousand people (Amnesty International et al., 2008). By December 2007, less than two hundred factories still had their doors open. The implications of this "man-made" economic implosion have been dire (Amnesty International et al., 2008). Standards in everything from primary education[43] to healthcare[44] have plummeted. In this way, Israel's containment policies have directly undermined many of the hopes for economic recovery in Gaza.

More recently, the economic crisis has sunk to drastic levels. Following Gaza's internecine fighting that ended in June 2007, leaving Hamas with unopposed control of the Gaza Strip, Israel placed Gaza under total closure—sealing it off completely by halting virtually all freedom of movement and limiting the shipment of food and humanitarian supplies. Between May and June 2007, wheat flour, infant formula, and rice became scarce in Gaza, and prices rose 34 percent, 30 percent, and 21.5 percent, respectively (Amnesty International et al., 2008). This shortage has occurred primarily because the number of supply trucks delivering commercial and humanitarian supplies has dwindled under the conditions of Israel's closure of the Strip; whereas 250 trucks entered Gaza daily prior to the 2005 disengagement, the crossing is only able to deal with a maximum of forty-five today—and most days, not even this number is reached (Amnesty International et al., 2008). In September 2007, Israel declared Gaza a "hostile entity," thereby justifying further cuts in supplies, including energy resources (Urquhart, 2007). The results have been harsh and dramatic. Gaza now receives the highest ratio of food aid to population size in the world, and approximately 80 percent of the population is reliant on handouts from the World Food Program (WFP) to survive—a tenfold increase in the last decade alone and an increase of 17 percent since 2006. The recipients of this aid "would literally starve without food aid from international agencies" (B'Tselem, n.d., "Tightened Siege …").

The economic and humanitarian consequences of disengagement for the Gaza Strip have been devastating, literally strangling the population with Israel's strict military containment of the territory. Yet, as we have described, this policy has contributed to greater suffering on both sides of the conflict, leading to an increase in bloodshed all around and entirely contradicting its justification as a path to peace. Not only has Israel's implementation of disengagement according to the philosophy of separation undermined hope for peace by making life excessively difficult for the Gazan population, it has rendered that population more hostile and abject, while exposing its own population to increased Palestinian attacks—a tragic outcome that is beneficial for neither side.

Conclusion: A (Not So) New Approach

In itself, the disengagement of Israel's presence in the Gaza Strip can be seen as a positive step. It has significantly improved the freedom of movement for Palestinians within the Gaza Strip and has granted them a degree of autonomy where before there was none. Yet Israel did not disengage with any illusions of ceding power in Gaza. Its military control merely shifted to the periphery, where it has remained ever since. Israel's treatment of Gaza in this way is nothing new (Zionism's historic record of exclusion and control clearly illustrates the point) but the retooling of separation as a peace philosophy is wholly unprecedented in the history of the conflict and we have analyzed Israel's actions in this context. If it has brought about any changes besides an intensified security crisis and a dramatic plunge in Gaza's already intolerable conditions, Israel's use of the philosophy of separation has altered the *conceptual* relationship between occupant and occupied by replacing the colonization principle with the application of the philosophy of separation (Gordon, 2008). This has been a change of justification, but not of practice. The specific use of disengagement in this case provided Israel with the guise of peacemaker—of a country exercising considerable restraint and making painful concessions for the sake of peace. But this observation largely ignores Israel's history of brutally enforcing control in the OPT and makes the crude assumption that partial compliance with international law constitutes a sacrifice, rather than a delayed and insufficient fulfillment of numerous United Nations resolutions calling a full withdrawal from the OPT.

Israel unquestionably remains the dominant military power in the Israeli-Palestinian conflict, and as we wrote in the introduction to this chapter, it holds the key to the conflict's resolution. Yet even if the Israeli political establishment must inevitably accommodate any future resolution; simply acknowledging the massive imbalance of power between occupant and occupied does not imply that a resolution to the conflict must germinate from within the Israeli political establishment. Our analysis has taken a rather dim view of Israeli policy-making in this regard, but it should be clear that there are alternatives to Israel's misleading justification of ethnic separation as peace philosophy. Despite the overwhelming international consensus on the illegality of Israel's occupation and the ongoing expansion of Jewish settlements, very little progress has been made over the years toward a peaceful resolution of the conflict. Rather, as we have discussed throughout this chapter, Israel has consistently gone to great lengths to conceal extreme policies under a veil of legitimacy. Given the grim picture we have outlined, it seems appropriate to now look at a potential alternative to the status quo. Thus, as we close this chapter, we wish to discuss the past application and future potential of nonviolent civil resistance toward achieving a just and lasting peace to the Israeli-Palestinian conflict.[45]

Nonviolent resistance is nothing new to Palestinians.[46] The first intifada was by and large a nonviolent grassroots movement aimed at overthrowing the apparatuses of control Israel had for so long enforced in the Palestinian territories (Dajani, 1995). As one academic put it at the time, "nonviolent forms of struggle" made up "perhaps 85 percent of the total resistance" with stone throwing constituting the remaining 15 percent of violent activities (Sharp, 1989, p. 3). Using a multifaceted strategy of symbolic nonviolence (including the waving of Palestinian flags and political demonstrations), noncooperation (including labor strikes, economic/social boycotts, and the resignation of tax collectors), and nonviolent intervention (including the creation of an independent civil society and en masse violations of Israeli-imposed restrictions, such as curfews) the Palestinian national movement during the first intifada demonstrated impressive restraint in the face of harsh repression from the Israeli military (Sharp, 1989). Israel's brutal response to the uprising evoked international outrage and testified to the serious potential for nonviolent resistance as a valid approach to peacefully resolving the conflict. It is widely accepted that the Israeli military was unknot prepared to react to nonviolent struggle and preferred instead to counter Palestinian violence, which was far more easily justifiable as retaliation (Sharp, 1989).[47] Given Israel's intimidation and disarray in the face of the Palestinian uprising, why did the intifada fail to bring about lasting change? Among many others, academic and activist Norman Finkelstein (2009) has argued that Yassir Arafat stifled the momentum of the intifada by subordinating it to a "dead-end diplomatic game" (p. 26) and by entering into the Oslo Accords process, thereby contributing to the establishment of a Palestinian pseudo-government that was inferior to the Israeli authorities—the Palestine National Authority (PNA)—effectively allowing the occupation and expansion of settlements to continue. This argument is compelling, and there is no way to know what difference could have been made had the Palestinians embraced 100 percent nonviolence. Still, it is unfair to dismiss the nonviolence of the first intifada as a failure. True, it ultimately failed to bring about Palestinian independence but at a minimum, the first intifada demonstrated the power and relevance of nonviolent struggle to the Israeli-Palestinian conflict by forcing Israel to substantially reorganize the prosecution of its occupation—Gordon's (2008) shift from the colonization principle to the separation principle.

If we attempt to reapply the doctrine of nonviolent civil resistance to the Israeli-Palestinian conflict today, we must understand the factors that determine the efficacy of nonviolence as a strategic choice.[48] In order to be effective, any form of resistance—nonviolent or otherwise—must be part of a larger strategy aimed at achieving explicit goals. These goals must be recognized as valid, at least to some degree. As Finkelstein (2009) writes, "it is not suffering alone that touches but suffering in the pursuit of a legitimate goal" (p. 17)—a goal that is already, latently or blatantly, recognized as legitimate. In the Palestinian case, the goals were and remain uncontroversial in the eyes of the international community: an end to the occupation and the implementation of a two-state solution based on the 1967 borders, negotiation over East Jerusalem, and negotiation over the return of refugees. And in Israel, while debate over Jerusalem and the refugees remain sticking points, if Palestinians regained the impetus of the first intifada with 100 percent nonviolence, the renewed movement would be less "likely to arouse Israeli fear and rage (and hence brutality)" by "[removing] the 'justification' for Israeli repression" (Sharp, 1989, p. 13). Furthermore, during and since the first intifada, we have witnessed how the Palestinians' gradual shift to more and more violent tactics diminished Israeli sympathy for their domestic peace movement (Kaminer, 1996). The more violent the Palestinian resistance has become—especially during the waves of suicide attacks during the second intifada—the weaker Israeli sympathy has become, and the legitimacy of Palestinian goals has consequently received secondary consideration to the Jewish collective memory of pogroms and mass persecution. This has also severely diminished the clout of the Israeli peace camp when compared to the first intifada's outpouring of solidarity and sympathy for the Palestinian cause.

Moreover, for any nonviolent movement to succeed, there is also a geopolitical aspect to the conflict that cannot be ignored. Just as a revitalized Palestinian movement must aim itself at shifting Israeli policies, it must also struggle for the goodwill of international public opinion. In the present case, the United States has played a particularly influential role, and the Obama administration has signalled a new approach toward its relationship with Israel that may yet lead to positive change on the ground. Nevertheless, in the battle for the hearts and minds of world public opinion, Israel has historically been well poised to gain acceptance of (or acquiescence to) its policies, while sympathy and understanding for the Palestinian cause has been negligible—especially in the West. In more recent years, the Israeli political class has hijacked the American-initiated concept of "war on terrorism" as the rationale for its attempts to preclude Palestinian national aspirations.[49] In this vein, the demand that Palestinians renounce violent resistance without similar reciprocation from Israel has echoed positively in the foreign ministries of Western countries. Indeed, this crisis of Palestinian legitimacy in the eyes of Israel and the international community now colors the very discourse of peace talks. As Sara Roy observed during the aftermath of Israel's 2005 withdrawal from Gaza,

> Palestinian powerlessness is arguably more acute now (with Gaza disengagement) than before (with Oslo)... [T]he Palestinians' continued dispossession is regarded as the price of peace, not as a reason for conflict. So defined, Palestinian legitimacy, at least for parts of the international community, no longer derives from the justice and morality of its cause but from Palestinian willingness to concede to terms largely if not entirely imposed by Israel. (Roy, 2005, pp. 71–72)

So how can it be nonviolently demonstrated with that Palestinian legitimacy derives "from the justice and morality of its cause"? Sharp (1989) has argued convincingly that for a Palestinian nonviolent movement to be effective at accentuating the legitimacy of its goals in the eyes of Israeli society, then it must appeal to the Jewish national sense of victimization. This seems reasonable, for we should also not forget the extreme imbalance in military power and the devastating effect of Israeli military strikes "justified" by Palestinian violence. This imbalance must somehow be reconciled by any serious attempt at a just peace. Polls regularly indicate widespread support for peace among Israelis and Palestinians; this is beyond question.

Indeed, we must remember the distinction between peace and justice. "It is worth recalling," writes Chomsky (personal communication, July 28, 2009) "that everyone wants peace, even Hitler. The question always is: on what terms?" If there is to be true peace in the Middle East based on principles of justice, it cannot be defined merely by an end to hostilities. For example, as this paper has argued, Israel's unilateral withdrawal and military containment of Gaza is not a valid peace philosophy because it seeks no deeper goal than military containment. With regard to the Israeli-Palestinian conflict, "there [isn't] anything that merits the term '[peace] philosophy'" Chomsky (personal communication, July 28, 2009) continues, "and the only lessons of history are the maxim of Thucydides: the strong do as they wish, and the weak suffer as they must. Of course, that's not an iron law, and it can be overturned by dedicated popular activism." Today, some would argue that the crisis of Palestinian legitimacy has returned us to a previous phase of the conflict, when the international community implicitly accepted Israel's occupation of the Palestinian territories as a marginal issue. Thus, the dilemma for the Palestinian national movement today is that a "back to the future" strategy is problematic to the extent that the gains achieved during the first intifada neither led to the creation of a viable Palestinian state nor to a substantial increase in Western goodwill toward Palestinian legitimacy. Still, it is evident that nonviolence was used to a powerful effect by courageous Palestinian and Israeli activists at the time, and there is no reason to believe that a renewed mass movement of dedicated nonviolence would not at least provide a compelling alternative to the destructive policies of the status quo. Yet, any movement aimed at achieving a just and lasting peace must be buttressed by expanding the Israeli and international perception of Palestinian legitimacy "from the justice and morality of its cause." How this can be achieved is not for us to say, but is surely limited only by the creativity of those willing to work tirelessly and sincerely toward bringing an end to this dark chapter in human history.

Notes

1. This discussion enjoys a very robust and active debate, much of which addresses the paradox of Israeli democracy and the struggle to maintain a Jewish ethnic identity. For more on this ongoing debate, see Al Haj, 1995; Gavison, 1999; Ghanem, Rouhana, & Yiftachel, 1998; Kretzmer, 1990; Lustick, 1980; Rabinowitz, 1997; Rouhana, 1997; Rouhana & Sultany, 2003; Smooha, 1997; Yiftachel, 1997; Yiftachel, 1998; Yiftachel, 2006.

2. This philosophy commonly envisions separation from the occupied Palestinian population as a worthy objective, but there are some who would like to see separation extend also to Israeli Arabs, who constitute approximately 20 percent of the Israeli population and are technically entitled to all rights as full citizens of the state. This chapter focuses solely on separation from the occupied Palestinian population, for while some reactionary politicians within Israel have called for the deportation of Israeli Arabs, there is no serious intention of doing, so as far as we are aware.
3. Morris's seminal work is credited with precipitating the Israeli 'new historian' or 'revisionist' movement, enabled by the declassification of Israeli military archives in the 1980s. Although his own work often relies heavily on military records, his research has helped to dispel a great many of the myths regarding the events of 1948 and challenged the guiltlessness of Israel's entrenched national narrative. Other influential scholars belonging to the "new historian" movement include Ilan Pappé, Avi Shlaim, and Tom Segev among others.
4. Theodor Herzl, revered in Israel as the father of modern Zionism, wrote his famous book Der Judenstaat in 1896 (Herzl, 1997). It should be noted that throughout his life, Herzl never believed that the specific geographical entity of Palestine should be the only consideration for a Jewish state; however, he clearly understood that other lands, such as Argentina or parts of Uganda, did not inspire comparable national zeal when compared to Palestine. In his own words, "you must have a flag and an idea. You cannot make those things only with money...With money you cannot make a general movement of a great mass of people. You must give them an ideal" (as cited in Gilbert, 1998, p. 21). All prospects other than Palestine died with Herzl in 1904, at which point Zionism was essentially synonymous with establishing a Jewish national home in Palestine exclusively (Pappé, 2006, p. 10).
5. For more on the activism of these proto-Zionists, see Hess, 1995; Ravitzky, 1996; Shimoni, 1995; Waxman, 1987.
6. The most common solution proposed for to this question was the "transfer" of Palestinians (a euphemism for forced expulsion) outside the borders of Mandatory Palestine. For an excellent overview of "transfer" in Zionist thought, see Masalha, 1992.
7. It is beyond the scope of this paper to thoroughly review the politico-historical emergence of Zionism and we limit the discussion here to the aspects of Zionism most relevant to our central argument: that exclusionary elements within the ideology have contributed to the contemporary emergence and implementation of the philosophy of separation.
8. Zionism was a fringe movement at the time and did not inspire significant levels of support throughout much of Europe or the United States. For an overview of Zionism's influence on European and American Jews during this period see Berkowitz, 1997.
9. Perhaps the most obvious example was the successful revival of the Hebrew language spearheaded by Eliezer Ben-Yehuda. See Fellman, 1973; Rabin, 1963; St. John, 1972.
10. As Morris has written, "the logic of a transfer solution to the 'Arab problem' [was] ineluctable; without some sort of massive displacement of Arabs from the area of the Jewish state-to-be, there could [have been] no 'Jewish' state" (Morris, 2004, p. 43).
11. We refer to the oft-quoted passage from Theodor Herzl's diaries: "We shall try to spirit the penniless [Palestinian] population across the border...Both the process of expropriation and the removal of the poor must be carried out discretely and circumspectly" (Herzl, 1960, p. 88). It should be noted that Herzl rarely raised the issue of "transfer" and this short citation constitutes his only diary entry on the matter. Morris attributes this to a tactful awareness that public discussion of the matter would cause unrest and antagonism among the Palestinian Arab population (Morris, 2004).
12. Expressing his opinion on the matter, Ben-Gurion wrote that "the possibility of a large scale transfer of a population by force was demonstrated, when the Greeks were transferred [after World War I]. In the present war the idea of transferring a population is gaining more

sympathy as [a solution to]...the dangerous and painful problem of national minorities" (as cited in Masalha, 1992, p. 128). Also see Morris, 2004, pp. 42–43.
13. Schechtman positively cites the India/Pakistan case to justify his own support for a retroactive Jewish-Arab population exchange in Palestine.
14. At a 1905 talk in England, Zangwill stated that "[We] must be prepared either to drive out by the sword the [Arab] tribes in possession as our grandfathers did or to grapple with the problem of a large alien population, mostly Mohammedan and accustomed for centuries to despise us" (Zangwill, 1937, p. 210). Masalha (1992) has pointed out that Zangwill was unusually outspoken in his support for the expulsion of the Palestinians compared to his contemporaries; most Zionists at the time "expressed the same ideas in euphemistic, discreetly formulated terms, stressing the peaceful nature of the operation that would be initiated by Zionist land acquisition and economic incentives" (p. 10).
15. Even among the "new historians," there is substantial debate. Morris (2004), for example, does not find evidence to support that "transfer" proposals translated into a policy or "master-plan of expulsion" during 1948. "But," he continues, "transfer was inevitable and built into Zionism" (p. 60). Nur Masalha (1991) and Norman Finkelstein (1991) have criticized Morris for what they perceived as his tendency to reach conclusions incompatible with his research—a charge against which Morris (1991) has vehemently defended himself. More recently, Ilan Pappé (2006) has accused Morris of largely ignoring Arab sources and oral histories in his research, thereby preventing him from grasping "the systematic planning behind the expulsion of the Palestinians in 1948" (p. xv).
16. The term Yishuv refers to the Jewish political leadership in Palestine during the British Mandate period. Upon statehood in 1948, it became the functional government of the state of Israel.
17. Interestingly, the United States issued a strong message to Israel in May 1949 demanding that repatriation of the Palestinians be a precondition for peace and even withheld a loan when Israel refused to agree (Pappé, 2006).
18. It should be noted that his colleagues labeled Shertok a so-called Arab appeaser for his perceived sympathy regarding the Palestinians' fate.
19. Because of a difference in definitions concerning what constituted a Palestinian village, Pappé (2006) lists 531 villages destroyed by the Yishuv, while Khalidi (1992) reports 418. For a more in depth look at the events of 1948, also see Benvenisti, 2000; Masalha, 1992; Morris, 2004.
20. Expressing this perspective, Benny Morris has controversially argued that "if [David Ben-Gurion] had carried out a full expulsion—rather than a partial one—he would have stabilized the State of Israel for generations...when one has to deal with a serial killer, it's not so important to discover why he became a serial killer. What's important is to imprison the murderer or to execute him" (Shavit, 2004). Addressing the feasibility of expelling Arab citizens of Israel, Morris claimed that "The Israeli Arabs are a time bomb...If the threat to Israel is existential, expulsion will be justified" (Shavit, 2004).
21. Masalha (2000) writes, "Since the occupation of the West Bank and Gaza, with their solid Palestinian population, demography and the so-called Arab 'demographic threat' has obsessed leaders in Israel...[T]he demographic concern remained an ever-present subject in public debates and political speeches" (pp. 200–202).
22. For example, toward the end of his term in office, President Bill Clinton began referring to East Jerusalem as "disputed" rather than illegally annexed—an almost complete reversal of previous U.S. discourse—in consideration of the now decades-old Israeli settlements around the city's periphery (Smith, 2004). More recently, former U.S. President Jimmy Carter assured residents of the Gush Etzion settlement bloc that he did not believe Israel would withdraw. "This is part of the close settlements to the 1967 line that I think will be here forever" (Ha'aretz Service & News Agencies, 2009).

23. Several members of the government live in the settlements themselves, including the hard-right Israeli foreign minister Avigdor Lieberman.
24. The Fourth Geneva convention states that an occupying power "shall not deport or transfer parts of its own civilian population into the territory it occupies." Yet, since 1967, the Israeli government has recognized 120 so-called communities in the West Bank (B'Tselem, n.d., "Land Expropriation and Settlements").
25. Many restrictions also apply to Israel's Arab population ("A Survey of Israel," 2008; Schocken, 2008).
26. Jimmy Carter's (2007) book, Palestine: Peace Not Apartheid, precipitated a furious reaction in some circles for his use of the term "apartheid" and led to allegations of anti-Semitism and bigotry, despite that fact that Carter presented an overall argument that was more sympathetic to the Israeli position than that of many mainstream scholars (Bosman, 2006). Several prominent South Africans have drawn the apartheid comparison (long before Carter discovered the term), including erstwhile Special Rapporteur for the United Nations Commission on Human Rights John Dugard, Nobel Peace Prize winner Desmond Tutu, and former South African Minister for Intelligence Services Ronnie Kasrils (McCarthy, 2007; Tutu, 2002; Tutu & Urbina, 2003). Furthermore, many Israelis have themselves used the term, including the historian Ilan Pappé, former Attorney General Michael Ben Yair, deputy mayor of Jerusalem Meron Benvenisti, and peace activist Uri Avnery among others (Barat, 2008; Lelyveld, 2007; Mearsheimer & Walt, 2007).
27. It is interesting to note that Israel has never constitutionally defined its borders, "since doing so would necessarily place limits on them" and effectively preclude the ambitions of the Greater Israel movement (Whitbeck, 2007). Moreover, as Israel continues to colonize the West Bank, the demographic implications of a negotiated settlement potentially threaten the Jewish nature of the state. For this reason, much has been made of Israel's "right to exist" and the Palestinian acceptance or refusal of this "right," despite the ambiguity of what this actually acknowledges. More recently, Israeli Prime Minister Benjamin Netanyahu has demanded the Palestinians not only recognize Israel's right to exist but also recognize Israel as a specifically Jewish state (Keinon, 2009). This is controversial because it would preclude discussions over the right of return for the 1948 refugees and because it trivializes the existence of a large Arab minority in Israel.
28. At the time this paper was drafted, it remained to be seen how far the Obama Administration was willing to push the issue.
29. The Gaza barrier was erected in 1994, while construction of the WBB began in mid-2002 and continues today.
30. For a detailed map of the WBB, visit http://www.btselem.org/download/separation_barrier_map_eng.pdf
31. In a 2009 speech, Obama said "[t]he United States does not accept the legitimacy of continued Israeli settlements. This construction violates previous agreements and undermines efforts to achieve peace. It is time for these settlements to stop" (White House, 2009).
32. For the text of the Roadmap to Peace see Department of State, 2003.
33. For example, the Israeli Defense Ministry decided to include the Israeli settlement of Alfei Menashe within the barrier's domain, thereby physically preventing the Palestinian town of Qalqiliya and the village Halba from growing into one another. The decision was especially devastating for Qalqiliya, which now finds itself entirely surrounded by the WBB, sealed off from the rest of the West Bank apart from a single military checkpoint. Consequently, 600 of Qalqiliya's businesses have closed and 20 percent of the population has left the city (United Nations, 2004).
34. Historically, Israel has preferred to refer to the territory as "administered" and not "occupied". For an excellent look at Israel's legalistic history in the occupied territories, see Kretzmer, 2002.
35. There is a small airport in Gaza, but it was only functional for a few years before it was bombed by Israel during the second (al-Aqsa) intifada.

36. Mortar shells are far less accurate than regular artillery and in a densely populated territory like the Gaza Strip, are likely to cause more civilian casualties. According to one Israeli officer, "I don't recall when we ever fired mortar shells in Gaza before" (as cited in B'Tselem, 2009, p. 7).
37. The practice of targeted killing by the IDF, also known as extrajudicial assassination, was granted legal approval by the High Court of Israel in 2006, though the Court has recently added stipulations requiring an investigation into each specific case. See, respectively, Izenberg, 2006; Segal, 2008.
38. As of January 17, 2009 (the end of Operation Cast Lead), nineteen Israelis have been killed by Palestinian rocket/mortar fire, and over 400 have been wounded (B'Tselem, n.d., "Rocket and Mortar Fire Into Israel").
39. Samhouri ascribes Gaza's economic collapse, among other causes, to "the very restrictive terms of the Israeli disengagement plan" (Samhouri, 2006, p. 1).
40. There remain Israeli video monitoring systems at the Rafah crossing and the IDF works closely with the Egyptians to ensure the border does not open without Israeli approval. There have been controversial exceptions to this, however—most notably the bombing of the Gazan border wall which resulted in an open border between Gaza and Egypt for a period of 11 days before being resealed.
41. After the failed coup in Gaza and Hamas's subsequent seizure of control, Israel resumed distribution of this money to the Palestinian Authority leadership in the West Bank.
42. The project had originally promised to create 3,000 new jobs and raise $50 million annually (Office of the Special Envoy for Disengagement, 2005).
43. Gaza primary schools now cope with an 80 percent failure rate from grades four through nine and a 90 percent failure rate in mathematics specifically. Moreover, Gazan schools have begun to cancel high energy-consumption classes such as Physical Education and Science Labs because the children are too malnourished (Amnesty International et al., 2008).
44. The closure has also restricted access to basic medical supplies. Gazan hospitals now barely carry 80 percent of the World Health Organization's recommended 437 essential medications. Vital immunization services have halted in more than three of Gaza's districts and sometimes children must be immunized with adult sized syringes due to a lack of supplies.
45. Historically, the Palestinian version of nonviolent struggle has modeled itself after Mahatma Gandhi's thought but has often stressed values common to Abrahamic religious tradition, such as respect for human dignity and concern for the weak and downtrodden.
46. See the first chapter of Dajani, 1995, for a good discussion of the roots of Palestinian nonviolence, going back to the British Mandate period.
47. At the time and to this day, Israel placed restrictions on the travel of human rights activists and proponents of nonviolence.
48. By using the term "reapply" we do not wish to ignore or trivialize the brave actions undertaken by Palestinian, Israeli, and international activists engaged in various forms of nonviolent resistance. Nevertheless, while these actions are praiseworthy, they are minor when compared to the massive public participation during the first intifada and do not constitute a coherent peace strategy.
49. The late Israeli sociologist Baruch Kimmerling coined the neologism "politicide" to define a series of Israeli actions he perceived as intended to preclude the emergence of a feasible Palestinian political structure (Kimmerling, 2003).

References

A survey of Israel. (April 3, 2008). *The Economist.* Retrieved June 25, 2009 from www.economist.com

Al Haj, M. (1995). *Education, empowerment, and control: The case of the Arabs in Israel.* Albany: State University of New York Press.

Al-Haq. (2006). *One year after the "disengagement": Gaza still occupied and under attack.* Retrieved June 25, 2009 from www.alhaq.org.
Amnesty International, CAFOD, CARE, Christian Aid, Medecins du Monde, Oxfam et al. (2008). *The Gaza Strip: A humanitarian implosion.* Retrieved June 25, 2009 from www.oxfam.org.uk.
B'Tselem. (n.d.). *Hostilities in the Gaza Strip since disengagement.* Retrieved June 25, 2009 from www.btselem.org.
——— (n.d.). *Land expropriation and settlements.* Retrieved June 25, 2009 from www.btselem.org.
——— (n.d.). *Rocket and Mortar Fire into Israel.* Retrieved June 25, 2009 from www.btselem.org.
——— (n.d.). *Sonic booms in the skies over Gaza.* Retrieved June 25, 2009 from www.btselem.org.
——— (n.d.). *The Gaza Strip after disengagement.* Retrieved June 25, 2009 from www.btselem.org.
——— (n.d.). *Tightened siege and intensified economic sanctions.* Retrieved June 25, 2009 from www.btselem.org.
——— (2009). *Guidelines for Israel's investigation into Operation Cast Lead.* Retrieved June 25, 2009 from www.btselem.org.
Barat, F. (June 6, 2008). An interview with Ilan Pappé and Noam Chomsky. *Counterpunch.* Retrieved June 24, 2009 from www.counterpunch.org.
Benvenisti, M. (2000). *Sacred landscape: The buried history of the Holy Land since 1948.* Berkeley: University of California Press.
Berkowitz, M. (1997). *Western Jewry and the Zionist project, 1914–1933.* Cambridge; New York: Cambridge University Press.
Bosman, J. (December 14, 2006). Carter's view of Israeli "apartheid" stirs furor. *The New York Times.* Retrieved July 22, 2009 from www.nytimes.com.
Carter, J. (2006). *Palestine: Peace not apartheid.* New York; London: Simon & Schuster.
Chomsky, N. (1999). *Fateful triangle: The United States, Israel, and the Palestinians* (Second edition). Cambridge, MA: South End Press.
Cook, J. (2006). *Blood and religion: The unmasking of the Jewish and democratic state.* London; Ann Arbor, MI: Pluto Press.
Dajani, S. R. (1995). *Eyes without country: Searching for a Palestinian liberation strategy.* Philadelphia: Temple University Press.
Department of State (2003). *A performance-based roadmap to a permanent two-state solution to the Israeli-Palestinian conflict.* Retrieved June 25, 2009 from www.mfa.gov.il.
Erlanger, S. (March 14, 2007). West Bank sites on private land, data shows. *The New York Times.* Retrieved June 24, 2009 from www.nytimes.com.
Fellman, J. (1973). *The revival of a classical tongue: Eliezer Ben Yehuda and the modern Hebrew language.* The Hague: Mouton.
Finkelstein, N. G. (1991). Myths, old and new. *Journal of Palestine Studies* 21(1), 66–89.
——— (2009). *Resolving the Israeli-Palestinian conflict: What we can learn from Gandhi.* Retrieved July 22, 2009 from www.normanfinkelstein.com.
Fisher, I. & Erlanger, S. (June 28, 2006). Israel: Troops move into Gaza. *The New York Times.* Retrieved June 24, 2009 from www.nytimes.com.
Gavison, R. (1999). Is Israel democratic? A rejoinder to the "ethnic democracy" debate. *Israel Studies* 4(1), 44–72.
Ghanem, A., Rouhana, N. D., & Yiftachel, O. (1998). Questioning "ethnic democracy": A response to Sammy Smooha. *Israel Studies* 3(2), 253–268.
Gilbert M. (1998). *Israel: A history.* New York: Morrow.
Gold, Dore. (2008). *Israel's war to halt Palestinian rocket attacks.* Jerusalem: Jerusalem Center for Public Affairs.

Goldberg, S. (May 30, 2001). Israel defies US with settlement expansion plans. *The Guardian*. Retrieved June 24, 2009 from www.guardian.co.uk.
Gordon, N. (2008). From colonization to separation: Exploring the structure of Israel's occupation. *Third World Quarterly 29*(1), 25–44.
——— (2008). *Israel's occupation*. Berkeley: University of California Press.
Gorni, Y. (1987). *Zionism and the Arabs, 1882–1948: A study of ideology*. Oxford; New York: Oxford University Press.
Ha'aretz News Service & News Agencies (June 15, 2009). Carter: Israel won't need to give up Gush Etzion settlements. *Ha'aretz*. Retrieved June 25, 2009 from www.haaretz.co.il/.
Haberman, C. (June 27, 1992). Shamir is said to admit plan to stall talks "for 10 years." *The New York Times*. Retrieved July 22, 2009 from www.nytimes.com.
Herzl, T. (1960). *The complete diaries of Theodor Herzl*. Translated by H. Zohn. New York: Herzl Press & T. Yoseloff.
——— (1997). *The Jews' state: A critical English translation*. Translated by H. Overberg. Northvale, NJ: Jason Aronson.
Hess, M. (1995). *The revival of Israel: Rome and Jerusalem, the last nationalist question*. Translated by M. Waxman. Edited by M. I. Urofsky. Lincoln: University of Nebraska Press.
Human Rights Watch. (2009). *Rain of fire: Israel's unlawful use of white phosphorus in Gaza*. New York: n.p.
Intelligence and Terrorism Information Center (2007). *Rocket threat from the Gaza Strip*. Retrieved June 25, 2009 from www.mfa.gov.il.
International Court of Justice (2004). Legal consequences of the construction of a wall in the occupied Palestinian territory. Retrieved June 25, 2009 from www.icj-cij.org.
Israel completes Gaza withdrawal (September 12, 2005). *BBC*. Retrieved June 24, 2009 from news.bbc.co.uk.
Israel Ministry of Foreign Affairs (2004). *Excerpt from speech by PM Sharon after government approval of the disengagement plan*. Retrieved June 25, 2009 from www.mfa.gov.il.
——— (2005). *Israel's disengagement plan: Renewing the peace process*. Jerusalem: Israel Information Center.
——— (2006). *The nature and extent of Palestinian terrorism, 2006*. Retrieved June 25, 2009 from www.mfa.gov.il.
Izenberg, D. (December 14, 2006). High Court allows conditional targeted killings. *The Jerusalem Post*. Retrieved June 24, 2009 from www.jpost.com.
Kaminer, R. (1996). *The politics of protest: The Israeli peace movement and the Palestinian Intifada*. Sussex: Sussex Academic Press.
Katz, Y., Abu Toameh, K., & Keinon, H. (January 3, 2008). PMO: Katyusha "strategic threat." *The Jerusalem Post*. Retrieved June 24, 2009 from www.jpost.com.
Keinon, H. (2009). Netanyahu wants demilitarized PA state. *The Jerusalem Post*. Retrieved June 25, 2009 from www.jpost.com.
Keinon, H. & Katz, Y. (May 19, 2008). Barak hints Gaza incursion imminent. *The Jerusalem Post*. Retrieved June 24, 2009 from www.jpost.com.
Khalidi, W. (1992). *All that remains: The Palestinian villages occupied and depopulated by Israel in 1948*. Washington, DC: Institute for Palestine Studies.
Kimmerling, B. (2003). *Politicide: Ariel Sharon's wars against the Palestinians*. London: New York: Verso.
Kretzmer, D. (1990). *The legal status of the Arabs in Israel*. Boulder: Westview Press.
——— (2002). *The occupation of justice: The supreme court of Israel and the occupied territories*. Albany: State University of New York Press.

Legitimization of land theft [Editorial]. (February 27, 2007). *Ha'aretz*. Retrieved June 25, 2009 from www.haaretz.co.il.

Lelyveld, J. (March 29, 2007). Jimmy Carter and apartheid [Review of the books *Palestine: Peace not apartheid* and *Prisoners: A Muslim and a Jew across the Middle East divide*]. *The New York Review of Books*. Retrieved June 24, 2009 from www.nybooks.com.

Lustick, I. (1980). *Arabs in the Jewish state: Israel's control of a national minority*. Austin: University of Texas Press.

MacKinnon, I. (October 7, 2004). Gaza withdrawal aims to "freeze" peace process. *The Times*. Retrieved June 25, 2009 from www.timesonline.co.uk.

Makovsky, D. (2004). How to build a fence. *Foreign Affairs 83*(2), 50–64.

Masalha, N. (1991). A critique of Benny Morris. *Journal of Palestine Studies 21*(1), 90–97.

—— (1992). *Expulsion of the Palestinians: The concept of "transfer" in Zionist political thought, 1882–1948*. Washington, DC: Institute for Palestine Studies.

McCarthy, R. (February 23, 2007). Occupied Gaza like apartheid South Africa, says UN report. *The Guardian*. Retrieved June 24, 2009 from www.guardian.co.uk.

—— (March 5, 2008). Hamas rockets bring Israeli city in range. *The Guardian*. Retrieved June 24, 2009 from www.guardian.co.uk.

—— (June 23, 2009). Israel defies US with plan for 240 new homes on Palestinian land. *The Guardian*. Retrieved June 25, 2009 from www.guardian.co.uk.

McGirk, T. (April 22, 2005). Israel bolsters security before Gaza Strip pull-out. *Jane's Defence Weekly*.

Mearsheimer, J. J. & Walt, S. M. (2007). *The Israel lobby and U.S. foreign policy*. London: Penguin.

Morris, B. (1986). Yosef Weitz and the transfer committees, 1948–49. *Middle Eastern Studies 22*(4), 522–561.

—— (1988). *The birth of the Palestinian refugee problem, 1947–1949*. Cambridge; New York: Cambridge University Press.

—— (1991). Response to Finkelstein and Masalha. *Journal of Palestine Studies 21*(1), 98–114.

—— (1999). *Righteous victims: A history of the Zionist-Arab conflict, 1881–1999*. New York: Knopf.

—— (2004). *The birth of the Palestinian refugee problem revisited*. Cambridge; New York: Cambridge University Press.

Office of the Prime Minister (2004). *Cabinet resolution regarding the disengagement plan*. Retrieved June 25, 2009 from www.mfa.gov.il.

Pappé, I. (2006). *The ethnic cleansing of Palestine*. Oxford: Oneworld.

Peace Now (2006). *Breaking the law in the West Bank: One violation leads to another*. Retrieved June 25, 2009 from www.peacenow.org.il.

Physicians for Human Rights (2006). *Report: Harm to children in Gaza*. Retrieved June 25, 2009 from www.phr.org.il.

Rabin, C. (1963). The revival of Hebrew as a spoken language. *Journal of Educational Sociology 36*(8), 388–392.

Rabinowitz, D. (1997). *Overlooking Nazareth: The ethnography of exclusion in Galilee*. Cambridge; New York: Cambridge University Press.

Ravitzky, A. (1996). *Messianism, Zionism, and Jewish religious radicalism*. Chicago: University of Chicago Press.

Reuters. (September 16, 2006). UN human rights envoy says Gaza a prison for Palestinians. *Ha'aretz*. Retrieved June 25 from www.haaretz.co.il/.

Rouhana, N. N. (1997). *Palestinian citizens in an ethnic Jewish state: Identities in conflict*. New Haven: Yale University Press.

Rouhana, N. N. & Sultany, N. (2003). Redrawing the boundaries of citizenship: Israel's new hegemony. *Journal of Palestine Studies 33*(1), 5–22.
Roy, S. (1987). The Gaza Strip: A case of economic de-development. *Journal of Palestine Studies 17*(1), 56–88.
——— (2005). Praying with their eyes closed: Reflections on the disengagement from Gaza. *Journal of Palestine Studies 34*(4), 64–74.
——— (October 4, 2006). The economy of Gaza. *Counterpunch*. Retrieved June 24, 2009 from www.counterpunch.org
Samhouri, M. (2006). Gaza economic predicament one year after disengagement: What went wrong? *Middle East Brief 12*, 1–7.
Schechtman, J. B. (1949). *Population transfers in Asia*. New York: Hallsby Press.
Schocken, A. (June 29, 2008). Citizenship law makes Israel an apartheid state. *Ha'aretz*. Retrieved on June 24, 2009 from www.haaretz.co.il.
Scobbie, I. (2006). Is Gaza still occupied? *Forced Migration Review 26*, 18.
Segal, Z. (November 27, 2008). Court ruling sees IDF targeted assassinations as last resort. *Ha'aretz*. Retrieved on June 24, 2009 from www.haaretz.co.il.
Sharon, A. (2004). The Sharon unilateral disengagement plan. *Journal of Palestine Studies 33*(4), 5–107.
Sharp, G. (1989). The Intifadah and nonviolent struggle. *Journal of Palestine Studies 19*(1), 3–13.
Shavit, A. (January 8, 2004). Survival of the fittest? An interview with Benny Morris. *Ha'aretz*. Retrieved June 24, 2009 from www.haaretz.co.il.
Shimoni, G. (1995). *The Zionist ideology*. Hanover: University Press of New England for Brandeis University Press.
Smith, C. D. (2004). *Palestine and the Arab-Israeli conflict: A history with documents* (Fifth edition). Boston: Bedford/St. Martin's.
Smooha, S. (1997). Ethnic democracy: Israel as an archetype. *Israel Studies 2*(2), 198–241.
St. John, R. (1972). *Tongue of the prophets: The life story of Eliezer Ben Yehuda*. Westport: Greenwood Press.
Tutu, D. (April 29, 2002). Apartheid in the Holy Land. *The Guardian*. Retrieved June 24, 2009 from www.guardian.co.uk.
Tutu, D. & Urbina, I. (June 27, 2003). Against Israeli apartheid. *The Nation*. Retrieved June 24, 2009 from www.thenation.com.
United Nations (2004). Profile: Qalqilya town update, July 2004. *The West Bank barrier*. Retrieved June 24, 2009 from www.un.org.
Urquhart, C. (September 20, 2007). Israel declares Gaza Strip hostile entity. *The Guardian*. Retrieved June 24, 2009 from www.guardian.co.uk.
Usher, G. (2005). Unmaking Palestine: On Israel, the Palestinians, and the wall. *Journal of Palestine Studies 35*(1), 25–43.
Waxman, C. I. (1987). Messianism, Zionism, and the state of Israel. *Modern Judaism 7*(2), 175–192.
Whitbeck, J. V. (February 2, 2007). What Israel's "right to exist" means to Palestinians. *The Christian Science Monitor*. Retrieved June 24, 2009 from www.csmonitor.com.
White House (2003). *President Bush welcomes Prime Minister Abbas to the White House*. Retrieved July 22, 2008 from georgewbush-whitehouse.archives.gov.
——— (2009). *Remarks by the President on a new beginning*. Retrieved June 25, 2009 from www.whitehouse.gov.
Wilson, S. (August 16, 2005). Eviction notices are served in Gaza. *The Washington Post*. Retrieved June 24, 2009 from www.washingtonpost.com.
World Bank (2004). *Disengagement, the Palestinian economy and the settlements*. Retrieved June 25, 2009 from lnweb18.worldbank.org.

World refugee survey (2003). Washington, DC: U.S. Committee for Refugees.

Yiftachel, O. (1997). Israeli society and Jewish-Palestinian reconciliation: "Ethnocracy" and its territorial contradictions. *The Middle East Journal 51*(4), 505–519.

——— (1998). Democracy or ethnocracy? Territory and settler politics in Israel/Palestine. *Middle East Report 207*, 8–13.

——— (2006). *Ethnocracy: land and identity politics in Israel/Palestine*. Philadelphia: University of Pennsylvania Press.

Zangwill, I. (1937). *Israel Zangwill, Speeches, Articles and Letters*. London: The Socino Press.

PART 2

Curricular Applications

Curriculum has as a foundation the belief that schools can shape their society through student preparation for life in it. Where the society evidences trends that are harmful, educators respond with instruction that may help the students identify and analyze its causes. Curriculum that enables this process has a theoretical base. It is conducive to purposeful as well as contextually responsive learning. Lessons that have theoretical bases evidence a belief about the goal of education. For example, hermeneutics has a communicative purpose in preparation for understanding others while pragmatism has a practical purpose of learning how to solve problems in society. Culturally responsive curriculum facilitates accomplishment of these purposes through inclusion and accommodation of diversity. In the context of social studies, the responsive curriculum represents all members of the society while respectfully presenting their beliefs, which facilitates understanding of diverse practices. While applying hermeneutics theory, understanding developed through curriculum fosters awareness of multiple perceptions and interpretations. The inclusiveness of multiple stories in social education enables perceptions of situations, including explanations of a situation as being detrimental or beneficial to one or more groups. Recognition of harm is essential for analysis of its causes and ways to counter as well as avoid it.

The chapters in this part of the book describe actions in curriculum design that responded to conflict within education or the societies where the instructional preparations occurred. The authors explain the theories that they used in development of lessons as well as the implementation of the curriculum for education that might contribute to peace development. Their examples of philosophically grounded instruction may inspire further design of curriculum that has potential for improving society through carefully designed lessons.

CHAPTER FOUR

History Curriculum with Multiple Narratives

ESTHER YOGEV

The Israeli-Palestinian conflict exists in a psychological context that influences its dynamics and has been an impediment to the attainment of a truly peaceful resolution. Where continuous and violent conflict exists, cultivating the conditions for conciliation is crucial for achievement of peace. This chapter examines the means by which an ethno-national conflict can be utilized in history education to promote a sober dialogue for the development of a conciliatory consciousness. To meet this challenge, I utilize the approach of the existentialist philosopher Hans-Georg Gadamer who proposed humanistic hermeneutics as a method for achieving a better understanding of individual consciousness and group narratives, thereby creating a culture of communication.

The chapter reviews the challenges Israeli society faces vis-à-vis peace education and then focuses on the need to change the study of history. It then describes Gadamer's humanistic and historical-hermeneutic perception and the implications of the sociopolitical context of the Israeli-Palestinian conflict on history studies. It suggests that Gadamer's insights are useful for developing methods of history instruction. It concludes with a description of an experiment that applied this approach in the development of a history curriculum that included multiple narratives for a peace-focused education. The curriculum may serve as a trial-and-error model for applied hermeneutics in other situations of continual conflict.

The Challenge of Peace Education in Israel

Two societies, Jewish and Palestinian, have been in conflict for centuries over objectives and interests such as land, self-definition, establishment of a sovereign entity, natural resources, economic achievement, and personal and collective security. Frequent acts of violence dictate the character of the conflict and weaken the chance of its resolution.

This "intractable conflict," according to Daniel Bar-Tal's definition (Bar-Tal, 2007), stamps its mark on the daily life of all those involved.[1] Every day the media presents fresh information on the conflict, and the subject is almost always first on the public agenda. The Jewish-Palestinian conflict touches upon all the national-political components and is embedded in the collective identities and the founding ethos of both protagonists; it affects the beliefs, the perception of values and of "justice," and the morality of each group's behavior.

This psychological-social state of mind, which was and is part of the culture of each of the adversaries, became a serious impediment on the road to resolving the conflict. In both societies, a collective identity developed which intensified the perception of an anxious and defensive "I" (the in-group) and created the image of the "other" (the out-group) as negative and threatening. In intractable conflicts the enemy is always described as faceless, immoral, and malicious. One's identity motivates attitudes of constant distancing and differentiation. Membership in one side is always bound up with delineating it and forming a perception of conflict and a belief that "my side is right." The perceptions combine a collection of ideas and beliefs, collective historical memories of painful experiences and the feeling of victimhood which these perceptions perpetuate (Rouhana & Bar-Tal, 1999). Collective memory frequently provides a succinct, biased, and black-and-white historical justification for the stance of the group. Collective memory focuses on specific events that are compatible with its principal themes and constantly ignores events that contradict them. Collective memory is the raison d'être to justify actions of the past, create solidarity, and mobilize society to contend with the challenges that the conflict presents. Perpetuating conflict through a repertoire of rival historical narratives serves as an underground shelter of the consciousness for survival and immortalizes the ceaseless conflict which will be virtually inescapable even after the conflict is mitigated.

Meron Benvenisti stressed the importance of the psychological basis in the context of the Israeli-Palestinian conflict in his book *Intimate Enemies: Jews and Arabs in a Shared Land*:

> Discussion of the Israeli-Palestinian conflict from a purely political point of view is simplistic and misleading...A hundred years of violent conflict have left residues of fear, hatred, revenge, dehumanization, and brutalization of values. A century has produced dichotomous, tribal, militant worldviews, psychological fixations and irrational perceptions.
>
> On those foundations, saturated with blood and hatred, educational systems, destructive myths, despicable stereotypes, organs of coercive control, dual legal and administrative bodies, terrorism and counterterrorism were created and fostered...Intimate enmity has made the two communities into mirror images, swaying in a dance of death, clutched in a fatal embrace. (Benvenisti, 1995, pp. 198–199)

The longer the conflict continues, defensive memory as an exclusive "historical truth" becomes even stronger and the difficulty in considering different historical narratives increases. This reality burdens attempts of tolerance and represses hope of possible conciliation. Its implications for young people are likely to be harsh: They will only know one view of history; they will develop a negative stance toward the "other" and will justify the dehumanization of, and the use of force against, the "other." These circumstances will perpetuate the cycle of violence and the brutal reality in which we live.

Johan Galtung, one of the founding fathers of the International Peace Research Institute, differentiated between "negative peace," i.e., the absence of violence and acts of hatred, and "positive peace," i.e., harmonious cooperation. Later, he added the concept of peace as "the absence of structural violence." By definition, structural violence comprises inequality, discrimination, and persecution, which are built into social life. The goal of education toward peace is to diminish these elements (Galtung, 1996).

Gavriel Salomon, a noted researcher of peace-education in Israel, differentiates between three different sociopolitical contexts of education toward peace: (1) a continuous violent conflict between nations or different ethnic or religious groups (Israel, Northern Ireland); (2) tension between different groups in the absence of violence, for example, as in Belgium and Quebec, and (3) a peaceful sociopolitical context in which any discussion of education toward peace is, to a large extent, academic and unrelated to any specific opponent, such as in Sweden (Salomon, 2000, pp. 41–42). This differentiation determines the kind of challenges which confront education toward peace, its objectives, and the methods by which it will be taught. A worldwide scrutiny of different programs devoted to education toward peace shows that in peaceful regions devoid of all conflict the programs largely underscore the aspects of "positive peace," cooperation and the creation of a "culture of peace," that does not address specifics. On the other hand, programs devoted to peace education in regions of active conflict largely underscore the prevention of violence ("negative peace"), effecting changes in the perception of the opponent, its culture and collective narrative, and achieving greater equality in society. Therefore, education toward peace in a region devoid of active conflict emphasizes the support of peace as an abstract matter. The development of individual skills for resolving conflict and enhancing communications in the context of relentless conflict will stress changes in the perception of the "other" as a collective entity (Bar-Tal & Salomon, 2006).

Following this insight, I contend that effective education toward peace in Israel will occur only when young people understand that, in an incessant conflict, each side has its own interpretation of history, and each group bases its collective identity on those interpretations. To this end, it is imperative to create an educational process and to generate educational material that will offer perspectives to young people that differ from the ones they are familiar with.

The teaching of history is an exceptionally appropriate field for promoting education toward peace. By its very nature, history deals with humanistic stories and therefore offers young people specific contents that can assist them, by analogy, in viewing themselves and what is happening to them. The distance in time from the historical incident allows students to extract from human experience a repertoire of possibilities and insights in a somewhat less emotional manner. I believe that developing history curriculum with multiple narratives as a common method of education may mitigate the demonization of the "other" and enable a less threatening means of coping.

Niens and Cairns (2005) as well as Barton and McCully (2006) found that multiple perspectives can encourage students to go beyond merely accepting or resisting an historical text. They studied the perceptions of history students in Northern Ireland, where history plays a contentious role in popular discussion and community conflict, and where one purpose of the school curriculum is to provide alternatives to the sectarian historical perspectives students may encounter elsewhere. They found that the students were aware of events and incidents that affected their understanding of the past which, in turn, governed their inclination to consider the opposing perspective.

In order to examine the hypothesis regarding the potential of history education to foster a multiperspective view, I employ the hermeneutic-humanistic approach of Hans-Georg Gadamer (Gadamer, 1960/1999).[2] Gadamer proposed humanistic hermeneutics as a resource for achieving better understanding of individual consciousness, group narrative, social ethos, and the culture of communication. His point is that human beings are historical and cultural creatures with primordial perspectives and judgments that are shaped by contextual and cultural conditioning. In a society embedded in a constant violent conflict, much importance is attributed to an approach that underscores the interpretive dialogue between the cultural horizon of the student and the horizons of "others" as a key to complex understanding and the creation of a need for conciliation (Yogev, 2007).

This chapter ends with a description of an experiment conducted under the auspices of the Peace Research Institute of the Middle East (PRIME) that applied this approach. The experiment brought Palestinian and Israeli teachers together. They developed a unique curriculum according to a model that presented conflicting historical narratives as a learning method. The preparation and teaching of this curriculum is a trial-and-error model which may be used in other situations of continual conflict. The majority of teachers who participated in the experiment were trained or working as instructors of novice teachers between 2002 and 2010 in the History Department of the Kibbutzim College of Education in Tel Aviv. Training in this department is based on humanistic hermeneutics perception, enabling novice teachers to engage in multiple narratives experience.

The Hermeneutic-Humanism of Hans-George Gadamer: A Language of Human Encounter

In his book *Truth and Method* Gadamer asks, "How is understanding possible?" And answers, "All understanding is interpretation!" (Gadamer, 1999, p. 295). Human "being," posits Gadamer, means understanding and creating meaning at every moment, both at the level of everyday existence, when we seek to understand what is happening around us, and when we are trying to understand an historical text, a work of art or a spiritual tradition. All man's actions, including the use of language and its world of images, are nothing but interpretations for man's perception and understanding of the world. This intermediary role is in the hands of the interpreter, who live is in the present. Human understanding does not work in accordance with a general regularity that is dissociated from the individual, but rather through a constant reciprocity between his or her life in the present and his or her cultural tradition. This intermediary role is in the hands of the interpreter, who live is in the present. "In this between is the true place of hermeneutics," writes Gadamer, "and its aim is the actualization of the infiniteness of knowledge in a complete fusion of past thoughts with the present" (Gadamer, 1999, p. 338). In this space between past and present, understanding is always a dynamic action taking place in time and never begins with a *tabula rasa* (Gadamer, 1999).

Gadamer further claims that understanding itself is always an applied act, an action within the world: we do not observe something but participate in it. The essence of understanding is not domination over reality, as in the scientific method, but is part life experience and dialectic of question and answer. Man's search for generalizations to explain human reality is understandable but unsatisfactory. The conclusions we draw from events, human behavior, and societal processes may aid us in imposing order in the chaos of consciousness, but they give us no more than a contextual framework. The human story is always concrete and exists in an authentic-subjective reality, and not a predefined pattern given, so to speak, to a final deciphering. Thus in order to explain a human phenomenon Gadamer proposes examination of a different viewpoint: instead of searching for the "truth" by means of positivism or its negation by deconstruction (Derrida, 1976; Megill, 1997; White, 1987) we should emphasize that understanding is an act of human encounter and dialogue. As we can see, the process of understanding is not passive but a situation wherein the object of the interpretation "talks" to us in a way likely to influence our consciousness. "In our understanding," says Gadamer, "... the other presents itself so much in terms of our own selves that there is no longer a question of self and other. In relying on its critical method, historical objectivism conceals the fact that historical consciousness is itself situated in the web of historical effects" (Gadamer, 1999, p. 300). This two-way dialogue is the co-existential essence of the generation of meaning. It is closer to "doing" than to "finding" or "discovering," it has no end point and its results vary in time and space (Warnke, 1987).

History Curriculum, Multiple Narratives   85

Let us take as an example books that interpret a painting by an artist. The explanations they contain deepen and enrich the reader's and viewer's understanding of the artist's work, but the painting itself always remains open to further understanding and thought. It is open to interpretations in the future even though it was completed in the past and is no longer touched. The work will have different readings and meanings that are not mutually exclusive. They relate to the same painting and thus become an integral part of it.

Following these hypotheses, Gadamer presents his observation of the historian's work. How can a historian, who like anybody else is not a tabula rasa, interpret and understand history in which he does not live? In an attempt to answer this question Gadamer presents three key concepts for historical understanding: "Prejudgments" (*Vorurteile*), "Effective Historical Consciousness" (*Wirkungsgeschichte*) and "Fusion of Horizons" (*Horizontverschmelzung*). These three concepts are interrelated and together constitute the interpretative process.

I shall describe them briefly, and from them derive the implications they have on the objectives of teaching history and particularly appropriate practices in conflict situations.

Prejudgment

In the face of the principles of a positivism that demands impartial inquiry and rejects presuppositions, Gadamer presented the concept of "prejudgments." These are categories of consciousness that are derived from culture, through which we assimilate the world. The term "prejudgments" refers to concepts and perceptions in our society that construct our cultural world. Our ability to understand reality or a text is bound up with the recognition of this inner knowledge and our awareness of it.[3]

Gadamer claimed that the historian must separate legitimate prejudgment, which enables an initial connection with the phenomenon he is investigating, from becoming entrenched in an arbitrary prejudice that locks his understanding. The reflective observation of the existence of boundaries is the first step toward crossing them. From a dialogue with a historical document, a monument, a contemporary work of art or a historiography written up to its time, the prejudgment-conscious historian can refer to them as temporary, put them to the test of critique and replace them with new and better judgments, the fruit of his informed and inquiring thinking (Gadamer, 1999). On the other hand, if the researcher-learner adopts his judgments without reflection and critique, he remains stuck with his "preconceptions" (as these were rejected by Enlightenment thinkers). Ignoring preconceptions will weaken his openness to the world, shape him as a "man without qualities" and will pull the rug from under the necessary basis for an understanding of himself and his fellow man (Gadamer, 1999, p. 360).[4]

Gadamer is aware that culture not only shapes humans but is also created by them. In other words, our meaning-generating process is cyclic: the categories of culture and the tradition in which we have grown constitute our perceptions of consciousness, while the course of our life creates new categories of culture. Our focus of interest also changes over time and in accordance with our life circumstances. When interpreting human figures, positions and situations in the historical story, we shall not relate to the story of the past dissociated from our life but will participate in an actively applied process of its understanding. The criteria of the interpretive process will be affected by the horizons of history and our own culture on the one hand, and by the reality of our life in the present on the other (Gadamer, 1999).

Like any researcher-learner, the historian must therefore be self-aware and develop reflective skills that will help him to understand his place in the interpretive process and to open up to other concepts and ideas. Also necessary in this process of understanding is that the researcher-learner develops a dual relationship toward his own culture: he should view it as a way of life in which he lives and feels comfortable with the life patterns it dictates, while at the same time he should be capable of critically assessing its patterns and preferences.

Effective Historical Consciousness

In the much-loved TV series *The Time Tunnel* (1966), the two heroes, Dr. Tony Newman and Dr. Doug Phillips, travel back in time with the accumulated knowledge of the present and become involved in historical events. This situation may be used as a metaphor for the inner, thorny issue preoccupying the historian who travels down the time tunnel into the past and back. Gadamer argues that every desire to learn is motivated by a relevant matter and not simply by a desire to seek neutral knowledge. Interest in the historical story therefore grows from within a question that is troubling us and from that interest seeks answers to questions of here and now. The authentic question, the search, and the intentionality to understand, are the "materials" forming the dialectical connection between the interpreter who is rooted in the reality of his life and his spiritual horizon, and the historical story that is in a different horizon. In other words, the reading of every text is of topical significance. It is Effective Historical Consciousness that drives the student's interest in the historical story and builds up his or her basic curiosity and understanding.

The nature of Effective Historical Consciousness is conscious movement from the present to the past and back. The historical story deals with a different reality of time and space, but in fact, it indirectly relates to the reality of our life in the present (Gadamer, 1999, pp. 299–302, 358, 374–375). Effective Historical Consciousness requires the historian to be keenly aware of the context in which his understanding takes place, and so observation of the historical story will always be reflective and rational. It will raise questions of why we are interested in this subject, why have we focused on it and not another, what this story actually tells us about ourselves, and why is it significant for us.

To complete the process of inculcation of meaning into historical interpretation, Gadamer adds the concept "Fusion of Horizons." This is essential to the process of understanding in general and the educational process in particular, as it focuses attention on the ethical aspect of the encounter of the partners to learning with conflicting narratives, and on the dialogue itself.

Fusion of Horizons

Gadamer states that the understanding of history means understanding the forces acting on human beings, and to understand them we must look into ourselves. Gadamer employs the horizon metaphor to explain the interpretive process. A horizon is the space of observation within us. Our ability to understand something derives from the fact that we have a horizon, but our understanding is not captive to the limits of the horizon. The horizon, claims Gadamer, is not a rigid, methodical borderline; instead, it can contract and expand and is not actually closed: "A horizon is something into which we move and that moves with us" (Gadamer, 1999, p. 245). According to Gadamer, hermeneutics is contending with our tradition and the horizon of our experience by means of a dual human story from another horizon. In this encounter the horizons fuse and the fusing process creates the meaning in our consciousness. The premise underlying the "Fusion of Horizons" concept is that human experience possesses its own language, and this language is common to all humankind. Even if one lives in different "horizons" of place, time, and culture, he can understand other people's stories. These areas of human similarity prepare people for similar experiences and situations and for contending with similar problems (Gadamer, 1999, p. 302).

Fusion of Horizons seeks a human relationship which is ready to deal with and understand another's different horizon through a new look at the interpretive horizon. Unlike scientific research in which the researcher is both the questioner and the one who answers the question, the essence of Fusion of Horizons is a dialogue between the interpreter and the interpreted: Both question and both answer, each from within his real world. The relationship between them is therefore not one of questioner-questioned as subject-object, but one between two human beings, one of "I-Thou."

The added value of Fusion of Horizons is realized in the "expanded self" that provides us with a wider panorama for observing the world, containing not only our own horizon but also the other's. "Openness to the other," says Gadamer, "involves recognizing that I myself must accept some things that are against me, even though no one else forces me to."(Gadamer, 1999, p. 361; Ricoeur, 1981). This intentionality of understanding, personal deviation, self-recognition, as well as the irony that sometimes accompanies them, express an essential change in our approach to the processes of understanding and knowing: We accept that our understanding is bound up in a dialogical encounter between two subjects living in different horizons, and thus a language of human engagement is formed between us. In this chain, says Gadamer, it is our willingness to enable different horizons to challenge our "pre-judgments" and even reject them that opens for us doors to complex understanding, tolerance, and containing (Gadamer, 1999, p. 367).

In a society entrenched in a constant violent conflict, historical education conducted in the spirit of the Gadamerian dialogue may heighten conciliatory awareness and constitute an effective tool for education toward peace. The process of fusing horizons will make it possible for young people to deal with the components of the culture of conflict which characterized their collective identity, abandon their prejudgments, and develop a new stance toward the components in their identity that are no longer relevant. Thus a conciliatory awareness may develop which will prepare the hearts and minds for the transition to a culture of peace.

The Dilemma of an Active Past in Israeli History Education

As mentioned earlier, education toward peace assumes that at the basis of an ethno-political conflict lie contradictory collective narratives, replete with painful historical memories that serve as a backbone for the collective identities of those involved in the conflict. The principal objective of education toward peace is to engender the acceptance by each opponent of the legitimacy of the other's narrative and the recognition of the responsibility of both parties in the conflict. When a relentless conflict in which the historical past is still active, this is a demanding process that is both rational and emotional.

In the first 30 years after the establishment of the State of Israel, Israeli society developed a set of beliefs, stances, and emotions that matched the conflict, justified it, and prepared the state for its struggle for survival. The collective memory that was consolidated within the education system was monolithic, highlighting the need to enlist Israeli society in the mission of establishing the Jewish state. One must not forget that all this took place following the trauma of the Holocaust in World War II and after an extremely brutal battle for survival against seven Arab countries in 1948. The peace agreement with Egypt, and later with Jordan, led to a change in attitudes regarding the conflict.

Since the mid-1970s Israeli-Jewish society has undergone a significant change. An alternative culture, which proposed contents that negated the central themes of the initial conflict, gradually began developing in the Israeli society. Writers, playwrights, cinematographers, and intellectuals began presenting the image of the Arab in a more human and personal way, together with his needs and legitimate objectives. They began asking trenchant questions about the part Israel played in perpetuating the conflict, its military culture, the mistaken decisions of its leaders, and they proposed peaceful relations between Jews and Arabs as their supreme objective.

Changes also took place in Israeli historiographical research that examined the roots of the conflict and even in some of the curricula that were written within the education system as of the 1990s. The first generation of Israeli historians took upon themselves the mission of writing the Zionist narrative and incorporating this narrative into the system of education. However, from the early 1980s, a new generation of historians published numerous studies that questioned the traditional narrative, criticized its interpretation, and promoted a far more reflective and even critical perspective toward the Zionist project (Naveh, 2007).

In May 1994, the Ministry of Education announced its "peace education policy" specifying the knowledge, attitudes and skills required of teachers and students for this new centre of attention. It also declared that the year 1994–1995 would be dedicated to "the peace process: Israel in the Middle East," and published a catalogue that comprised over 400 booklets and teaching devices (Ministry of Education and Sport, 1995).

In spite of the official Israeli policy, the majority of religious Jewish schools, including all the ultra-Orthodox Jewish schools and a majority of the Arab-Israeli schools, did not participate in the previous coexistence trend or in the "peace process years" (Firer, 2008).

The Palestinian National Authority (PNA) did not allow any direct relations between Israeli and Palestinian academic institutes; it also forbade Palestinian public schools from participating in joint programs with the United Nations Relief and Works Agency schools (resulting in many NGOs on both sides working as mediators). Therefore, most of the joint peace-education projects were carried out between the Israeli state schools (mostly non-religious) and the few private schools in the PNA (which were usually supported by Christian agencies). As a result, nearly all the encounters during those days took place within the state of Israel, among the Israelis of both ethnicities, and were informal in nature (Maoz, 2000).

Doubtless, in present-day reality there is still a great deal of asymmetry between the parties. As shown in the study of Maoz about the meetings of Jewish and Palestinian students in informal education, each party in the conflict is guided by a different agenda. The Israeli side is more interested in planning a shared future of peace based on its achievements, and therefore it does not relate to the problematic parts of the conflict. The Palestinian side seeks a preliminary investigation about what it regards as the wrongs of the past and their rectification (Maoz, 2000).[5]

In view of these understandings, I suggest that it is both feasible and constructive to use the ethno-political conflict as an effective tool in development of a more complex and rational historical thinking. This can be achieved by tackling the roots of the conflict and exposing students to the existence of the conflicting historical narratives in history classes.

The Gadamerian Dialogue: Cognitive and Emotional Implications of Teaching of History

As mentioned earlier, Gadamer proposed "prejudgments," "effective historical consciousness," and "the fusion of horizons" as key concepts that form the process of understanding. I wish to derive from these concepts possible applications for teaching history in formal education as an effective way of educating toward peace, and give one experiment as an example.

Departure from Prejudgments during History Instruction

Understanding the departure from prejudgments within the teaching of history is essential to the teaching process. The working assumption in teaching is that a learning dialogue that brings together a group of peers with contradictory historical narratives is likely to bring young people to new understandings regarding the historical story, and also to its role in their life.

We assume that history students coming to the classroom are not a tabula rasa, from the standpoint of an empty personality seeking to be filled. They have active working assumptions on the process of history, positions on causes and effects, and sometimes even on the historical figures to be discussed in the lesson. These prejudgments will affect both the way the lesson is given and its discourse. The history teacher will want to clarify how these judgments direct the young peoples' learning, what is meaningful in their views, their attitude toward the various historical figures, and how they absorb the knowledge. In other words, the teacher must recognize the students' thinking when they "think history" and when they formulate historical arguments (Stearns et al, 2000; Wineburg, 2001; Barton & Levstik, 2004).

This point of departure in their thinking will constitute a starting point for the paths of critical historical literacy and observation of cultural materials, and the way they are shaped. The teacher will draw students' attention to the way in which historical knowledge is created and handed down. He will sharpen the students' sensitivity and ability to identify the conceptual lenses of historians and especially to be aware of the incompleteness of their interpretation.

The dialogue with prejudgments enables students to discuss the complexity of the components of their collective identity and develop a new position regarding the components of their identity that are no longer relevant. This observation is a developmental process that seeks to develop young people as thinkers who are aware of the incompleteness of the information reaching them, making them more resistant to the sweeping propaganda of their society, which may exacerbate the conflict. There is a high degree of probability that they will then be able to more maturely discuss similar complexities in the identities of others. This is only possible by virtue of Effective Historical Consciousness, which does not view the historical text as a foreign body but examines its demands and its message.

Memory as History

A possible teaching track emphasizing the teaching of the past can open a discussion in class on shaping the culture and memory of communities and peoples: the way people in the past created their images of homeland and land, death and birth, of assumptions of what is just or unjust, what is moral and what is despicable, and how these images affect life in the present. This approach demands consideration of the circumstances, assumptions, and time at which the memory was formed, but it also heightens awareness of the act of understanding at the time of learning. In other words, a dialogue between the past and present during the studying of history requires constant reflection on the seam lines between past and present by the teacher and the students alike.

Classes of older students can focus on evolution of memory. For example, an examination of attitudes toward the Holocaust and its survivors during various periods, from the disregard and silence of the 1950s; the arousal of consciousness and openness to the survivors' stories in the 1970s; the visits to the death camps in Poland after the fall of the Berlin Wall; the shaping of the camps as preferred memorials during the 1990s; and the desperate clutching at memorial as a cohering force from the end of the 1990s to the early years of the present century shows an evolution of perception. Thus, a question can be posed: Does the aging and gradual demise of the Holocaust survivors drive the need to preserve the memory or is it possible that there is a connection between the heightening of Holocaust memory in Israeli space and the continued occupation of the Palestinian territories? Does the Holocaust possibly serve as a kind of latent contrition vis-à-vis the occupation, or alternatively, is its increased awareness due to a need to justify the occupation? Does an increased awareness serve different, even ambivalent, purposes in the contemporary Israeli political arena? All of the above are examples of difficult questions that tend toward the fusion of contemporary context and historical memory.

This teaching process heightens young peoples' awareness of the way in which their preconceptions act upon the formation of historical memory, empowering their critical capabilities: They create their knowledge "from the inside," but at the same time observe its creation "from the outside." Historicization of memory opens up to young people the essential understanding of the Gadamerian dialogue: A historical discourse deals with another's human story, but it is in fact also an observation of the student's life.

Fusion of Horizons: The Ethical Aspect of Learning

The Fusion of Horizons concept is suitable for use in history instruction in situations of conflict and societal schism because it accepts multiplicity of interpretations of an historical event as an existential situation: It emphasizes the language of encounter and does not seek the bottom line of scientific truth.

As in human reality, a dialogue takes place in an existential sphere for which we need a language of existential meaning and not an "objective" structural language that imprisons the individual in a category and thus restricts his thought. Education operating in the spirit of the Gadamerian dialogue does not seek to camouflage the national, ethnic, class, or gender components of the students' identity; rather, its working assumption is that these components, important as they might be, are only partial dimensions of a much broader identity-human milieu of man qua man.[6]

We therefore occasionally guide the history lesson to the discussion of deeper and more personal aspects and then dwell on them. The group narrative leaves the stage to the students' personal narratives and life stories, and they in turn gain structured and sensitive attention.

The teaching process will present to the class conflicting narratives derived from unquestioned facts on which there is agreement and focus the discussion on the tension between those narratives. The discussion in class will concentrate on the meanings that are ascribed to the different narratives and the feelings of injustice, anxiety, and anger they engender; it will examine the language they use, their mutual demonization, and it will attempt to understand the historical context in which they were formed. The students may accept the new historical narrative in full or in part, or they may reject it completely, but most importantly, they will understand its importance, its seminal place for those who believe in it, and its real effects on the conflict and the everyday lives of all concerned (Yogev, 2007; Batson et al, 2007; Torsti & Ahonen, 2008).

Now that I have described the possible applications of the hermeneutic humanism in the teaching of history as a possible way of education toward peace, I wish to examine one interesting experiment that provides an example of such instruction.

An Attempt to Evoke Conciliation Awareness within a Culture of Conflict

A unique attempt to promote education toward peace through a history dialogue in the spirit of the Gadamerian dialogue is offered by the Israeli and Palestinian academics of PRIME. The Institute works on projects focused on education toward peace.[7]

PRIME brought together a group of 12 teachers, two historians, and 6 observers, which met between 2002 and 2008, to work on a highly ambitious project: The group developed three textbooks that tell the historical story of the Israeli-Arab conflict from both the Israeli and Palestinian points of view.

It is note worthy that seven of the Israeli teachers who participated in the project were students who attended teacher-training workshops that were conducted according to the humanistic hermeneutics approach at the Kibbutzim College of Education. Two of them also worked in the Department of History as lecturers or instructors of teachers' trainees between 2005 and 2008. The selection of teachers suitable for this project was not accidental. Some are kibbutz members who are moderates in the Israeli political spectrum. In addition, the majority of schools that used the unique learning materials developed by the team were kibbutz schools. These schools were more open to what was a fundamentally radical experiment. The study materials had not been approved by the Israel's minister of education at the time, Limor Livnat, and teaching the program was tantamount to an act of dissidence.

Based on the creators' understanding that it is impossible to write a conciliatory narrative in the midst of the conflict, the textbooks comprise two separate narratives that deal with the milestone events in the history of the conflict (*Learning Each Other's Historical Narrative*, booklet I, II, III). The narratives appear on the same page throughout the book, connected with blank lines designated for the students' comments. The students–Jews and Arabs alike–read both narratives and record their responses on the blank lines; they also talk about them in classroom discussions.

The assumption was that the students' daily coping with different narratives that represent different collective "truths" would render a basic change in their prejudgments: In the first stage, they develop an

History Curriculum, Multiple Narratives   95

attitude toward the totality of "the true history" and the reasoning underlying its formation; in the second, they will develop an attitude of mutual respect, tolerance, and sensitivity to the other party's pain (Adwan & Bar-On, 2006).

From the early days of the project it became clear that the definition of the components of success was overly optimistic. The historian Eyal Naveh, one of the project's leaders, describes the difficulties involved in writing the booklets and using them in the experimental classes:

> The participants themselves had to overcome personal reservations and group crises in order to continue their work. Suffice to mention that from the six original Palestinian teachers, only two continued up to the present while other members were frequently replaced. Even the historian who served as the professional facilitator to the Palestinian team did not always keep up with the various stages of the project... The Israeli group was more stable but also experienced moments of crisis and fierce internal disputes. The gap between the enthusiastic international responses outside the region, and the inability to use the material officially in Israel or Palestine, leads to frustration and disappointment. (Naveh, p. 188)

The fifth meeting of Israeli and Palestinian teachers took place in 2003. The teachers who developed the first PRIME project booklet reported on their experiences teaching the two narratives in their (non-mixed) classrooms. The teachers did not teach in mixed classroom, They were mixed as writers. As teachers they only taught in their own national school. The reactions of the majority of the Palestinian students were affected by the harsh reality of their lives under Israeli occupation and detentions, and they related to the narrative from this perspective.[8] Bar-On inform about one of the Palestinians' teachers report that some of the students' reaction to the Israeli narrative related the Balfour Declaration (1917): "They have no place on our land. If they were persecuted, why are they persecuting us? It's our natural right... it is the land of our forefathers... It's a British conspiracy to bring Jews to Palestine. They shouldn't have done that... why do we have to pay the price of their suffering in their Holocaust?" The teacher told that he tried to "defend" the Israeli narrative: "... It is their story ..." His students wanted to know what he thought about the validity of the Israeli arguments, and he felt himself to be a "traitor" (Bar-On, 2006, p. 100).

The Israeli teachers also reported on harsh and angry reaction of their students. One reported:

> The children said that the Palestinian narrative is not history but rather propaganda or tall tales.... the narrative always attacks the Israelis' view—we see how many "wrongs" the Israelis have committed but not one word on the Palestinian part in the conflict...the Palestinians see themselves only as victims and offer no solution...why do we have to study Palestinian propaganda in class, particularly in view of the violent conflict...? (Bar-On, 2006, p. 101)

Bar-On claimed that the dynamic meeting of the Israeli and the Palestinian group came in the fifth workshop over the issue of whether to continue the project and resulted in a defining moment: The teachers agreed to replace the term "propaganda" with the term "a partial picture." The national flags would be removed from the booklets, and the teachers also expressed their willingness to change the original texts in the booklet. In the thirteenth meeting, held in Germany during the summer of 2004, an Israeli teacher asked his Palestinian colleague: "When I teach your narrative...what do you feel is the most important thing that you want me to convey to my students?" (Bar-On, 2006, p. 104). It had taken thirteen meetings to articulate the question.

The example presented above indicates the extent to which the Israeli and Palestinian societies are still yearning for differentiated categories of identity and culture. In view of the findings so far, I believe that it is imperative to continue the process with greater resolve and to refrain from despair—even when the flames of the conflict continue to burn. During intractable conflicts, different interpretations of the historical story are created and each nation bases its collective identity on its own interpretations. I believe that instead of fighting this process, it is better to reinforce an educational process that focuses on the recognition of these different interpretations and their underlying logic, and at the same time respects those differences. Studying history through conflicting narratives enables a dialogue and a sharing of life stories, clarifies the differences between narratives by neutralizing the humiliating parts or the parts that undermine the other, and at the same time maintains their distinctions. Encountering this type of learning environment is threatening, and it can create a temporary schism in the students' consciousness. In such a situation, the young person will analyze positions of his or her parents and immediate environment, including the sincerity of his or her own position in the face of social pressure for conformism.

Along with the resolution to commence history education that confronts conflicting narratives, it would be useful to study the extent to which children and young adults are capable of coping with two solutions to the same problem and the extent to which this ability may be transferred to intractable conflicts. Interesting research about challenges encountered by teachers and students attempting to deal with conflictual historical narratives in integrated bilingual schools in Israel showed that those involved in the educational initiative drew selectively from formal and informal sources in order to support their identification and sense of belonging within their particular political, national, and religious communities. The vignettes in the studies presented a complex picture that is not necessarily encouraging in terms of the potential of education to help overcome situations of intractable conflict (Bekerman, 2009). These are not optimistic findings, but I think that learning environment in which the presence of conflicting narratives in educational materials is the norm renders the different narratives as history, dismantles the mythical dimension of the sense of victimhood that is rooted in them, normalizes their existence, and increases the young student's capability of containing them.

Summary

It may be said that every society maintains a biased and distorted collective memory, but the collective memory of an inflexible and continuous conflict has greater significance and effect than any other memory. As one that is so relevant to and functional in the present, it channels the view of reality into extremely narrow straits, and does not enable complex understanding of the past which could shed new light on both present and future.

The development of a conciliatory awareness demands a change in the psychological-social state of mind that developed over the period of conflict. It particularly mandates a change in the social objectives, including reversing the de-legitimization of the enemy as well as removing fear, distrust and hatred. This kind of change is by nature prolonged and complex during which progress and withdrawal will continually alternate. The process of conciliation demands the creation of a new ethos, embedded in the culture of peace, which mandates an extremely significant turnabout in society. New norms of values, opinions, symbols, and collective memory must be created. One of the ways recognized as having a strong effect on promoting psychological conciliation is education toward peace (Harris, 1999; Markova, 2003; Kilpatrick & Leitch, 2004; Barton & Levstik, 2004; Bar-Tal & Salomon, 2006; Batson et al, 2007; Torsti & Ahonen, 2008; Bekerman, 2008).

As stated earlier, education toward peace assumes that the basis of ethno-political conflicts is contradictory collective narratives, replete with painful historical memories, which serve as the backbone of the collective identities of those involved in the conflict. Its principal objective is to bring about the acceptance of the legitimacy of the narrative of the adversary. Consequently, it is imperative that education toward peace aspires to develop new stances and skills among students, inculcate tolerance, self-control, sensitivity to the needs of the other, critical thinking, and openness.

The history lesson is a most suitable space for nurturing education toward peace because it offers young people the opportunity to discuss the components of the culture of the conflict that characterizes their collective identity. Such can foster development of new dispositions.

The Gadamerian Hermeneutic-Humanism that this chapter presents may serve as a strategy for promoting conciliatory awareness between conflicting collective identities through rational historical education. The concept is suitable for teaching history in conflict situations because:

- It adopts a pluralistic position and enables conflicting stories as an existential state.
- It accepts the partiality of the speaker's interpretive view.
- It suggests treating the other's historical story as a human truth rather than a scientific truth and it focuses on listening and the resulting action.

The implementation of teaching in the spirit of the Gadamerian Dialogue might constitute a good resource for evoking conciliation awareness in any society which experiences a state of a prolonged conflict. The challenge of teaching history in such a society resides in navigating wisely between the contradictory goals of history teaching in the right dosage. For that purpose, we need to agree that fostering learners as historical thinkers is the first necessary step on the way to an enlightened conciliation. Instead of delivering a unilateral monolithic knowledge during history classes, we should consider them as a cultural and political deed, illustrating the nature of comprehension and the learners' share in constructing historical knowledge. Learning classes should become an experiential space, whose goal is: acquaintance with the collective memory, development of a democratic culture and an encounter with a multitude of narratives which respond to the components of society.

In order to allow education for history to cope with its contradictory goals in a state of an intractable conflict and to position it as a foundation for evoking a conciliation awareness, teaching should develop in three stages: at young age, teachers will choose the "good story" for the purpose of nurturing the collective memory element as well as use it in a way worthy of education for values (the epic narrative of a national revolution, struggle for human rights, the story of outstanding heroes, various dilemmas of valued choice, etc). In junior high, teaching of history will present stories with different interpretative versions (similar to the movie "Rashomon"—mutually contradictory stories or a flashback within a flashback) in order to illustrate the analytical element in historians' work and the fact that history is an interpretative discipline. In high school, history teachers will demonstrate the function of memory in forming identity, illustrate how it changes with time and how different groups use it distinctly. In order to attain these goals, teachers will present to the class primary sources in an accessible dosage as well as internet knowledge, contemporary cinematography, visual art and classic literature.

Another possible accomplishment of history teaching according to the humanistic-hermeneutic perception is encompassed in its ability to allow the group to perform an intra-conciliation with its historical narratives, even in their less heroic moments. Getting acquainted with the shadows in the historical narrative and acknowledging them as an existential component requiring reference and revision, might expand the adolescents' capability to view the complexity of the state of conflict and their group's share in the conflict.

This process of teaching can never reach a "bottom line," and its very existence is largely Sisyphean. However, I believe that teaching history while emphasizing its multi-perspectives is likely to serve as a good basis for education toward the tolerance and openness that Israeli society so desperately needs.

Notes

1. "An intractable conflict" is defined as a violent conflict related to existential objectives which continue over numerous years, with not hope to resolve it. It involves a high security, social and economic price, and confronts society with arduous challenges of adjustment to life under conditions of incessant pressure, security stress, and continuous loss to people and property (Bar-Tal, 2007).
2. Gadamer, Hans-Georg (1900–2002) was a disciple of Heidegger, one of twentieth century's most important philosophers, and made a significant contribution to philosophical hermeneutics. His principal ideas appear in his great work, *Truth and Method*, published in 1960. Despite the book's title Gadamer deals but sparingly with the methodological aspect and is mainly interested in the epistemological aspect of understanding per se: clarification of the conditions under which understanding exists, and particularly its connection with the historical context. The book was published in several editions and translated into numerous languages. The task of hermeneutics, Gadamer claims, is to assist in the understanding of the true meaning of texts, works of art, and spiritual traditions. In his writings he deals extensively with the processes of creating human meaning through dialogue and human encounter, and in this sense he advances the concept of intelligence located in societal and cultural contexts, and which varies in space and time. Gadamer conducted trenchant debates with notable philosophers that gained wide attention, like Jürgen Habermas, Jacques Derrida, and Emilio Betti.
3. With this assertion Gadamer rehabilitated a concept that had been a thorn in the side of philosophers since the Age of Enlightenment. Historical understanding, he claimed, could only rely on the cultural materials that had developed up to its time. The constant variation of the historical context and the new thought categories it produces prevent the attainment of the objective knowledge sought by the cultural heritage of the Enlightenment. "Insofar as we understand it all," says Gadamer, "we understand differently" (Bernstein, 1983).
4. Most of the theorists, who questioned Gadamer's hermeneutical philosophy, led by J. Habermas, held reservations regarding his rejection of the need for scientific methods and claimed that he accepted, too hastily, the authority of tradition thus diminishing the critical dimension required for the act of understanding. Habermas argued that the role of hermeneutics is to be at the service of the humanities and society as a method that would expose the ideological elements of tradition that had been blurred and then vanished from the figures that acted in the historical situation. To free himself from the constraining influence of tradition the interpreter must adopt a critical stance toward it and reflect the dominating relations that shaped the worldview of the studied figures, and also that of the interpreter himself (Habermas, 1988; Mootz, 1988).
5. See also another critically evaluated case study from Israel: Zelniker, T., Hertz-Lazarowitz, R., Peretz, H., Azaiza, F., Sharabany, R. (2008). Arab and Jewish Students' Participatory Action Research at the University of Haifa: A Model for Peace Education, in: McGlynn, C. M., Zemblas, M., Bekerman, Z., Gallgher, A. (Eds.). *Peace education and post-conflict societies: Comparative perspectives*. 199–214, New York: Palgrave Macmillan.
6. Arising from Gadamer's philosophy is that people living in Israel in the framework of different cultural groups can define other people living in other cultural groups, and their connection with them, in far broader ways than the way in which political leaders and sometimes even academics and clerics define people living in different cultural groups, and the appropriate relationships between them.
7. The project is managed under the auspices of The Peace Research Institute in the Middle East (PRIME), a joint Israeli and Palestinian initiative ngo. Its co-directors are Sami Adwan, Prof. of Education, Bethlehem University and Dan Bar-On, Prof. of Social Psychology, Ben Gurion University. They are assisted by two history professors, Prof. Adnan Massallam

History Curriculum, Multiple Narratives

(Bethlehem University) and Prof. Eyal Naveh (Tel-Aviv University and the Kibbutzim College of Education. Dew to the death of Dan Bar-On on September 2008, Naveh is currently the Israeli Director of Prime). This section is based on the narratives of five teachers and lecturers participating in the experiment who related it to me and elaborating articles written by the principal researchers who directed the project.

8. Most of the Palestinians teachers came from Hebron region and East Jerusalem.

References

Adwan, S & Bar-On, D. (2006). PRIME's sharing the History Project: Palestinians and Israeli teachers and pupils learning each other's narrative. In S. Mcoy-Levy (Ed.), *Troublemakers or peacemakers?* 217–234. Notre Dame, IN: Notre Dame University Press.

Bar-On, D. (2006). *Tel your story: Creating dialogue between Jews and Germans, Palestinians and Israelis*, 82–123. Beer-Sheva: Ben-Gurion University of the Negev Press (Hebrew).

Bar-Tal, D. (2007). *Living with the conflict: Socio-psychological of the Jewish Society in Israel, Jerusalem: Carmel (Hebrew).*

Bar-Tal, D. & Salomon, G. (2006). Israeli-Jewish narratives of the Israeli-Palestinian's conflict: Evolvement, contents, functions and consequences. In R. I. Rothberg (Ed), *Israeli and Palestinian's narratives of Conflict: History's double helix*, 19–46). Bloomington, IN: Indiana University Press.

Barton, K. C. (2005). History and identity in pluralist democracies: Reflections on research in the U.S. and Northern Ireland. *Canadian Social Studies 39*(2). Retrieved October 1, 2007 from: http://www.quasar.ualberta.ca/css/Css_39_2/ARBarton_pluralist_democracies.htm.

Barton, K. C. & Levstik, L. S. (2004). *Teaching history for the common good*. Mahwah, NJ: Lawrence Erlbaum.

Barton, K. C. & McCully, A. W. (March 2006). Secondary students' perspectives on school and community history in Northern Ireland. *The European Social Science History Conference*, Amsterdam.

Batson, C. D., Eklund, J. H., Chermok, V. L., Hoyt. J. L., & Ortiz, B.G. (2007). An additional antecedent of empathic concern: Valuing the welfare of the person in need. *Journal of Personality and Social Psychology 93*(1), 65–74.

Bekerman, Z. (2009). The complexities of teaching historical conflictual narratives in integrated Palestinians-Jewish schools in Israel, *International Review of Education 55*, 235–250.

Benvenisti, M. (1995). *Intimate enemies: Jews and Arabs in a shared land*, 198–199. Berkeley: University of California Press.

Bernstein, R. J. (1983). *Beyond objectivism and relativism: Science, hermeneutics praxis*. Philadelphia: University of Pennsylvania Press.

Derrida, J. (1976). *Of grammatology*. Baltimore, MD: Johns Hopkins University Press.

Firer, R. (2008). Virtual peace education. *Journal of Peace Education 5*(2), 193–207.

Gadamer, H. G. (1999). *Truth and method* (Second edition). Translated by J. Weinsheimer & D. Marshall. New York: Continuum.

Galtung, J. (1996). *Peace by peaceful means: Peace and conflict, development and civilization.* Oslo: International Peace Research Institute.

Habermas, J. (1988). *On the logic of the social sciences*. Cambridge, MA: MIT Press.

Harris, I. M. (1999). Types of peace education. In Amira Raviv, Louis Oppenheimer, & Bar-Tal, Daniel (Eds.), *How children understand war and peace: A call for international peace education*, 299–317. San Francisco, CA: Jossey-Bass.

Kilpatrick, R. & Leitch, R. (2004). Teachers' and pupils' educational experiences and school-based responses to the conflict in Northern Ireland. *Journal of Social Issues* 60(2), 563–586.

Leman, J. (1997). Undocumented migrants in Brussels: Diversity and the anthropology of illegality. *New Community* 23(1), 25–41.

Lowenthal, D. (2000). Dilemmas and delights of learning history. In P. Stearns, P. Siexas, & S. Wineburg (Eds.), *Knowing, teaching and learning history: National and international perspectives*. pp. 63–82. New York: New York University Press.

Maoz, I. (2000). Power relations in inter-group encounters: A case study of Jewish-Arab encounters in Israel. *International Journal of Intercultural Relations* 24(2), 259–277.

Maoz, I. B., Bekerman, D. Z., & Jaber-Massarwa, S. (2004). Learning about "good enough" through "bad enough": A story of a planned dialogue between Israeli Jews and the Palestinians. *Humans Relations* 57(9), 1075–1101.

Markova, I. (2003). *Dialogicality and social representations*. Cambridge: Cambridge University Press.

McGlynn, C. (2008). Negotiating cultural difference in divided societies: An analysis of approaches to integrated education in Northern Ireland. In C. McGlynn, M. Zemblas, Z. Bekerman, Z., & A. Gallgher (Eds.), *Peace education and post-conflict societies: Comparative perspectives*, 9–26. New York: Palgrave Macmillan.

Megill, A. (1979). Foucault structuralism and the ends of history. *Journal of Modern History* 51, 451–505.

Mootz, F. (1988). The ontological basis of legal hermeneutics: A proposed model of inquiry based on the work of Gadamer, Habermas and Ricoeur. *B.U.L Review* 68, 523.

Naveh, E. (2007). Recognition as preamble to reconciliation: A two narratives approach in a Palestinian—Israeli history textbook. *Horizons Universities* 3(4), 173–188.

Niens, U. & Cairns, E. (2005). Conflict, contact, and education in Northern Ireland. *Theory into Practice* 44(4), 337–344.

Ricoeur, P. (1981). *Hermeneutics and the human sciences*. Translated by J. B. Thompson. Cambridge: Cambridge University Press.

Ross, L. & Ward, A. (1996). Naïve realism in everyday life: Implications for social conflict and misunderstanding. In E. S. Reed, E. Turiel, & E. Brown (Eds.), *Values and knowledge*, 103–135. Mahwah, NJ: Lawrence Erlbaum Associates.

Rouhana, N. N. & Bar-Tal, D. (1998). Psychological dynamics of intractable ethno-national conflicts: The Israeli-Palestinian case. *American Psychologist* 53, 761–774.

Salomon, G. (2000). Rashomon is not a Film. *Panim* 15(1) (Hebrew), 41–42.

——— (2002). The Nature of peace education: Not all programs are created equal. In G. Salomon & B. Nevo (Eds.), *Peace education: The concept, principles, and practices around the world*, 3–13. Mahwah, NJ: Lawrence Erlbaum Associates.

Seixas, P. (2000). Schweigen die kinder! Or, does postmodern history have a place in the Schools? In P. Stearns, P. Siexas, & S. Wineburg (Eds.), *Knowing, teaching and learning history: National and international perspectives*, 19–37. New York: New York University Press.

Torsti, P. & Ahonen, S. (2008). Deliberative history classes for a post-conflict society, theoretical development and practical implication through international education in United World College in Bosnia and Herzegovina. In C. McGlynn, M. Zemblas, Z. Bekerman, & A. Gallgher (Eds.), *Peace education in post-conflict societies: Comparative perspectives*, 222–226. New York: Palgrave Macmillan.

Warnke, G. (1987). *GadamerHermeneutics, tradition and reason*. Stanford, CA: Stanford University Press.

White, H. (1987). *The content of the form: Narrative discourse and historical representation*. Baltimore: Johns Hopkins University Press

Wineburg, S. (2001). *Historical thinking and other unnatural acts: Charting the future of teaching the past*. Philadelphia: Temple University Press.

Yogev, E. (2007). Promoting understanding through teaching history. In P. A. Bartolo, A. M. Lous, & T. Hofsass (Eds.), *Responding to student diversity: Teacher education and classroom practice*, 295–314). Qawra: Malta University.

Zelniker, T., Hertz-Lazarowitz, R., Peretz, H, Azaiza, F, Sharabany, R. (2008). Arab and Jewish Students' participatory action research at the University of Haifa: A model for peace education. In C. McGlynn, M. Zemblas, Z. Bekerman, & A. Gallgher (Eds.), *Peace education in post-conflict societies: Comparative perspectives*, 199–214. New York: Palgrave Macmillan.

CHAPTER FIVE

Pluralism and Transformative Social Studies "Us and Them": Challenges for the Indian Classroom

TEESTA SETALVAD

The Indian subcontinent is unique in its pulsating diversity of faiths, languages, and cultures, challenging the educationist's creativity and commitment to pluralism within the classroom. India has 22 official languages and dozens of other dialects. It is a vast region with interwoven and competing traditions and beliefs. The transaction within the classroom, especially through textbooks, poses a great challenge for the educator. Hegemonizing tendencies have painted a monochromatic vision of the past that is influenced by a political agenda for the present and future. This monochromatic vision has consolidated within history and social-studies textbooks and, especially, in teaching. In a country that is the size of many continents, the vision and narrative reflected in the history and social-studies texts need to negotiate a delicate balance between regional and national histories. A lived experiment with pluralism can be seen in the multiple cultures of the subcontinent, but it is absent from its teaching methodology and textbooks. Despite sharp hegemonizing tendencies, however, India continues at a fundamental level to celebrate its own diversity.

Hundreds of years of negotiation in the business of living and power sharing in India have produced a robust coexistence of faiths and cultures that challenges attempts at monocultural hegemony. Two parallel phenomena are unique to this subcontinent. A negotiation and assimilation of many faiths through the centuries has resulted in shared spaces and a multireligious and multicultural experience unparalleled anywhere else in the world, giving us a unique sense of lived negotiation and coexistence. In parallel, this eclectic and unique phenomenon has been marked by the existence and consolidation of a cruel side of the organized Hindu faith, the phenomenon of caste that for centuries has brutally denied and discriminated against a fourth of its own people.

Yet there are further complications for the educator besides this multitextured reality. The challenges thrown by the proponents of harsh right-wing ideologies over the past decades—ideologies that advocate a narrow and exclusivist vision of the past in the hope that it will give them control over the present and future—challenge the educationist to creatively enlist India's pluralist traditions in order to help young minds embrace an understanding of diversity within a democracy committed to critical reasoning, dialogue, and nonviolence. Within India, the overarching tendency in the past decades is to blatantly promote a right-wing Hindu nation-building exercise through the education project. This Hindu nation is at once inherently antidemocratic and hegemonizing, thus denying India's pluralist past and also promoting a narrow upper-class, upper-caste vision of reality.

Such a hegemonizing project that manipulates history and controls the content and share of education is not only inherently antidemocratic; it is not unique to South Asia. The brutal suppression of the history of the original and indigenous peoples on the North American continent, American Indians, and the glaring absence of the narrative of their oppression from modern textbooks is comparable. So is the reluctant negotiation with Maori history a contribution to modern Australia's culture and ethos. France, a nation that prides is itself on its secularism, has a strange tradition within history teaching: Modern French textbooks in history are whetted by the country's Ministry of Defense. The period between the first and second World Wars is glossed over to avoid the embarrassment of the Vichy regime's transparent collaboration with the Nazis. Even the historic image of Charles de Gaulle addressing the French resistance from the British Broadcasting Corporation (BBC) studios in London barely conceals the fact that the black Algerian soldiers, who were the core body of that resistance, were denied French citizenship at the time.

A genuine open exploration of every modern country and of the history of civilization history inevitably reveals dominant and prejudicial denials and distortions (Leahey, 2009; Lowen, 2009). Work in peace education pries open these spaces to enable all people an equal and legitimate share in the past, and through this the future, such as the efforts of the Peace History Society (2009).

Such an analysis of history and social-studies teaching that the project KHOJ (Quest): Education for a Pluralistic India has developed could positively impact the negative fallout of the "separation strategy" being adopted by Israel. Conversations with Arab-speaking Christians, let alone Muslims who travel to Jerusalem, reveal sad levels of antipathy that include the refusal of pizza parlors in the holy city to serve the popular fast food to any who speaks the "alien" Arab tongue!

The Historic Context

Denial and discrimination as the source or the core of conflict is not easily institutionally acknowledged and pedagogically given its due. In the Indian, or the subcontinental (or South Asian) context, the historicity of denial and consequent discrimination is thousands of years old, sanctioned socially and scripturally through the organized system of caste.

In the otherwise wider and often repugnant descriptions that illustrate what the caste system is, and what it does—practices of segregation, ostracism, and relegation of "menial" tasks to a section of people ordained through birth not to perform any other function—its core, has been the rigid denial of the right to knowledge gathering, learning, and education to a whole segment of the Indian people.

Confronting inequality and discrimination head on, even the inequality of a social system and of a religious system that is often sanctioned by scriptures has therefore meant, historically, reclaiming the right to knowledge and to history itself, such knowledge gathering being kept in an exclusivist preserve, "owned" by a powerful few, through the system of caste. The history of education in the Indian subcontinent has therefore meant the rediscovery and acknowledgement of the contexts of this struggle through the contextualization and contours of this debate.

The terrain of education is therefore a deeply complex and contested territory within South Asia. A philosophy for peace education in the modern Indian context needs to both historicize this conflict and simultaneously develop a pluralistic content and the inclusive approach that is necessary to a democracy. Consequently, acknowledgements of these denials and discriminations include eliminating the shadows and silences of our history and social-studies teaching and books through restoring content; the emergent peace education philosophy needs to adapt to the continued denial of access to primary education for disadvantaged sections (quantitatively) in modern-day India while qualitatively addressing the lacunae in perspective and content. The student is an active agent in this process of relearning, along with the teacher, parents, and active accomplices. The goal is to challenge education policy and textbooks that have (with the notable exception of recent efforts by the National Council for Educational Research and Training (NCERT) doggedly refused to respond to demands for change.

From ancient to early medieval periods in South Asia to modern periods of history, strong philosophical struggles challenging the restrictions put in place by caste denials have been key to the growth of resistance to this oppressive practice A language of resistance that is at once theoretical and practical has evolved, articulating itself through the voices of poet saints, reformers, and finally, in modern times, radical humanists and rationalists.

A myriad of emergent philosophies and discourses have, apart from being diverse and pluralistic, challenged the hegemonies of the caste system in a nonviolent way, through discourse, alternate-faith systems, and literature. Our history is replete with these examples. The birth of Jainism and Buddhism in the ancient period was among the first challenges to this man-made segregation. In the early medieval periods, the voice and writings of poets, saints, and philosophers like Namdeo (1270–1350 AD), Thiruvellar (first century BC), Dnyaneshwar (1275–1296 AD), Eknath (1533–1599 AD), Tukaram (1577–650 AD) and Kabir (1398–1518 AD) resonated among the people creating a mass consciousness on issues of social justice. The emergence of these poet discourses and their rapid spread among the people created an accessible system of people's peace education.

Observations like this polite, yet prescient, comment by Dnyaneshwar that "the Vedas (religio-philosophic texts of caste Hinduism) are rich in knowledge, but also miserly because the information contained within is available only to three *varnas (*castes)" (Women and Culture, 1985) give a sense not simply of the philosophy, but also the deep scholarship of the poet saints. The dialogue between a man of indigenous origin and a Turk of aggressive temper, Eknath (the Hind Turk Samvad, Eknath, 1533–1599) is another example of an intellectual grappling with the challenges of intercultural coexistence. Saint Tukaram, another poet born in the region that is modern-day Maharashtra, came to symbolize the acclaimed Varkari tradition.

As Jayant Lele and Rajendra Singh (1984) explain, the Warkaris belong to a distinct stream of critical reflection with an established framework for the institutionalization of critical thought and activity, and Tukaram was an outstanding example of them. The ability to critique traditions and question inequity and discrimination is deeply rooted in the historical discourses of the subcontinent. The absence of this exploration from our history texts denies young minds access to the richness of this past.

The propagation of the worship of an impersonal deity by many poet-philosophers among the non-Brahmanical population also produced what is known as the Nirguna tradition. The words of the poet saint Kabir, who was born to a weaver, are among the most illustrious of this tradition. His couplets, however, have had a universal appeal, and they resonate through the villages and small towns of north India to this day.

Along with these subaltern struggles against caste, Indian history is also replete with examples of monarchies and oligarchies practicing a practical pluralism. King Asoka of ancient India (Thapar, 1961), who converted to Buddhism after a bloody conquest and war, spoke to the people through inscriptions in the local languages—bypassing the upper-caste language of Sanskrit. King Akbar, who after Asoka controlled the vastest unified territory in the sixteenth century, not only practiced pluralism, he withdrew discriminatory taxes like the *jazziya* tax, which before its repeal was applied to non-Muslims alone, and he also evolved his own version of a syncretic form of belief, *Din-E-elahi* (Ali 2006; Habib 1995). Shivaji, the Maratha ruler from the peasant castes who commandeered a huge guerrilla army, challenged latter day Moghul rule and the excessive taxes. He also had Muslims among his most trustworthy ministers and general lieutenants (Pansare, 1998; Sabhasada & Sen 1977). Ironically, a ruler like Shivaji has been appropriated in many parts of western India as a symbol of "Hindu" pride and hegemony, providing a clear example of the religio-political right's blatant manipulations of history. In 1953, a prominent trade unionist, S. A. Dange, wrote a powerful lecture titled "Their Shivaji, Our Shivaji" to the working class presenting a lucid essay about this appropriation. Contemporary sources like the Sabhasad Chronicles provide evidence of the same. Similarly, rulers like Tipu Sultan, ruler of Mysore in the south, and Shahu Maharaj (1874–1922) both implemented and practiced a system of affirmative action allowing students from among the depressed castes learning and job opportunities, thereby articulating democratic needs and responding with political solutions that reflected rare maturity and vision.

Romila Thapar (1997) explains in *Communalism Combat* that

> when we study Indian history, we also need to examine Religion in Indian history which was quite different from the way religion evolved through the history of Europe. Indian or subcontinental history is replete with instances, from the ancient period on, of the patronage by rulers of religions other than their own. The ruler or the monarch had to observe a policy of pluralism. This is unheard of in European history where you would never hear of a Christian monarch ever building a mosque. Various eras in Indian history are full of such examples: during the rule by the Kushans, there was evidence of a coexistence of Shaivism and Buddhism, during the medieval period; the Moghul kings provide examples of this. So we need to ask ourselves the motive or reason behind this multi-purpose patronage? Because it was good political policy? Pragmatic for a pluralist society? (p. 2)

With the advent of colonialism and its consequent oppressions, an interesting change was that through missionary education working classes and castes were for the first time given the opportunity for dignified education and allowed entry to schools. This practice was not popular with everyone: South India particularly experienced full-fledged riots as the privileged sections resisted this widening of opportunities to their countrymen. But these developments, among other consequences, sharpened the discourses, challenges. We saw the emergence of protests demanding education for all, schools for castes dubbed "lower" came up and for the first time, girls received formal schooling. Jyotiba Phule's Gulamgiri writing about slavery (1873) was a scathing exposure of the social economic and political dimensions of caste (Gulamgiri, as published in Deshpande, 2002). It sounded a clarion call to wage a struggle against the scripture-sanctified social system of Hindus. Phule's wife, Savitri Phule, opened one of the first schools for girls in the country (in Pune in western India) and its work among Brahmin widows was path breaking. This period, the nineteenth century, saw the emergence of strong movements of protest amongst western India's "low" and "untouchable castes." The government of Maharashtra has published Phule's Collected Works in two volumes. The book *Caste, Conflict* and *Ideology: Mahatma Jotirao Phule and Low Caste Protest in Nineteenth-Century Western India* is also a thorough study of this period (O'Hanlon, 2002).

It is out of this rich and diverse tradition of critical rational discourse and pluralism that the struggle for independence against the British was born. Hindu social reformers of the nineteenth centuries also began to speak out against practices such as child marriage and for the right of the "upper-caste" widow to remarry (Robertson, 1999). Reforms among the Muslim community, severely hampered by the British following the first war of independence in 1857, took the shape of drawing the community into education through English. Sir Syed, whose vision helped establish the Aligarh Muslim University, was the pioneer in this direction.

The Indian Constitution, the core document that defines the Indian nation, was authored by an advocate and mass leader of the untouchables (who now prefer to go by the emancipatory term *Dalit*—"broken people"), Dr. B.R. Ambedkar was also a strong advocate for radical social reform including the abolition of caste as an unfair and racist construct. When the final draft was completed, however, after eighteen months of rigorous debate in the Constituent Assembly led by ideologues of all hues, including those from within the "Hindu" fold, it settled for "abolishing the practice of untouchability," but not caste (*Constituent Assembly Debates,* December 1946-January 1950). (Today, many Dalits prefer the broader, and politically more empowering term of "Bahujan" a term that literally means the majority. Bahujan includes, apart from the "Untouchables" other castes and sections that were not among the privileged caste hierarchy).

Sixty-two years of our experiment with secular democracy has still not removed some of the wide disparities and denials within education, policy, the classroom, and texts. While the policy of affirmative action for the Dalits has resulted in two generations gaining limited access to education and employment in the government sector, the continued lack of access to primary and secondary education for large numbers of rural and urban Indians, especially those who are poor, tribal, Dalit, and among the religious minorities, points to an institutionalization of historic bias against these sections (Rajinder, 2006). Just as in Japan the prowar movement for the abolition of Article 9 has created a strong resistance movement in support of its continuation, the movement for peace education within India is strongly rooted in modern constitutional values of equality and nondiscrimination (see chapter two).

How We Understand the Past

KHOJ Education for a Pluralistic India Project has for 15 years created innovative and successful techniques and content materials for such a lasting engagement.

When we speak of India, the rich, the poor, the rural, the urban, the tribal, the nontribal, the Dalit, the Hindu, the Muslim, the Christian, the Keralite, the UP-ite, the Gujarati, the Assamese, the task of an creating an education that is committed to pluralism and diversity raises several questions. For instance, how do the student and the teacher of history reconcile the vastness of regional and linguistic distances and locations, the variety and contradictions in community lore and literatures, and the differences of approach and nuance in the varied religious traditions and their symbols, and thereafter put it all together in the study of the one big whole: India and its history?

The excitement and the challenge lies in the need to preserve all these nuances and differences, the variations and the shifts, and gift to the young mind with its infinite capacity to wrangle with multipolar, and varied, senses of history. It also requires that we not be concerned, as the more rigid adult world usually is, with offering certitudes; on the contrary, we encourage contradictions and complexities. Children should be encouraged to doubt, to question, and perhaps, to twist and turn beliefs and practices on their heads.

Our history, literature, culture, and politics are witness to the contribution of a myriad of faiths, beliefs that have woven their own traditions on this soil, or of the manifold peoples who have found for themselves a home on this land. Various traditions touched this land, become enmeshed, flowered, and have grown, and even flourished. How do we approach this plurality within the classroom? The first step is coming to terms with a harsh reality.

The Reality

Equal and fair access to primary and secondary education and high quality textbooks are two levels at which the Indian state has yet to deliver. Poor literacy rates and an underemphasis on planning and finance and on quality primary education, together with the privileged sections benefiting more and more has meant that even today, a wide section of the Indian population is not even first-generation learners. Indian history and social-studies textbooks, excluding the recent attempts, still in an experimental stage, by the National Council for

Educational Research and Training (NCERT) to recast the social studies text, continue to reflect bias. Equally serious, there has been little engagement with the revitalization of history or social-studies teaching in the classroom.

Within this broader framework, we face problems related to classrooms that are increasingly segregated along the lines of religion, language, and social class, which pose a specific challenge for educators who are committed to interreligious understanding. The right to education exists within the Constitution. The first and most basic issue, providing free and fair primary education to every child between ages 0–14, as well as the second issue of parity in quality is mandated in the Constitution in Chapter 4, the "Directive Principles of State Policy." Articles from 14 to 31, that is, the "Fundamental Rights" chapter, Chapter 3 mandates equality and nondiscrimination before the law in matters of public employment, freedom of movement, expression, faith, and so on. After nearly six decades of Independent and Democratic functioning, these two chapters should have already ensured the eradication of illiteracy, and granted basic and good quality education—one that is free of race, caste, and community driven or gender bias. Low and disparate literacy rates and falling school enrollment among young, poor children are testimony that these fundamental rights remain on paper only.

Quality texts would have ensured the broadening of mindsets and have helped to generate a genuinely pluralist and democratic polity. This failure on the education front has compelled the government to pass the recent Education Act specifically mandating the right to education. However, this legislation is severely contested by serious educationists, including KHOJ as it is prescribes a noninclusive and profit-oriented approach (Sadgopal, 2004).

Instead, we have the huge lacunae cause in state-run education explained above. That leaves meaningful education initiatives up to the private sphere. At independence in 1947, the largest number of private schools in India were run by Christian missionaries. For a few hundred years before that, the only major private enterprise in the area of education was the church with its schools and colleges in far-flung parts of the country. Data evidence the church's institutional control (Setalvad, 2005). The Catholic Church has run more than 7000 primary schools, 3000 secondary schools, 150 colleges, 1500 technical and training Institutes, two engineering colleges and two medical colleges, 1700 hostels and boarding houses and over 1000 orphanages. In addition, about 3500 community-centered service institutions such as hospitals, rehabilitation centers, homes for the aged, for the destitute, and for the handicapped are also directly under the care of the church.

Today, the situation has altered drastically. The sharp rise to dominance of the Hindu rightwing in the socio-political sphere is the result of systemic organizational work and consolidation in the field of education for over eighty years, at least since 1922. This is the year that the ideological fountainhead of the right, Rashtriya Swayamsevak Sangh (RSS), which calls itself a cultural organization even though its agenda is downright political, was born. This systemic organizational works in primary and secondary education through the establishment of their own private schools and with textbooks and extracurricular activities that actively promote supremist and racist attitudes in young minds. As of March 2002, Vidya Bharati had 17,396 schools (both rural and urban), 2.2 million students, over 93,000 teachers, 15 teacher-training colleges, 12 degree colleges, and 7 vocational and training institutions (Sundar, 2004). With the state reneging on its main duty to provide free and compulsory primary education, the section of privately controlled education, which dominated by organizations for which education is a tool to generate cadres for its movement toward a Hindu nation. Exclusivism and the ideal of Hindu (upper-caste) supremacy are evident in the texts used by these organizations, which promote enmity and hatred toward other religions. Thus education is the means to a political goal.

The Textbook

Creative interventions toward the learning and teaching of history and social studies on the Subcontinent are a hotly debated issue today. This is after three days of further deterioration in both the Indian and Pakistani history and social studies text over the past three decades (Aziz 1998; Kumar, 2003; Mubarak Ali Papers, 1974–2005).

This selective rendering of the past has also been sharply visible in the "emerald isle," Sri Lanka, which has been racked by bitter war and conflict since the early eighties. Two sharply different renderings of history are taught in the country's Sinhala (and Buddhist) and Tamil (read Hindu and Muslim) medium schools. The genesis of the sharp division within Sri Lankan society goes back to its birth as an independent state, which was accomplished in a way that denied its shared past and history.

In "Will Buddhist Lions Make Peace with Tamil Tigers?" Setalvad (1997) writes,

> Two thousand five hundred years ago, a radical and non-violence challenge to tyrannical and oppressive Hindu Brahmanical practices was posed by the Gautama Buddha who espoused a new spiritual and religious doctrine with a strong secular element Buddhism. The Stupas of Bodh Gaya and Sanchi within India are historical reminders of the location of the birthplace of Buddha, and Buddhism. But the sad historic reality is that Buddhism and Buddhists were driven away from the land of their birth—a testimony to the tenacity and the tyranny of Brahmanism.

Tragically, at the southern tip of the Indian peninsula, this doctrine of the oppressed has metamorphosed itself and assumed a rigid and tyrannical form of its own. The Sinhalization of Sri Lankan Buddhism—seventh century A.D. historical texts speak of many a Tamil-speaking, Buddhist scholar translating ancient works from Pali—was critical in linking a religion with the language of the majority of Sri Lankans.

Today, no Buddhist in Sri Lanka speaks any language but Sinhala. Appropriating historical myths in constructing a superior Sinhala race with Aryan antecedents (due thanks to the European Orientalist tradition) which has prior claim to the land and soil of Sri Lanka is matched by the project for the Tamil state of Eelam (homeland that in no less measure advocates an exclusivist and communal construction of its citizenship...

The dominant community, Sinhala Buddhists who's religious body, the Buddhist Sangha (monastic order of Buddhist monks) was given advisory status to the government after Sri Lanka attained independent status in February 1948, followed by Sinhala (only) as the official language policy adopted through the Language Bill passed by Parliament in 1956 gave successful political expression to this deep rooted exclusivism.

Dr. K. D. Arulpragasam, the former vice chairman of the Sri Lanka's National Education Commission, invited the KHOJ director, Setalvad to address the government and bureaucrats on the criticality of an inclusive and democratic history and social studies curriculum (Setalvad, September 1997). The occasion was a national workshop to review the curriculum being taught with Sri Lanka's schools. The influential educationist Dr. K. D. Arulpragasam spoke hauntingly of what it meant to be a Tamil in Sinhala Buddhist—dominated Sri Lanka.

R.A.L.H. Gunawardana, then vice chancellor of the University of Peradiniya, in a 1997 interview in *Communalism Combat,* expanded on the reconstruction of a dominant exclusivist path followed by both the separatist Tamil Eelam and the Sinhala Buddhist chauvinist movements. A renowned anthropologist, Gunawardana also wrote *Historiography in a Time of Ethnic Conflict: Construction of the Past in Contemporary Sri Lanka* (1995).

The Eelamist interpretation of history and the Sinhala interpretation of history can be seen as two sides of the same coin. They in fact support each other, socially and politically.

The historiographical project undertaken by some Sinhala ethnonationalists has been the construction of a past in which the Sinhala language and the Sinhala ethnic identity has always been present. In this imagined past, all the Sinhala ethnics are Buddhists; their enemies, who invaded to create disruption and occupy their land, are the Tamil-speaking Hindus.

On the other hand, the Tamil ethno-nationalist project is the invention of a "classical age" for the Tamils of the Jaffna Peninsula. It is presented as a time when the peninsula was united under a Tamil kingdom centered on Kantarotai, independent from "Sinhala hegemony."

The political swing toward the right on the subcontinent has left its indelible mark on the teaching of history and social studies, posing a specific challenge to peace educators. As explained in detail by Setalvad in the 1998 Keynote Address es to the Catholic Bishop Conference of India, this tendency in textbooks has progressed from noncreative treatment of community histories to an actual exclusion of leaders' personalities and movements that challenge the unidirectional and fascist interpretations of the past. The manipulation of history within India and Pakistan, for example, has been critical for the political project of a creating a religion-based nationhood that scoffs at notions of inclusion and multireligious understanding and in fact seeks to redefine the contours of the history of the subcontinent—misinterpreting conflict as solely based on religious identity and also denying critical and rational challenges to hierarchies in the past. Political projects that have as their goal the fundamental change of the Indian state from a secular democratic republic to a Hindu Nation in India and the further Islamization of the state in Pakistan rely critically on controlling the teaching of history and social studies. This political thrust is reflected in state-controlled curricula within India taught by persons trained in this political mindset, who enter the system and reshape policy and content of education. It is more crudely seen in the material used in the schools run by the rightwing (Setalvad, 1998).

We certainly cannot blot the presence of Hedgewar, Golwalkar, and Savarkar from the historical landscape. Nor should we attempt to do so. Generations must study them, just as students of history need to study Hitler and the ideology that he represented. The politics of exclusivism are practiced by votaries of a Hind (RSS, Hindu Mahasabha) and a Muslim nation (the Muslim League).

Following nationwide movements in the 1990s that squarely challenged this tendency through mass protest and mobilization, and in which this author took part, the newly elected United Progressive Alliance's government in 2004 reconstituted the Central Advisory Board of Education (CABE) committee (2004–2005) that through a separate subcommittee.

This subcommittee of CABE, 2005 under the mandate "Regulatory Mechanisms for Textbooks and Parallel Textbooks Taught in Schools outside the Government System" was set up with the following terms of reference:

> a) To study and report on textbooks in government schools not using the central government syllabus; b) to study the textbooks and curriculum of schools outside the Government system, including those run by the religious and social organizations; c) To suggest an appropriate regulatory mechanism for institutionalizing the issue of preparation of textbooks and curricular material (Ministry of Human Resources Development, Government of India, 2005, p. 3).

Even before this, the bigotry taught in the privately-run right-wing schools was studied and exposed by the Government of India through the NCERT. NCERT's National Steering Committee, 1992–3, on textbook evaluation found that the RSS-run Vidya Bharati schools were being clearly used for the dissemination of blatantly sectarian ideas. As this extract from National Steering Committee on Textbook Evaluation, Recommendation and Report II, NCERT (National Council for Educational Research and Training) reports, publications of Vidya Bharati (Section VI of the report): The Committee shares the concern expressed in the report over the publication and use of blatantly communal writings in the series entitled, *Sanskriti Jnan* in the Vidya Bharati Schools which have been set up in different parts of the country. Their number is reported to be 6,000. The Committee agrees with the report that much of the material in the so-called *Sanskrit Jnan* series is "designed to promote bigotry and religious fanaticism in the name of inculcating knowledge of culture in the young generation." The Committee is of the view that the Vidya Bharati schools are being clearly used for the dissemination of blatantly communal ideas. In its earlier report (January 1993), the Committee had commented on publications which had been brought out with similar objectives by the Saraswati Shishu Mandir Prakashan and Markazi Maktaba Islami and had recommended that they should not be allowed to be used in schools. The *Sanskriti Jnana* series are known to be in use in Vidya Bharati schools in Madhya Pradesh and elsewhere. The Committee recommends that the educational authorities of Madhya Pradesh and other states should disallow the use of this series in the schools. The state governments may also consider appropriate steps to stop the publication of these materials, which foment communal hatred and disallow the examinations which are held by the Vidya Bharati Sansthan on the basis of these materials. A valuable reference to this disturbing phenomenon can also be found in Sarkar (2002), *Beyond Nationalist Frames: Relocating Postmodernism, Hindutva, History.*

The Challenges

One of the fundamental flaws in textbooks relates to the way periods in history are presented—the ancient, medieval, and modern that is dominated by colonial periodization. As Romila Thapar says,

> within colonial historiography, we have as two distinct trends the Orientalists and the Utilitarians; the first that presented a sympathetic image of a golden age but this image had a double edge that pitted the great Indian civilization with the rationalisation for the British conquest; and the Utilitarians that moved away from this romantic vision of a glorious Indian past and presented "Hindu" and "Muslim" periods in a more or less static sense with Oriental despots at their helm. The unkindest legacy left by James Mill, one of the Utilitarians was the periodisation of Indian history into three periods, Hindu, Muslim and British (not Christian). This was a meaningless categorization as it no way reflects or characterizes an age.
>
> Nationalist historians, in the early part of this century, in their search for an identity harked back to descriptions and imagery

of golden ages of the past. To fight colonialism these interpretations of history pointed to a backward looking utopia. All these streams show a close link between ideology and history writing. And it was in the 1920s, 1930s and 1940s that the culmination of this link, this time in the form of communal ideologies and history writing became transparent. This clash of communalisms continues with us (Hindu and Muslim communalist history writing). Communal interpretations of history have crept into regional histories as well (Sikh communalism, etc.). (Thapar, 1997, p.2)

As discussed above, in the decades since independence, the content of textbooks has reflected the political changes on the subcontinent. In India, it was the 1980s that saw the earlier written "nationalist" history being replaced, not by more a vibrant treatment of the subject that reflected plurality, but by content that promoted even sharper and more sectarian and divisive interpretations of the past.

For two decades after Partition (1947) of the subcontinent, history teaching and textbooks within Pakistan were not significantly different from Indian textbooks in either periodization or content. Pakistan's loss in the 1965 war with India, however, changed all that. Until then, only political heroes had been emphasized, but following its humiliating defeat by India, the weakened Pakistan state introduced the study of the army and military heroes in the classroom through its textbooks. Since then, ancient history has been blotted out in all school- and college-level education in Pakistan. It exists merely as an option for postgraduate students (Ali 2006; Aziz 1998; Kumar 2003).

Extremist observations (see Appendix B) on Islam and Christianity can be clearly seen in excerpts from the books conceived by the RSS and used for "teaching" in the schools run by these organizations. What is equally or more disturbing is the fact that textbooks produced by state boards of education under the control of the state governments also contain prejudicial perceptions and contentions.

Under the Indian Constitution, which seeks within its unitary framework to have a distinctive federal character, "education" is a field in which the central Indian government and the state governments both have a say and some control. The overwhelming majority of schools within the state sector are, however, run by state education boards. The Central Board of Secondary Education (CBSE) comes under the Government of India's human resources development ministry. Other Boards include the Indian Certificate for Secondary Education (ICSE) and, more recently, the IGCSE and IB boards (which have international affiliations).

Anomalies and misconceptions in history and social-studies texts range from the construct of ancient India as "Hindu," to the myth of the Aryan invasion. Colonial historiography is largely responsible for the mythical construct of the people who spoke the Indo-Aryan language as a race of distinct and superior Aryans. It has been alternately used by Hindu Indian, Sinhala Buddhist, and Tamil Sri Lankan chauvinists to "prove" (or establish) their claim of superiority and more legitimate citizenship on "indigenous" soil. The construct of medieval India as "Muslim" and interpreted as one of conflict, denial of the syncretic traditions of Bhakti and Sufi, evasion of the impact of both caste and the strong rational and critical movements that contested caste-driven denials and discrimination from the thirteenth century onward and were sharply evident in the nineteenth and twentieth centuries. Gender, too, is treated indifferently and even prejudicially within this wider construct. In the more modern era, the communal interpretations include limiting understanding of the forces that were successful for the partitioning of the subcontinent. In Indian texts, while the right-wing Muslim League gets the most blame, the contributions by the Hindu Mahasabha, which was born in 1904–1905, and the RSS to the sharpening of the identity divide, are downplayed. For example, Indian texts are reluctant to engage the young mind in an exploration into the forces responsible for the assassination of Mahatma Gandhi on January 30, 1948 (Setalvad, 1997). In most texts, a single line addresses the killing, but nowhere is the curious young mind encouraged to ask why forces like the Hindu Mahasabha (Nathuram Godse, Gandhi's assassin belonged to this organization and was a former member of the RSS) felt that a man like Gandhi, who spoke above all of Hindu-Muslim unity and who was so devastated by Partition that he vowed to spend the rest of his days in Pakistan, was such a threat to the Hindu right. (Dalton, 1993). Incidentally, the organization Rashtriya Swayamsevak Sangh was banned after the killing. The ban only lifted in 1950. India's first minister for internal security commented in an official communication that "RSS men distributed sweets after Gandhiji's assassination."

> All their speeches were full of communal poison. As a final result of their poison, the country had to suffer the sacrifice of the invaluable life of Gandhiji...RSS men expressed joy and distributed sweets after Gandhiji's death. (Sardar Vallabhbhai Patel, Union

Home Minister, to Guru Golwalkar, RSS chief, in an official letter as minister for home affairs on September 11, 1948.)

(Similarly, Indian texts generously ignore the ideological threat of fascism that the Hindu rightwing represents.) The ideologues of the RSS, theoretically and practically, lionized Hitler and fascist Germany (Casolari, 2000; Golwalkar 1939).

Every civilization has a myth, and a country's myth can console and knit together men and women of different needs, carry them through different times, explain sorrow and defeat, as well as locate them in the world. But the myth can also hide the country from itself, from scrutiny. One of the myths surrounding the glorious, golden, thousand-year old Indian (read Hindu) civilization, which many of us fall easy prey to, is about its essence. We believe, or would very much like to go on believing, that it is one of the world's most nonviolent and tolerant civilizations, whereas a critical look back would reveal a violent past at conflict with our capacity to assimilate plural realities and construct diverse realities. Do we by this very assertion hide ourselves from scrutiny?

Challenges for South Asia, the Indian Subcontinent

South Asia has over centuries collectively experienced common links and trends: cultural, economic, and social links. These links and shared experiences suddenly, but surely, got severed when each state within the region dominated the teaching of history, especially through the creation of course syllabi and the writing of textbooks.

Over the past 100 years, a period that encompasses both nation building and the emergence of independent nations in the South Asian region, historical construction and history teaching and its dissemination have legitimized certain groups, defined in terms of the "majority" and therefore conversely, the exclusion of others. The construction of this "minority-majority" discourse has also meant locating identities exclusively within a religious context and ignoring the multifarious facets of identity that reflect historical and practical realities. For example, the Urdu language was crushed through a political post-Independence act under the influence of the RSS and the Jana Sangh, whereas in Pakistan it was used as an aggressive hegemonizing force identified with the new state in which regional languages and scripts were obliterated! Today the rebirth of Urdu in India is a conflict for progressive secular traditions and sections within the Muslim community that see it as a "Muslim" language.

There have also been other distinct phases behind this majority-minority construct that are not only crucially linked to the emergence of these nation states, but also have a direct impact on the type of nation state—its inherent composition and commitment—that was formed, in all three countries, within this region. What are the theories of origin and identity in pre-and post-colonial South Asia? How have they been appropriated by exclusivist tendencies within nations? In 1997, KHOJ organized the first ever workshop of South Asian historians in Mumbai that raised some critical questions, such as:

- How has the teaching of distorted versions of history been used to achieve this legitimization and exclusion of sections within the nation states of South Asia?
- How did Partition impact on the consolidation of these theories? What was the role of the Hindu right wing during this period?
- What was the discourse within the northeastern regions of India at the time of independence and partition that have since been marginalized from mainline Indian history learning?
- How has language been used by communal forces within the South Asian region to impose hegemony and kill diversity?
- What can be done by educational initiatives to push governments toward less intransigence between governments in the region? (The Aman/KHOJ initiative)
- Can a group of South Asians, scholars, teachers and writers conceive of building a history beyond the national boundary, encompassing the wider region and hereafter, beyond the region as well?
- Can we conceive of textbooks without absolute truths, suggesting different theories about events in the past, conveying to the student of history the inherent dynamism of the discipline?
- Can the history textbook contain an implicit recognition of fluidity between past and present, so events don't end or finish and have continuing implications for the future?
- Should not even the most elementary of textbooks attempt to trace, for the child, the growing mind, history from different routes and different sources?

Responsive to these challenges has been peace oriented education that employs pluralism.

Peace Philosophy in Action

The KHOJ Vision

The KHOJ experiment with plural education is firstly committed to a multidimensional approach, at the center of which is the young learner who is equipped through our sessions to negotiate the inner, emotional, and explorative world of the child, or adult in education, including explorations of preconceptions and prejudice while he or she learns about this rich and multilayered past along with the complex present. Sessions covering local history run alongside explorations of the migratory histories of the students' own past, teaching them the value of examining sources and conflicting facts. Students learn both theory and practice preserve the fundamentals of learning. Education as a means of social transformation, toward the dream of equality and nondiscrimination as articulated by the thinkers of our past, Phule, Ambedkar, and Gandhi, combine to guide our vision.

Students sharing and learning the constitutional values of equality, nondiscrimination, negotiation, and nonviolence are central to the KHOJ project. We ask the school administration, "Are we schools that share and care?"—with the neighborhood whose children who cannot or do not go to school, where poor shanty homes sit side-by-side with plush buildings, that has civic problems of safe drinking water and decent public health. Civic values are not to be simply taught in books, but experienced as values by the learner.

It is, surely, impossible to speak about apartheid in the world context without linking it to the birth of South Africa as an independent nation under Nelson Mandela or to understand slavery in the modern context without understanding the role played by the colonial powers in Africa or, equally pertinently, the story of the American Civil War and Abraham Lincoln. Yet, Indian textbooks do not examine social inequality, specifically, the caste system as it emerged, was legitimized historically, and continues to exist today, perpetuating an exploitative and unjust social order. Such an approach would be invaluable to bring about dialogue between the conflict zones within South Asia. It could also open dialogue within countries and cultures where dominant themes have been thrust by totalitarian state regimes. An examination of history and social-studies texts and narratives of China, Taiwan, and Japan could be instructive.

To understand discrimination and inequality in the Indian situation, the young mind must understand the reality of caste. Several sessions on Caste, past and present, help introduce the Indian child who may not be a victim of this discrimination to a phenomenon that is deliberately avoided in the hegemonizing education project.

The world " Khoj" means literally to search and explore. Our aim is to equip young learners with the ability to critique, question and explore diverse realities. To help students appreciate the ideal of nondiscrimination, we employ the methods of dialogue, debate, and negotiation.

The Methodology: To help tomorrow's citizens experience schools as a place and learning as a process in which they are encouraged to not run away from but to express their feelings, to articulate and reflect on, individually and as a group, their experiences of conflict in a noncensorious environment. Only then do paths emerge for resolution and transformation of conflict (Carter, 2010).

The Belief: That if an atmosphere of genuine questioning and enquiry is offered to children, they will come to recognize received prejudice and preconceived notions, develop independent critical faculties that slowly but surely dismantle the myths and the stereotypes.

The Objective: To develop from the live experience of classroom engagements, a module for "Teaching Tolerance" and "Celebrating Diversity" that can be shared with the community of teachers and educationists in a country still struggling to come to terms with self.

The Content: Teaching materials and multidimensional modules that explore the emotional world of the child, introduce alternate social-studies and history teaching content and civic studies while also robustly engaging in media studies and critiquing.

Our Audience: The issues that KHOJ addresses—intracommunity and the class and caste prejudice that are found in our history and social-studies textbooks—finds relevance in both formal and informal instruction and even in community workshops with teachers, parents, and policemen. The lack of depth and low self-esteem today in both the Indian teacher and policeman often manifests in shallow prejudice. The division of our population, especially in urban ghettos, further aggravates the situation. Schools and even health clinics in certain areas are completely absent of cosmopolitanism.

KHOJ Modules

I would like to share our experience with children and adults on five linked modules that KHOJ includes and show how we use them with each new group of children. This is just one example of the KHOJ approach, using related modules that link a child's notion of and relationship to God. We begin with an exercise called, "Our God(s)." The student writes about or draws his or her vision of Divinity or the Divine. This is followed by the student's candid observations on ten different Indian communities (Hindu, Muslim, Christian, Sikh, Buddhist, Jain, Dalit, Brahmin, Jew, Parsee—*My perceptions*).

Our work with 8200 children (KHOJ Content Analysis, 2008) shows that, when expressing visually or in words their ideas, notions and relationships with God, children are idealistic, searching, and emotional. Searing, questions to "Him" (a majority of children relate to a male God) center on disturbing questions: why is there poverty, violence, disunity, and hatred? Surely, God must have answers, and any child in the modern world needs to ask these questions.

But the abstract response of young minds to God is, qualitatively, at odds with their observations about the different religious communities. It is this critical and qualitative difference in responses that we, as educators, need to understand very clearly if we are to make any real progress on imparting a sense of celebration of diversities and difference and succeed in our mission of peace education.

Following the exploration activity "Our God(s)" is the session, My Perceptions. During this module, the children listen to a short recording of diverse music—the Parsee *kushti* prayers, the *azaan* (*muezzin's call*), the Vaishnavajana (Hindu) *bhajana*, a church choir, , the recitation of verses from the Guru Granth Sahib. Then the teacher writes the names of the ten different Indian communities on the board and asks the children write a few words expressing their honest feelings about them.the children's responses to "Our God(s)" contain only very faint, sometimes barely noticeable, notions of nationalism or their own national identities. But the moment they share their honest impressions of different religious communities, stereotypes and a pronounced and narrow sense of supremacy are evident. Such preconceptions are clearly a challenge for anyone concerned with injecting an appreciation of diversity in young minds. They reflect confusions of religion and language, with some communities specifically being associated with religions that, for children, are "foreign," or "violent." for example:

> *Christian*: "Christians speak English and it is not an Indian religion."
> *Hindu*: "The majority in India"; "Hindi speaking"; "open and tolerant religion"; "an ancient community"; "the most important religion."
> *Dalit*: "abject poverty and illiteracy"

Muslim: "Islam is a good religion but its people are angry." "My friend is a Muslim, but everybody says if a Muslim is your friend, you are not an Indian, you are a Pakistani." "Muslim is the name of a religion. They are majority of people in India. First, when the British rule India they play along to create a fight between Hindus and Muslims. All Muslims keep weapons with them." "Muslims eat goats and hens and if we say something to the Muslims, they show a knife to us and we die." "Muslims are not Muslims, but they are Hindus." "They have been made Muslims by the Britishers. They have a fixed time of doing their prayers in their own language." "They wear black colored clothes." "Muslims pray very loudly. They go to their temple at night."

The sharpest misconceptions are about Muslims and Islam. Children on average barely have any knowledge of smaller minorities such as the Parsees, Jews, and Buddhists. Notably, there is no matching candor in articulating the violence and indignities perpetrated against at least 25 percent of our own population in the name of caste. Undignified mannal labour, like manual scavenging still remains a caste driven activity and the fact that articulate Indians have scant knowledge or acceptance of this reality is a reflection of the inherent bias in syllabus content.

Only after the children's genuine opinion on these questions has been sought and received do we enter into the final module in this section. This includes two sessions where students are introduced to the History of World Religions—how and in what social contexts they originated, how and where they spread, and their essential tenets, forms of beliefs, and rituals. The final module in this group is an exercise in creative articulation when the ten-year-old is asked to formulate, "My Ideal Religion" for the modern world.

The KHOJ Field Trip for Children

Most schools, big or small, undertake field trips with their children. But unfortunately, many of these, too, have been reduced to a mere formality. Today's zoo, the aquarium, or museum is sometimes nothing more than a construction site, where little attention may be paid to the lives and conditions of the construction workers.

We have found, however, that the field trip can be an effective means exposing children to how different communities and cultures live if it is conceived of as an extension of the theme and concerns of the social studies. For the past fifteen years, we have been taking the children on several field trips each year.

In Bombay, ten minutes away from one of the schools in which our project began in 1994 is a predominantly Muslim neighborhood. Our visit was planned in collaboration with a community organization that runs a library and conducts literacy classes there. Because of their efforts, we were able to visit two mosques, and in one of them the *Imam* (head priest) even explained the Muslim prayer rituals to each child.

The warmth of our welcome overwhelmed even the most skeptical among us. Many, including the teacher accompanying us, could not believe we would be entering the inside of a mosque. Seventeen little girls who were studying at the center welcomed us and gave us each a rose, while displayed banners and placards proclaiming intracommunity camaraderie made an impression on each child's mind. Songs sung by a local choir led off an experience that is bound to have made some impression on each child.

The spontaneity of personal experience is the best antidote to stereotype and prejudice. Does our learning system encourage this? In fact, the segregation of the Indian classroom due to the ghettoization (the Muslim minority is more or less forced into ghettos and is unable often to find living spaces in mixed localities) has created a dangerous situation in a society wracked by violence and the breakdown of the rule of law—children of different faiths mix less and less in urban India. For the peace educator, (re)introducing children of different faiths to each other has in a myriad of ways become both a challenge and a necessity.

As we entered the two mosques, a few children had exclaimed, "But it's so very clean!" The remark posed a challenge for the adults accompanying the children. Did the children mean that they did not expect a Mosque to be clean (an often-repeated stereotype of the Muslim is that he is "unclean," besides being "barbaric," quick to anger, and so forth), or was it in fact of the reaction of children who are used to temples that are more often than not, not spotless? How does a teacher parse the elements of the experience and respond without implanting preconceptions of her own?

When we were approaching the mosque, one of the girls from the local community had pulled at my tunic and asked in a soft conspiratorial whisper, "May I please enter? I have not seen my own Mosque?" That day many young Muslim girls got a glimpse of their own prayer house for the first time, a right unfortunately denied to many in several parts of India. Another layer and level of reality and challenge presented itself to the educator. How much we help close our children's minds by denying them the benefits of such firsthand experience. A few weeks later one student, whose drawing otherwise depicted very positive images of the trip, drew the Indian and Pakistani flags at the top of the page. Why did he draw the Pakistani flag, we wanted to know, when the mosque we had visited was barely fifteen minutes away from the school? Perplexed by the question, he answered, "Did not all Muslims originate from Pakistan?" Another community myth perpetrated about the Indian Muslim minority is that they are inextricably linked to Pakistan; this misconception places a heavy burden on Indian Muslims— responsibility for the Partition and, worse, questioned loyalty to India.

These are the words of school teacher Renu Koshy, who described the experience of this visit in "A Teacher's Ringside View" (1996).

> An unfortunate side effect of education in a "good" school may be an isolation of the students from the society of which they are a part. Opportunities seldom arise where children are enable to see and observe beyond their own families, friends and school mates. Verbal explanations and audio-visual aids do help in portraying various aspects, but not as effectively as direct exposure. This trip was therefore a welcome one.
>
> I had the luxury of being an observer (apart from the odd check now and then) and was able to see and note the reactions of both groups of children. The spontaneous welcome of the host group and the initially hesitant response of the guests which quickly turned to one of interest were obvious. Nothing like a spot of music to get things going—and this is precisely what happened. It was a pleasure to see some of my prim, self-conscious girls joining in with gusto. At that moment, watching all the children singing together, one saw harmony in all the sense of the word.
>
> KHOJ was able to organize a trip into two mosques. The children removed their shoes and with curiosity and with respect went in and looked around with great interest. They asked a great number of questions that ranged from questions regarding Islamic beliefs to the reasons for fish in the water tank.
>
> The bus ride and the walk through areas of Bombay to areas of Bombay to which they had never really gone, was an eye-opener. They threaded their way through narrow, crowded lanes, stepping over open drains and even peered into squalid dwellings. Do people really have to live here? was the astonished response.

At the end of the day, the students came away overwhelmed with the warmth of the response, taken aback by the poverty and squalor, buzzing with the details they had heard and seen inside the Mosques. The hospitality and the warmth extended to us superseded other aspects of the children's minds. The single rose given to us, the careful arrangement of seats for us, the sung—the overall delight in having us there—were the real highlights of the day.

It's difficult to tell exactly what the qualitative results of such trips are. Nor can a trip like this in isolation achieve anything from a single experience. But as a teacher of social studies, I have become growingly aware of the inadequacies of our systems of imparting information that detaches our children so completely. Knowledge is compartmentalized and relationships and connections rarely made between real life experiences and people.

KHOJ has over the years closely documented the effects of such efforts. Our analysis of over 10,000 responses to KHOJ sessions in the past 15 years offers rewarding glimpses of a greater appreciation of pluralism and diversity in our students. Poor Muslim children who go to state schools study in the Urdu language and often live in squalor made worse by conservatism. Their fascination with the Jain faith (which teaches nonviolence and vegetarianism) is humbling. The Hindu child, carrying the baggage of supremacy bordering on aggression is humbled when introduced to the inclusive, compassionate side of Sufi Islam, and intrigued or impressed when translations of rich Urdu poetry eulogizing Hindu religious icons are recited. Statistics show that while gender disparities and denials are an unfortunate fact of Indian Muslim life, the basic tenets of the faith has ensured that female feticide (a curse among richer, upper-caste Hindus and even Sikhs who have traditionally placed a high premium on the male child) is almost entirely absent among Indian Muslims. Understanding and appreciating this complexity furthered by discussion about it in the classroom counteracts stereotype and prejudice.

Revitalizing History and Social-Studies Teaching

Central Indian folklore and fables are filled with stories of the Bhil tribal boy Eklavya, a bright archery student who challenged the mastery of a favored, upper-caste student and then was forced by his caste-conscious teacher to chop off his thumb. The legend of Eklavya may or may not have the same resonance for a Muslim or Christian youth living on the margins of acceptability in a deeply polarized Indian polity today; but as a profound comment on the denials of education to lower castes in a rigidly caste-ridden society and tradition, it surely has lessons for any student or teacher attempting to grapple with notions of social equity, justice, and systemic deprivation in the past.

The vivid account of Gandhari's curse on Lord Krishna—the mythical image of a "mere" woman cursing a God—after the great war (*Mahabharata*) that left millions, including her eldest son, dead has been immortalized in Indian literature. This cannot but have profound meaning for women today grappling with ever-increasing indignities—familial and societal violence included—in a violent, modern India and world. KHOJ strives to introduce narratives from this rich tradition of denial and resistance that pulsates within India.

Journey of Faiths

Our history and social-studies texts are reluctantly silent on the journey of faiths to and fro from the Indian subcontinent, an account that is not just illuminating and rich. For over three thousand years, the greatest determinant has been the growing influence of caste Hinduism over large tracts of land on which tribes and peoples of indigenous faiths have lived for centuries. At least 110 years before military conquests brought Islam to the deserts of Sind, Arab settlers on Kerala's shores settled here, and a local king converted to a faith he perceived as attractive and egalitarian.

Maulana Abul Kalam Azad, India's first education minister said in this presidential address at the session of the 1940 Indian National Conference at Ramgarh,

> [A] full eleven centuries have passed by since then. Islam has now as great a claim on the soil of India as Hinduism. If Hinduism has been the religion of the people here for several thousands of years Islam also has been their religion for a thousand years. Just as a Hindu can say with pride that he is an Indian and follows Hinduism; so also we can say with equal pride that we are Indians and follow Islam. I shall enlarge this orbit still further. The Indian Christian is equally entitled to say with pride that he is an Indian and is following a religion of India, namely Christianity. (Kumar, 1991, p. 18)

The region of South Asia, of which India is a significant part, offers fascinating nuances from the past. Today we refer to the nation as "India" or "Hindu-sthan" (land of the Hindus). Five thousand years ago, knowledge of medicine as well as culture crossed lands and social barriers. The King of Persia received a copy of the book *Kalilavadamana*, which contained vital information on a medicine thought to grant immortality, from these shores. A fact often missed by Indian students is that ancient local wisdom and philosophy as well as mathematics and numerology were respected and even revered in the universities of Egypt and Mesopotamia. Colonial Christianity was preceded by the arrival, in 57 AD, of one Thomas, who brought Christianity to Indian shores. Early medieval times saw an expansionist phase under the Cholas when Hinduism travelled to the Far East and became firmly embedded in beliefs and in practices of worship there. The temples and monuments of Angkor Wat, Borobodur, and Prambanan are evidence of the lasting Indian influence there (Findlay & O'Rourke, 2007).

Every culture and most civilizations have had a tendency to look to the past for icons and symbols and to hark back to traditions from the days of yore before packaging such contents into history curriculum and syllabi. The question that needs to be asked is, which past or aspects of the past does the current Indian agenda seek to emphasize?

Is it the tradition that Jayabala and Gargi represented when they, as single women, held discourses on the sophisticated intellectual issues of the day described in the Upanishads, which form the core of Hindu philosophy and precede the demarcation of society into caste, a phenomenon that began with the Vedas. During this period of early pastoral society, articulate single women had many visible roles. Following the imposition of caste, women (even in the so-called upper castes) were relegated to positions that matched those of the "lower" castes; their sexuality was now suspect, their roles subordinated. Or is it the practice of *sati*—the burning of a woman alive on the funeral pyre of her husband—and the staunch defence of wife burning as "part of our glorious ancient traditions" by proponents of division, an act that is even mildly praised in some Indian social-studies textbooks?

The need to incorporate a study of the history and evolution of different religious faiths into school curricula is clearly evident. Needed is the vigorous and energetic study of the contexts and conditions behind the birth of faiths, the sets of belief held by the believers that changed over generations, the history of gods and forms of divinity, human engagement with the divine, and the festivals and other forms of festivities characteristic of current dominations and assertions.

The subject of the shifts and changes in different faiths is educative on the Indian subcontinent, simply because if it is fairly approached, the process will illuminate different sets of reasons and varying motivations for the changes of faith that people chose. The differences and variety would depend upon the period when the change took place, the region within India that we would be looking at, and finally, the method employed for the conversion itself. Many conversions to Islam or Christianity in the modern period of history have also coincided with the passage of emancipatory laws that liberated bonded labor and gave oppressed groups the freedom of choice in the matter of faith. These groups, then, exercised this choice, rightly or wrongly perceiving Christianity or Islam to be more egalitarian than Hinduism with its oppressive system of caste.

None of the mainline Indian textbooks sufficiently develop this subject. Wider dissemination of creative historical narratives on the journey of faiths is necessary for both the child and adult in South Asia. Banal, prejudicial misconceptions of each other's faiths have worsened with the disproportionate growth of business, management, and Indian Institute of Technology (IIT) schools—encouraging empirical syllabi with no social studies content. Of late, groups like the KHOJ Education for a Plural India project, together with the Institutes of Higher Education, have been pushing to include critical aspects of Humanitarian Studies and Options, especially Human Rights. According to Setalvad (1999) in the article "How Textbooks Teach Prejudice" in *Communalism Combat*,

> There were several instances of conversions during the second half of the 19th century, in Travancore for instance. Educational endeavors of missionaries and the resultant aspirations to equality of status encouraged many persons of "low" caste to change faiths and through this to a perceived position of equality. For example, the first "low" caste person, in 1851 to walk the public road near the temple in Tiruvalla in 1851 was a Christian. (p.16)

In about 1859, many thousands of converted to Christianity in the midst of emancipatory struggles that were supported by missionaries in the region, for example, the struggle of Nadars for the right of their women to cover the upper part of their bodies, which had been opposed by the upper castes! Large-scale conversions to Islam took place on the Malabar Coast, not just during the "invasions" by Tipu Sultan, but also during the 1843–1890 periods. These were directly linked to the fact that in 1843, under the British, slavery was formally abolished in the region. As a result, large numbers from the formerly oppressed castes, bonded in slavery to upper caste Hindus, moved over to Islam, in which they perceived a message of equality and justice.

Migratory Histories

One of the most enlightening sessions that KHOJ has created focuses on the migratory histories of the individuals in the group, whether they are students, teachers, community workers, or policemen. The module involves encouraging each person to explore his or her migratory history from region to city, town, or village; the period in which it happened; the changes it brought about; the links with the place of origin have been maintained, and so on. The session lasts several months, with the group (or class) returning every few weeks to each person's research and findings. The very process of individual and collective exploration transforms the group into a multihued and diverse collective of learners. The process of questioning and cross-checking facts adds precision to the exercise during which an understanding of life patterns slowly emerges.

Conclusion

Such an approach to the unraveling of history means that local histories are explored and legitimized. Historical denials and exclusions that perpetuate present-day inequalities are addressed, making the classroom a space for genuine dialogue. If the methodology is nondidactic, and the hierarchy between the teacher and the taught broken down, or even reversed, this transformation of the classroom can be electric, suddenly multilingual, with the migratory histories of the families of students and teachers enriching the understanding of each other's cultures, life styles, belief systems, and languages.

A huge challenge for KHOJ has been adapting modules to different sections of Indian society. KHOJ modules have been used for training educators, community workers, and policemen. It is often harder with adults to break through the barrier of stereotype, but when the effort is honestly pursued, the process can be elevating. We have used this in post-2002 Gujarat, a western Indian state that was racked by brute communal violence, which was even encouraged by the state and government in power. KHOJ has effectively used its modules among teachers and community workers to bridge the interreligious divide in Gujarat.

In fact, KHOJ was born out of the post–1992–1993 bitter conflicts in Bombay, when, after Hindu right-wing elements demolished a historic Mosque, violence was unleashed all over India. Even our classrooms resonated with hatred that had become widespread and seemingly legitimized there. Two and a half decades since, the negative euphoria of hatred may be ebbing, but the misuse of the project of education to divide, not dialogue, poses the single biggest threat to educator, the educated, and us today.

In approach and content, the KHOJ vision has found a wide resonance; some of its methodologies were incorporated by the Delhi's State Council for Educational Research and Training (SCERT) and later by the NCERT textbooks. The difficulties that Indian education faces, with the lack of universal access to education and the curriculum problems, make creating peace-supporting social studies a huge challenge. In the years to come, KHOJ will be actively engaged with action groups and mass movements to carry its message to a wider audience and to advance the policy of peace education.

Terminology

Hegemonizing. Dominance of one social group over another, such that the ruling group or hegemon acquires some degree of consent from the subordinate, as opposed to dominance purely by force.

Brahmanical/Brahman. A Hindu of the self-designated "higher" caste, traditionally assigned to the priesthood and conferring a monopoly on education, learning, and access to Hindu scriptures.

Communalism. The manipulation of religion and religious symbols for the purpose of political mobilization and as a route to political power (a uniquely South Asian term).

Appendix A

KHOJ Goals and Contents

Our Vision

An alternate approach
Radical change in content

Our Methodology

Interactive, discursive, practical
Media studies and media critiques encouraged
Creative exercises for greater engagement
Emotional world explored
Multi-dimensional methodologies
Emphasis on conflicts: personal, political and social

Our Aim

Analysis, strength, and strategies to enrich theoretical knowledge and practical application

Creating an alternate vision of social-studies teaching

Contents: Samples from a 45-Session Modular Intervention for Middle School

Modules 1 and 2: Self-Portrait and Problem Solving
Modules 3 and 4: History of Mumbai, Mine and Others
Modules 5 and 6: Religion—History of Religion and How Faiths Have Traveled
Module 7: Festivals of India—project work on the festivals of India and how they reflect India's diversity
Module 8: Equality and Justice
Module 9: Human Rights; Children's Rights
Module 10: Child Labor
Module 11: The Concept of South Asia—our neighbors, our climates, our common problems, some differences
Module 12: Dates in History—how to understand dates in history.
Module 13: Resources and Environmental Damage
Module 14: Civic Sense and Responsibility

Appendix B

Teachings Toward Hate

Some Examples from Indian Textbooks

Indian history and social studies textbooks have been subtly or more directly used to generate exclusion and hatred of the sections of our religious communities, women, and castes (Seltalvad, 1998 & 1999). They are also dismissive of and derogative about hard physical work. Details of the analysis of this exclusion and hate teaching in textbooks is available on the Web site http://www.sabrang.com. Following are brief examples of this trend.

About Islam, a textbook for final-year Bachelor of Arts students of history in Maharashtra, a state in western India, has a chapter titled "Invasion by Mahmud of Ghaznavi" in which the author launches a tirade against Islam. The official social-studies textbook of Gujarat, selected by the Gujarat State Board, labels Christians, Muslims, and Parsees (Zorastrians) as foreigners. For example, a chapter titled, "Problems of the Country and Their Solutions" has a section, "Minority Community," that labels Muslims and even Christians and Parsees, as "foreigners." It also falsely states that Hindus are in the minority in most states of India. Additionally, there is an attempt to glorify caste: "Caste is a precious gift." Meanwhile, Standard IX of the social-studies text denigrates women by stating that the practice of child marriage and widow burning was praiseworthy. The same textbook also teaches, in Standard X, positive aspects of both Fascism and Nazism.

Created by the RSS in 1978, the Vidya Bharati Akhil Bharatiya Shiksha Sansthan network focuses on moral, extracurricular, and physical education for "mind, body and spirit." The Vidya Bharati system supervises over 18,000 schools across India, with 1.8 million students and 80,000 teachers, with a shared curriculum used throughout the country. The Vidya Bharati operates 60 graduate institutions. About 5,000 Vidya Bharatis are endorsed by education boards, primarily in states where the Bharatiya Janata Party is in power. In recent years, the Ekal Vidyalayas set up in central and eastern Indian states where dominant tribal populations have been also operating as propaganda tools of the parent Vishwa Hindu Parishad (VHP), which was indicted for intracommunity violence. An example of materials used in the VHP's Ekal Vidyalayas include *Bapparawal*, a bimonthly Hindi magazine published by the Rajasthan Vanwasi Kalyan Parishad (RVKP) and freely circulated in tribal Rajasthan. Bappa Rawal was the name bestowed on Rawal Kalbhoj (AD 734–753), founder of Rajasthan's Mewar dynasty. In its January-February 2004 edition, *Bapparawal* carried an article titled, "Misuse of the Innocence of Tribals and Endeavour Required to Awaken One's Self" (Kashyapnath, 2004). The Kashyapnath article about Christian missionaries, drawn from interviews of "converted tribals," describes Christian goals personal and national conversion away from Indian culture such as use of Hindu names for Christian children (Kashyapnath, 2004).

"Us and Them"

The massive increase in private education funded by cash campaigns sponsored by political outfits of the Hindu right that has resulted in their establishment of many schools, has since the late 1980s begun to influence state textbook boards where the parliamentary wing, the Bharatiya Janata Party, has assumed power.

References

Ali, A. (2006). *Mughal India, Studies in polity, ideas, society and culture.* New York: Oxford University Press.

Armstrong, K. (1993). *A history of God: The 4000-year quest of Judaism, Christianity, and Islam.* New York: A. A. Knopf.

Azad, A. K. (1959). *India wins freedom: An autobiographical narrative.* Bombay: Orient Longmans.

Azad, A. K. & Chopra, P. N. (1990). *Maulana Azad, selected speeches and statements, 1940–47.* New Delhi: Reliance.

Aziz, K. (1998) *The murder of history: Critique of history textbooks used in Pakistan.* Delhi: Renaissance.

Carter, C. C. (Ed.). (2010). *Conflict resolution and peace education: Transformations across disciplines.* New York: Palgrave Macmillan.

Casolari, M. (January 2000). Hindutva's foreign tie-up in the 1930s: Archival evidence. *Economic and Political Weekly 35*(4), 218.

Chakravarti, U. (1998). *Rewriting history: The life and times of Pandita Ramabai.* New Delhi: Kali for Women in association with the Book Review Literary Trust.

Chakravartty, G. (1987). *Gandhi, a challenge to communalism: A study of Gandhi and the Hindu-Muslim problem, 1919–1929.* New Delhi: Eastern Book Centre.

Chopra, P. N. (1990). *Maulana Azad: Selected speeches and statements, 1940–47.* New Delhi: Allied.

Constituent Assembly Debates (December 1946–January 1950). Volumes 1–12. Lok Sabha Secretariat, New Delhi: Government of India, Reprint 1999, First printed 1950.

Dalton, D. (1993). *Mahatma Gandhi: Nonviolent power in action.* New York: Columbia University Press.

Deshpande, G. P. (Ed.) (2002). *Selected writings of Jotirao Phule.* New Delhi: Leftword.

Findlay, R. & O'Rourke, K. H. (2007). *Power and plenty: Trade, war and the economy in the second millennium.* Princeton, NJ: Princeton University Press.

Grewal, P. M. S. (2007). *Bhagat Singh, liberation's blazing star.* New Delhi: Leftword.

Golwalkar, M. S. (1939). *We, or, our nationhood defined.* Nagpur: Bharat Publications.

Gunawardana, R. A. L. H. (1995). *Historiography in a time of ethnic conflict: Construction of the past in contemporary Colombo, Sri Lanka.*, Social Scientists' Association of Sri Lanka.

Habib, I. (1995) *Essays in Indian history: Towards a Marxist perception.* New Delhi: Tulika.

Habib, S. I. & Singh, B. (2007). *To make the deaf hear: Ideology and programme of Bhagat Singh and his comrades.* New Delhi: Three Essays Collective.

Humayun, K. (1968). *Minorities in a democracy.* Calcutta: Firma K. L. Mukhopadhyay

Indian History Congress. (1994). *Papers on Indian history: Indian History Congress; 56th session 1994; Aligarh.* Aligarh: Centre of Advanced Study in History, Aligarh Muslim University.

India Parliament House of the People (1950). *Lok sabha debates.* New Delhi: Government of India. *Constituent Assembly Debates* (December 1946–January 1950). Volumes 1–12. Lok Sabha Secretariat, New Delhi: Government of India, Reprint 1999, First printed 1950.

Jhabvala, S. H. (1955). *Kabir:* Translated from Original Hindi into English, Published by S. H. Jhabvala.

Kuber, W. N. (2001). *Ambedkar, a critical study.* New Delhi: Shameem Faizee for People's Publishing House.

Kumar, R. (1991). *Life and work of Maulana Abul Kalam Azad.* New Delhi: Atlantic.

——— (2003). *Prejudice and pride: School histories of the freedom struggle in India and Pakistan.* London: Penguin Books.

Leahey, C. R. (2009). *Whitewashing war. Historical myth, corporate textbooks and possibilities for democratic education.* New York: Teachers College Press.

Lele, J. K. & Singh, R. (1989). *Language and society: Steps towards an integrated theory.* Leiden, The Netherlands: E. J. BRILL.

Lowen, J. W. (2009). *Teaching what really happened: How to avoid the tyranny of textbooks and get students excited about doing history.* New York: Teachers College Press.

Michael, S. M. (1998). *Anthropology of conversion in India.* Occasional papers of (IIC). Mumbai: Institute of Indian Culture.

Ministry of Human Resources Development. (2005). *Regulatory mechanisms for textbooks and parallel textbooks taught in schools outside the government system.* New Delhi: Government of India.

O'Hanlon, R. (1985). *Caste, conflict, and ideology: Mahatma Jotirao Phule and low caste protest in nineteenth-century western India.* Cambridge: Cambridge University Press.

Pansare, G. (1998). *Who was Shivaji?* Prakash Viswasrao. Mumbai: Lokvangmay.

Peace History Society (2009) Retrieved on January 13, 2010 http://www.peacehistorysociety.org/

Patel, S. V. B. (September 1948). Sardar Vallabh Bhai Patel, Union Home Minister of India, to Guru Golwalkar, RSS Chief, in an official letter as minister for home affairs on September 11, 1948.

Rajinder, S. (2006). *Social, economic and educational status of the Muslim community in India. A Report, Prime Minister of India's High Level Committee, Cabinet Secretariat.* New Delhi: Government of India.

Rammohun R. & Robertson, B. C. (1999). *The essential writings of Raja Rammohan Ray.* New Delhi: Oxford University Press.

Regulatory Mechanisms for Textbooks and Parallel Textbooks Taught in Schools Outside the Government System, Report of the CABE Committee (2005). Ministry of Human Resources Development, Government of India, New Delhi.

Renu, K. (December 1996). A teacher's ringside view. *Communalism Combat,* 11–14.

Research Centre for Women's Studies. (1985). *Women and culture.* Bombay: Research Centre for Women's Studies, Shreemati Nathibai Damodar Thackersey Women's University.

Sabhasada, A. K. & Sen, S. N. (Eds.) (1977). *Śiva Chhatrapati.* Extracts and documents relating to Marątha history, v.1. Calcutta: K. P. Bagchi & Company.

Sadgopal, A. (February 2004). *Globalization and education: Defining the Indian crisis.* XVI Zakir Husain Memorial Lecture. New Delhi: Zakir Hussain College, New Delhi.

Sarkar, S. (2002). *Beyond nationalist frames: Relocating postmodernism, Hindutva, history.* Delhi: Permanent Black.

Setalvad, T. (September 1997). *Are our schools those that care and share?* Meeting of Educationists and Bureaucrats, Colombo, Sri Lanka.

——— (October 1997). Will Buddhist lions make peace with Tamil tigers? *Communalism Combat,* October 1997 Retrieved January 13, 2010 from www.sabrang.com.

——— (November 1998). History preaching. *Communalism Combat, November,* 27–29.

Setalvad, T. (February 1999). Allah's army in Pakistan, Hindutva Brigade in India, Buddhist Lions in Sri Lanka. *Communalism Combat, February*, 8–16, Retrieved January 13, 2010 from http://www.sabrang.com/cc/ccthemes.htm.

——— (October 1999). How textbooks teach prejudice, *Communalism Combat, October*. Retrieved January 13, 2010 at http://www.sabrang.com/cc/ccthemes.htm

——— (January 2001). Education with values. *Communalism Combat, January*, 8–14.

——— (2005). *Constitutional mandate and education*. Central Advisory Board of Education (CABE) Committee, Government of India. Retrieved January 13, 2010 at http://www.sabrang.com/khoj/CABEReport.pdf

Sikand, Y. (2004). *Sacred spaces: Exploring traditions of shared faith in India*. Sydney: Penguin.

Singh, B. & Chandra, B. (2008). *Why I am an atheist*. New Delhi: National Book Trust.

Sundar, N. (2004). Teaching to hate: RSS's pedagogical programme. *Economic and Political Weekly 39*, 16.

Svd, S. M. (1998). *Anthropology of conversion in India*. Mumbai: Institute of Indian Culture.

Thapar, R. (1961). *A'soka and the decline of the Mauryas* (Third edition). London: Oxford University Press.

——— (March 1997). Past and prejudice. *Communalism Combat*, March 2.

Vaudeville, C. (1993). *A weaver named Kabir: Selected verses with a detailed biographical and historical introduction*. French studies in South Asian culture and society, 6. Delhi: Oxford University Press.

Veeramani, K. (1999). *Periyar and Ambedkar: Ambedkar endowment lectures (14, 15, 164–1986 Three Days)*. Chennai: Dravidar Kazhagam.

Westcott, G. H. (1907). *Kabir and the Kabir Panth*. Cawnpore: Christ Church Mission Press.

CHAPTER SIX

Peace Education in Elementary Teacher Education of Tamilnadu

SAVARIMUTHU VINCENT DE PAUL

In the twenty-first century, people all over the world are concerned about how to have peace. They are searching outwardly for peace, even though it resides first in one's inner mind and then manifests in the outer world. Teachers having efficacy for the commitment to peace education develop student knowledge, skills, and dispositions that support that visionary goal. This chapter discusses the actions that have been taken in elementary teacher education in the state Tamilnadu, India, for the advancement of peace. These efforts have been grounded in pragmatism and in conceptions of peace that have framed the actions of the last decade, and they resonate with notions of peace around the world.

Notions of Peace

The concept of peace has been construed in many ways. One may think that the absence of war reflects the existence of peace. It is more than that, as Table 6.1 demonstrates.

Joel Kovel (Harris & Morrison, 2003) defines peace as the

> state of existence where neither the overt violence of war nor the covert violence of unjust systems is used as an instrument for extending the interest of a particular nation or group. It is a world where basic human needs are met and in which justice can be obtained and conflict resolved through nonviolent processes and human & material resources are shared for the benefit of all people. (p.12)

Table 6.1 Typical Content of Peace Education

Resolving conflict without use of force
Stopping forms of violence, including structural
Following standards of justice
Living in balance with nature
Providing meaningful participation as members of social and political groups
Restoring well being after harm

Peace processes include people working together to resolve conflicts, respect standards of justice, satisfy individual and group needs, honor rights, and respect all human beings without discrimination or prejudice. The desire for peace has been expressed at different levels in response to the recognition of conflict in each one. These levels include: intrapersonal, interpersonal, institutional, national, global, and cultural. Comprehensive peace education teaches students to analyze conflict in each of those domains (Carter, in press). Voluntary standards for peace education help prepare teachers and school administrators about conflict management in each domain (Carter, 2008). Curriculum, the contents of a lesson, at all levels of peace education includes examples of peace enactments, including the peace history that Setalvad identifies in this book as needed. For example, the following events belong in social-studies lessons about international conflicts:

- Mahatma's nonviolent principles liberated India from one of the world's greatest empires.
- Citizens of the United States organized for peace in the decade between 1960 and 1970 and contributed to the end of U.S. involvement in the Vietnam War.
- From 1950 to 1960, citizen protests against atmospheric testing of nuclear weapons led to a partial test-ban treaty.
- Man Mohan Singh's nonviolent and assertiveness with peace principals has avoided an anticipated India–Pakistan War that could have resulted after the 2009 attacks at hotels in Mumbai, India, were linked to Pakistani citizens.

Necessity of Peace Efficacy

To maintain or sustain peace, every individual should have peace efficacy. The term refers to one's perceptions of one's own capabilities to

(1) choose peace: (2) work hard to achieve it; (3) persist in the face of adversity; and (4) maintain a vision of peace while bringing it about. Among other knowledge components supporting peace efficacy are awareness of peace concepts, the nature of conflicts, and the causes of violence as well as techniques of conflict resolution and transformation (Carter, 2010a). Peace efficacy develops among individuals and groups through informal systems (observation and experience) as well as through formal education. For instance, knowledge of three main peace strategies enables clarification of immediate goals for responding to different types of conflicts.

Peace Strategies

Most people have a desire for peace, but there is a considerable disagreement about how to achieve it. Methods of developing peace range from containment of destruction to fortification of existing peace structures. The three categories for describing this range of peace development are *peacekeeping*, *peacemaking*, and *peacebuilding* (Galtung, 2004).

Peacekeeping maintains international peace and security through the deployment of military forces in specific areas. This strategy does not bring about lasting peace. It indirectly creates conflicts within each individual. Peacemaking refers to the process of restoring peace where it has been lost, especially by reconciling parties who disagree, quarrel, or fight. Peacebuilding helps to strengthen existing peace, which history has demonstrated is fragile. Peacebuilding is an encompassing strategy that includes conflict transformation, restorative justice, trauma healing, reconciliation, and development and leadership, all underlain by peace principles. It highlights the difficult reality that ending violence does not automatically lead to peaceful and stable social or economic development.

Each strategy has its own merits and limitations, and the three are not mutually exclusive. The approach to peace a given society uses depend on the inclinations, experiences, and desires of those in power or on well-organized citizen movements. Table 6.2 lists examples of peace strategies that have been used for peacemaking and peacebuilding.

In most of the cases these strategies are not mutually exclusive. Rather, they interplay in addressing the complex problems of conflict and violence. However, peace education is valid throughout the world.

Table 6.2 Peace Strategies

Education
Sustainability
Justice
Institution-building
Pacifism
Strength (efficacy and connection)

Peace Education

The removal or minimization of aggressive behavior happens when humans understand peace, desire it, and work to achieve it. The desire should be deeply rooted in the individual's inner consciousness. Development of the requisite knowledge and disposition calls for new social structures that allow the cultivation of those characteristics. Peace education is one needed structure in formal schooling.

The term peace education has different connotations for different people, but all have the focal point of peace. Peace education is considered to be both a philosophy and a process involving certain skills, including the ability to listen, reflect, solve problems, cooperate, and resolve conflicts (Ndura-Quédraogo & Amster, 2009; Salomon & Nevo, 2002). Peace education involves empowering students with the skills, attitudes, and knowledge needed to create a safe world and build a sustainable environment (Wenden, 2004). It incorporates philosophies that include the concepts of nonviolence, love, compassion, and reverence for all life.

Through peace education, students learn how to solve the problems caused by violence. It inoculates students against the terrible effects of violence while teaching them skills to manage their conflicts without using violence and by motivating them to choose peace strategies when they recognize conflict.

The behavior of individuals can be modified because of the constructivist nature of the human being. Consequently, a peaceful environment for learning about peace is essential. Such environments not only promote a desire for peace, they also foster knowledge about it and teach skills for it.

In peace education the teacher, from the primary to tertiary level, provides an optimal learning environment and serves as a role model to the students and institution. The importance of nonviolence should be emphasized by evidencing the sources of the violence, their adverse impact on humanity, methods of analyzing conflict, and techniques for responding nonviolently to conflict.

Nonviolence

Many people in India appreciate and follow the long-advocated ways of nonviolence. The ancient sages believed that peace was the only way to achieve *Mukhi*, that is, "happiness." Many famous people, including Jesus Christ, Vardhamana Mahavira, Gautama Buddha, and Mahatma Gandhi, followed the principle of not doing evil to others.

Three domains in which transformation of conflict occurs nonviolently are self, society, and nature. Nonviolence first involves self-work, such as not developing jealousy and other negative dispositions that evidence personal needs. This self-work for peace evidences the spirit of love and acceptance of all as well as the absence of aversion to any living organism, from germinated seed to human being. From a state of cultivated inner peace one can have compassionate concern about others' needs and develop constructive responses to them.

It is crucial to teach children the concept of nonviolence practiced by Jesus, Gandhi, and others as a way to achieve peace. After schooling or college that does not include education about responding to conflict without violence, the individual graduates as an endangering citizen. Such youth often live as violent adults or complacent observers of harm, further promoting dysfunctional social and environmental behaviors. The culture of violence that reverberates in the media, the entertainment industry, politics, national policy, institutions, community, and the family cannot be changed without education for peace through nonviolence. The optimal school curriculum features avoidance of multiple forms of violence, and it creates a desire in students to learn how nonviolence can provide the basis for a just and sustainable culture. School authorities must model dispute-resolution techniques and support constructivist-learning environments so that students can learn to manage their own conflicts constructively, in real life as well as at school.

Educating about Conflict

Conflict is an inevitable and a naturally occurring event that is present in all significant relationships and environments. In school environments reflecting diverse values, beliefs, and attitudes, conflicts are bound to occur. Children need to learn techniques of conflict resolution, since resolution methods do not always seem to develop naturally. Johnson, Johnson, Dudley, and Acikgoz (1994) found that before the children in their elementary-school study population were taught to resolve conflict, the majority turned to teachers to settle conflicts using their adult judgment, or they attempted to use punitive or destructive strategies that escalated the conflict. The early child should know how to handle conflict without giving room to any kinds of violence. Conflict is a natural part of our daily lives and cannot be avoided. Every one should consider conflict in day-to-day activities and the positive responses to it, such as clarification of feelings and needs. Conflict is viewed from multiple perspectives: What one sees, thinks, feels, and believes may be different from what others see, think, feel, and believe. Conflict is thus a part of all human interaction, and it can have a positive impact. One can learn from one another and benefit from a variety of perspectives on issues. If managed wisely, conflict is a source of vitality and an opportunity for positive change.

Conflict education develops problem-solving skills in children and encourages their proactive propensities. They learn response skills such as constructive communication and cooperation as well as accommodation of diversity. Conflict-response strategies they learn are analysis, ideation, and risk taking—doing something they have not yet done or experienced.

Analysis means defining the conflict. It is the first step. The goal of analysis is to accurately and objectively describe the problem. Conflict becomes evident when two or more people interact and perceive that they have incompatible differences or feel a threat to their resources, needs, or values and response in accordance with these perceptions. The conflict can move in either of two directions, namely escalation (the conflict gets worse) or de-escalation (the conflict gets resolved).

Ideation in conflict resolution enables the peacemakers to step back, reflect, and present creative and positive responses to conflict situations for both parties. Ideation involves the creative formulation of alternative solutions to the problem. There are many possible ways to respond to a conflict. For long-lasting de-escalation, two conditions are essential. First, attention should be focused on the on the problem, not on the participants. Second, there should be a decrease in exposed emotion and perceived threat. Then meaningful discussion can take place, which normally follows a "cooling–off" period. In general, if the parties had experienced neutral or amicable relations before the conflict arose, and if the participants know how to make peace or have someone to help them do so, de-escalation will continue. A normal reaction to a conflict situation is to find the most practical solution. It often involves identification of what is perceived as right and wrong, followed by action on these determinations. However, the solution must meet all participants' needs.

The technique of reflective listening involves the capacity to hear and identify others' needs. Effective communication skills are the foundation stone for resolving conflicts and ensuring smooth relationships in any kind of social interactions. This means fair and impartial communication.

Risk taking refers to choosing to follow up with previously untried or unsuccessful solutions to a problem. Positive responses to the risk of new approaches are very beneficial for the risk taker, the peace partner in the conflict, and the observers, who learn from the different mode of conflict-response. Risk-taking is often most difficult in everyday interactions, which are habitual, with family and friends. The experience exemplifies the pragmatic nature of peace education.

Pragmatism and Peace Education

A child's mind does not absorb only what it sees and hears. It is also selects from the place where the child dwells and interactions there. In the *School and Society* (1899) and *The Child and the Curriculum* (1902), Dewey argued that the educational process must be built around the experiences and interests of the learner; it must facilitate an interplay of thinking and doing in the learner's interactions. Dewey explained that such a process should occur with the school organized as a component of the larger community; the teacher should be a co-worker with pupils as well as a guide, rather than a taskmaster assigning a fixed curriculum. The goal of education should be the all-around development of the child, rather than mere "banking" of knowledge (Freire, 1998). Thus, a child needs a situation that provides a forum for practicing the skills that are needed in society.

Pragmatism is a philosophy that holds, among other tenets, that means and ends are not dichotomous. Education for peace develops through means that are known to facilitate peace for individuals and groups. There is no dichotomy between living and working for peace. Hence, teachers have the responsibility to work for peace as well as live for peace. Pragmatism values practice. The teacher's role as an educator involves sustained practice by the self and students in social education. Both the pragmatist John Dewey and the educator Maria Montessori described the role of formal education in the lives of children as practical preparation for the enactment of social responsibility in local and global contexts.

Peace education includes focusing on the events of the past so that learners can understand the reasons and causes of the history. Knowledge of the past, combined with a forward-looking approach to problem solving and values clarification, are core components of the peace-focused curriculum. Dewey emphasized learner-centered concepts: "Historical knowledge helps provide such insight. The assistance which may be given by history to a more intelligent sympathetic understanding of the social situations of the present in which individuals share is a permanent and constructive moral asset" (Dewey, 1916, p. 217). A century ago, Dewey encouraged the cultivation of internationalism along with patriotism

> ...which will make it more difficult for the flames of hatred and suspicion to sweep over this country in the future, which indeed will make this impossible, because when children's minds are in the formative period we shall have fixed in them through the medium of the schools, feelings of respect and friendliness for the other nations and peoples of the world. (Dewey, 1923, p. 516)

Showing tremendous foresight, Dewey called for the development of a curriculum exploring the theme of nationalism within an international context (Howlett, 2008). In designing the curriculum, peace educators employ pragmatism to help students develop and put into practice foundations of peace.

Pedagogy and Curriculum

The central pedagogical goal of peace education is enabling students to find creative and nondestructive ways to settle conflict and to live in harmony with themselves, others, and their world. It has a protective component to keep children from falling into or becoming victims of violence in society. While it aims at the total development of the person, peace education tries to inculcate higher human and social values. In essence, it attempts to develop a set of behavioral skills necessary for peaceful living and peacebuilding from which the whole of humanity will benefit (Mukhopadhyay, 2005).

Table 6.3 Issues Included in the Curriculum

Commonality and diversity of human cultures
Population
Destruction of the ecosystem/pollution
Gender differences
World poverty
Trading relationship
Racism
Problem of war/terrorism
World cultures
Animal rights/animals threatened by extinction

Source: Mukhopadhyay, 2005, p. 12.

The curriculum typically provides opportunities for learners to realize and internalize the following: affirmation, positive thinking, empathetic listening and expression, critical thinking, decision making, and assertiveness for peace. Interactions in the school climate are part of the curriculum. Informal education about peace culture prevails throughout the school as well as the in the classroom environment.

The concepts of peace culture are integrated into the subjects the students study. The curriculum designers identify current issues to include in the curriculum that will encourage student discussions about the issues, which typically increases their global awareness as they learn about the structural nature of the international conflicts. Marmar Mukhopadhyay (2005) suggests that the curriculum include the issues listed in Table 6.3.

Peace education's aim is to develop an individual who will grow into a peaceful person—within the self and then in the society, nation, and world. UNESCO's World Heritage in Young Hands: An Educational Resource Kit for Teachers (1998) contains a section entitled, "Culture of Peace," which approaches the problem from the perspective of World Heritage. It includes competencies such as cooperation, teamwork, and confliction resolution, and the development of dispositions such as respect for other peoples and their culture (UNESCO's World Heritage in Young Hands: An Educational Resource Kit for Teachers, 1998, in Mukhopadhyay, 2005, p. 17).

India, a country with rich values adopted from the ancient *"Gurukula"* into modern education, incorporates moral values in the school curriculum—not as a separate subject, but integrating them into every subject. This provides multiple opportunities to reinforce the values being inculcated and also maximizes opportunities for developing alternative solutions to problems. In this way, peace education need not be imparted as a separate subject at school (Carter, 2004a). Rather, peace education adds dimension across the curriculum, like a concern that may be explored in different ways with any age group and subject. This calls for well-defined and appropriate curriculum. For example, a similar approach in Northern Ireland that involved integrating Education for Mutual Understanding did not last after a clearly articulated "citizenship" curriculum replaced it (Carter, 2004b). Marmar Mukhopadhyay (2005) suggests an appropriate curriculum that develops a knowledge base, including sources of violence and strategies for effectively handling it within and outside of the school. He recommends use of a curriculum that develops sensitivity, respect, open-mindedness, concern, critical thinking, commitment to justice and vision (p. 16).

Along with appropriate curricular design, appropriate teaching methods are also needed. Teachers should know the best way of creating the learning environments for peace education. These environments enable learners to apply peace concepts to real-life situations or problems. Empowering teachers' peace efficacy and pedagogy is therefore important. Peace culture can be learned effectively in a democratic classroom in which all voices are heard.

Conducive to learning about and for peace are democratic and constructivist processes. Student engagement with learning should be constructivist rather than depend on memorization that ignores the meaning of the concept. This enables the learners to comprehend real problems and construct new knowledge by identifying solutions to problems. The role of a teacher is not that of transmitter of knowledge. Rather, a teacher acts as a facilitator of knowledge and the skill building needed to use it. (Carter in press, Koshmanova, 2009.)

Peace Education in Teacher Education

Just as society is the reflection of its education system, education is the reflection of teacher preparation. Unless teachers having a strong knowledge of and commitment to education for peace, they cannot sow the seeds that students will harvest (Baker, Martin & Pence, 2008). This further underscores the importance of preparing teachers for peace education and the need to provide more information about it (Carter & Vandeyar, 2009; Carter, 2010).

Peace Education in India

India is a country characterized by the term "unity in diversity." It is home to many people of many cultures and languages. The National Council of Educational Research and Training (NCERT), which is under the Government of India's Ministry of Human Resource Development, has pointed out the importance of inculcating peace among the children in its National Curriculum Framework for School Education (NCF) (2005). It emphasizes that education must be able to promote values that foster peace, humanness, and tolerance in a multicultural society. The aim of education as envisaged in the NCF is developing in students a commitment to democracy and the constitutional values of equality, justice, freedom, secularism, and concern for well-being of others. India needs a system of education that enables students to eschew violence in their lives. The present school system has overloaded curricular expectations that contrast with the ability of the students. This structural conflict can result with violent responses. India's school system needs to be revised along the lines of the removal of systemic violence by education and the need to nurture the peace values among students. The NCF stresses education for peace (Ministry of Human Resource Development, 2005). Its position paper clearly argues that education for peace is different from peace education only in the manner in which it is delivered. That is, at the school level, education for peace is integrative rather than additive, which means that values are integrated into the curricular content and processes of education.

In order to develop peace knowledge, attitudes, and skills, peace education has been included in the teacher-education curriculum at both the elementary and secondary levels, as per the NCF (2005). The NCERT and National Council for Teacher Education (NCTE), which is an autonomous body that regulates teacher education in India, have taken several measures to develop peace education in the Indian teacher-education system. They have developed modules for peace education and teacher training.

Recently, the Regional Institute of Education Mysore, one of the constituent units of NCERT, has developed a Training Package for Teachers. It has two parts. The first part consists of modules for self-instruction, concentrating the contents, covering peace from the philosophical, sociological, and psychological perspectives. The package also includes suggestions for empowering self, understanding family dynamics, developing school-community linkages, understanding media's role, and having global concerns. The second part is the training package, which is a manual for school staff containing issues and concerns related to different levels and dimensions of peace. (National Council of Educational Research and Training, 2005.)

All the peace-education training programs and activities carried out by NCERT are aimed at raising teacher consciousness, helping them to understand their role as peace educators, and teaching them specific ways to integrate peace into the school curriculum and the teaching-learning context. In general, NCERT tries to put the theory of peace education in action by carrying out the following three major paths: extension, development, and training.

Every teacher should be a peace educator. The NCTE, visualizing the peace educator inside the teacher, introduced peace education into its teacher-education curriculum (2005). Unless teacher-educators, both pre-service and in-service, are educated about peace and its approaches, they cannot accomplish the aims of peace education in the classroom.

The University for Educational Planning and Administration (UEPA) in New Delhi, which is one of the national bodies for shaping education-policy decisions in India, has also worked on both national and international peace education. NIEPA and NCTE, in collaboration with United Nations Educational, Scientific and Cultural Organization (UNESCO) in New Delhi has developed an informative book titled *Peace Education—Framework for Teacher Education* (2005). Five chapters are particularly useful: "Peace Education: Meaning, Concept and Scope"; "Peace Education: Curriculum and Content"; "Pedagogy of Peace Education"; "Peace Education: Planning and Management Dimension."

Peace Education in Tamilnadu

The state of Tamilnadu has been a pioneer in providing peace education to students. The people of Tamilnadu have a concept of Internationalism. It has been expressed by the poet Kaniyan Poonguntrnar as *Yathum Oore Yavarum Kelir* (Every village is ours and so listens to all villages).

The education curriculum of Tamilnadu includes the concept of peace beginning in the primary classes. The Directorate of Teacher Education, Research and Training (DTERT) in Chennai, the apex body of Elementary Teacher Education in Tamilnadu. It has trained faculty at the District Institutes of Education and Training (DIETs) (the DTERT's constituent units) looking after the quality concerns in elementary teacher education and in the elementary schools of each district. Each revenue district has one DIET.

The DTERT, under the Eleventh Plan for Teacher Education 2007–8, has planned a peace-education program for the teacher-educators working in DIETs and at Block Resource Centers and the Coordinators of Cluster Resource Centers who are responsible for maintaining quality in elementary education at the District, Block, and Cluster levels, respectively. It has adopted the module developed by the NCTE in collaboration with the UNESCO and translated it to the regional language Tamil, Learning the Way of Peace: A Teachers' Guide to Peace Education. (UNESCO, 2001.)

Training Module

John Dewey perceived the educator's job as teaching the basic values of peace and nonviolence as correct social behavior (Howlett, 2008). The constructivist approach also enables the learner to understand the real situation and develop understanding of the concepts that are suitable for everyone in society. Therefore, the training module encompassed Dewey's pragmatic ideas and the constructivist approach based on the insights of Vygotsky (1978). By doing activities based on an actual situation, the trainees construct and acquire the concepts of peace and peace education. The training module includes the following topic areas:

- Peace Education—An Introduction
- Curriculum and Pedagogical Concerns for Peace Education
- Co-curriculum on Peace Education
- Think Positively, Think Critically
- Build Peace in the Community
- Respect for Human Dignity
- Care for the Planet

The developed training module adopted the themes prescribed in the UNESCO *Handbook on Peace Education* (2001. p. iv).

- Build Peace in Community
- Think Critically and Nonviolently
- Respect Human dignity
- Discover Inner Peace
- Think Positive

- Care for the Planet
- Resolve Conflict
- Be Your True Self
- Learn to Live Together
- Compassion and Do No Harm

Training with Module

The training module was used in the Elementary Pre-service Teacher Education Program. The faculty and the students of DIET, Perundurai, Erode District, Tamilnadu, conducted the pilot study under the direct guidance of experts from the NCTE and UNESCO. To facilitate an effective program, the principal of the DIET Perundurai attended workshops, one for instructors in the position of senior-lecturer one, and five for the Master Trainers' Program at the NCTE, New Delhi, during the last quarter of 2005. The UNESCO representatives, several eminent educationists drawn from various parts of India, two key educational administrators of NCERT and NIEPA, and a few practitioners of peace education from Pakistan and Sri Lanka took part in these workshops and trained the faculty. The NCTE assigned two observers and one evaluator for the field trial. The trial was conducted at DIET Perundurai from January 17–21, 2006. This training module formed the core resource material for the pilot study and was written along the lines of "Learning the Way of Peace: A Teachers' Guide to Peace Education" (UNESCO, New Delhi, 2001). It was again published for use in the Capacity Building Training on Peace Education under the Eleventh Five-Year Plan for Teacher Education 2007–8 (DIET, Perundurai, Tamilnadu, 2008).

Imparting Training

The state-level training of key resource persons was conducted at DIET Perundurai during three days of February 2008. The faculty members of all 30 DIETs of Tamilnadu were trained as resource persons for Zonal-level resource person training. At Zonal-level training, 150 faculty across the state participated in peace-education training.

At the DIET Pudukkottai, one of the leading DIETs in Tamilnadu, the author of this chapter was one of the faculty trainers, presented a

Table 6.4 Participants in Training

Site Number	DIET Name	Number of Trainees
01	Aduthurai	175
02	Chennai	98
03	Dharamapuri	–
04	G. Ariyur	85
05	Kalaiyarkoil	148
06	Kaliampoondi	80
07	Kilapalur	83
08	Kilpennathur	45
09	Kothagiri	–
10	Krishnagiri	243
11	Kumulur	Not available
12	Kurukathi	Not available
13	Manjur	159
14	Mannargudi	33
15	Mayanur	107
16	Munanjipatti	80
17	Namakkal	80
18	Oddanchathram	75
19	Palayampatti	80
20	Perundurai	80
21	Pudukottai	77
22	Ranipet	140
23	T.Kallupatti	85
24	Therur	79
25	Thirumoorthinagar	80
26	Thirur	77
27	UthamaCholapuram	159
28	Uthamapalayam	146
29	Vadalur	Not available
30	Vanaramutti	114

Source: State-level Documentation Report DIET Perundurai.

lecture on peace and its components to 77 selected Block Resource Teachers and Cluster Resource Center Coordinators of Pudukkottai District during November 2008. The author of this chapter also trained 100 selected Block Resource Supervisors, Block Resource Teachers, and Elementary School Teachers of DIET Manangudi, Thiruvarur Distict, during October and November 2008.

Similarly, in all 30 DIETs, training on peace education was given to Block Resource Teachers (BRT) and Cluster Resource Center (CRC) Coordinators who are providing academic support to primary school teachers at Block and cluster levels respectively. The district-wise details regarding the number of BRTs and CRC Coordinators attended training are given.

Many educators, including 30 DIET faculty in the first level, 150 DIET faculty in the second level, and 2608 teacher educators consisting of BRTs and CRC Coordinators have been trained across the State Tamilnadu in peace education, under the Eleventh Plan for Teacher Education for the school year 2008–9.

Feedback on Training

The training participants provided the following feedback at the end of the program (State Consolidation Report, DIET, Perundurai, Erode District, 2008).

- They felt that training imparted a peaceful mindset among the participants.
- It made the teaching faculty realize the importance to budding generations of peace education in schools.
- The training was felt as the need of the hour that would turn the present world of conflicts into a garden of harmony.
- The concepts in peace education dealt with in the training were highly relevant as well as comprehensible.
- The major components of peace education were experienced by the participants, and the participants were able to relate peace knowledge to their profession.
- The training had an impact on the trainees/participants, ensuring the application of what they learned in their real-life situations.
- The participants were informed of the history of peace education, and the well-known psychologists and educationists related to it.
- The participants felt that the training program would enable them to handle the boys and girls successfully in classrooms.
- The training program prepared the trainees to inculcate values such as discipline and diligence, time management, and courage into their day-to-day life activities.
- The training enhanced the participant's professional ability and knowledge of peace pedagogy..
- The training helped the participants to discern intrapersonal and interpersonal relationships.
- The training program helped the trainees to know their strengths and weaknesses in dealing with professional challenges in their daily activities.

- The participants were motivated to read books and learn about peace education.
- The trainees learned the ways and means of acquiring values such as kindness, friendliness, caring, and empathy toward students' needs.
- The training program helped the trainees to reflect on their personalities and realize that a teacher is a life-long learner.
- The training program acquainted the participants with the importance of life skills like *Yogasana* (Yoga) and meditation.
- The training program taught the participants to be resourceful in giving guidance and counseling by following the peace values in their lives and being role models to others, especially students, for their better future.
- The training program developed the trainees' self-confidence.

The feedback from the teachers evidenced an improvement in their attitude and interpersonal relationships. From observation during training and feedback, it was clear that their skills in providing environments to construct the concept of peace among the children improved.

UNICEF presumes about the benefits of peace education, including the process of promoting the knowledge, skills, attitudes, and values needed to bring about behavioral changes that will enable children, youth, and adults to prevent violence, both overt and structural; to resolve conflict peacefully; and to create the conditions conducive to peace, whether at an intrapersonal, interpersonal, intergroup, national, or international level.

Conclusion

The concept of Internationalism should exist in every human mind, as Dewy pointed out. It needs acceptance and the support of neighbors, begins at home and extends across the community to other regions, including counties. Expressions of love and affection for those near and far advance a sense of local and distant community. For this purpose, everyone needs knowledge of peace and conflict-resolution techniques. Teachers need empowerment and preparation to educate their students toward this goal. To put peace into action, more peace building techniques can be developed and integrated across teacher-education curriculum. Throughout the world, pragmatism can be the foundation of teacher preparation for peace education and a rationale for students' community experiences in peacebuilding.

References

Baker, M., Martin, D., & Pence, H. (2008). Supporting peace education in teacher education programs. *Childhood Education 85*(1), 20–25.

Carter, C. C. (2004a). Whither social studies? In pockets of peace at school. *Journal of Peace Education 1*(1), 77–87.

——— (2004b). Education for peace in Northern Ireland and the USA. *Theory and Research in Social Education 32*(1), 24–38.

——— (2007). Teacher preparation for peacebuilding in USA and Northern Ireland. In Z. Bekerman & C. McGlynn (Eds.), *Addressing ethnic conflict through peace education*, 245–258. New York: Palgrave Macmillan.

——— (2008). Voluntary standards for peace education. *Journal of Peace Education 5*(2), 141–155.

——— (Ed.). (2010a). *Conflict resolution and peace education: Transformations across disciplines*. New York: Palgrave Macmillan.

——— (2010b). Teacher preparation for peace education. In C. Carter (Ed.), *Conflict resolution and peace education: Transformations across disciplines*, 187–206. New York: Palgrave Macmillan.

——— (in press [a]). *Holding the world together: Visionary learning for peace through social education*. Charlotte, NC: Information Age.

——— (in press [b]). Peace-building education: Responding to contexts. In M. Nagler & M. Pilisuk (Eds.), *Building peace: Best practices, lessons learned*. Santa Barbara, CA: ABC-CLIO.

Carter, C. C. & Vandeyar, S. (2009). Teacher preparation for peace education in South Africa and USA: Constructing compassion and commitment. In C. McGlynn, M. Zemblas, Z. Bekerman, & A. Gallgher (Eds.), *Peace education and post-conflict societies: Comparative perspectives*, 373–396. New York: Palgrave Macmillan.

Dhammakaya Foundation. (2005). A manual of peace. Patumthani, Thailand: Dhammakaya Foundation.

Dewey, J. (1899). *The school and society*. Chicago: University of Chicago Press.

——— (1902). *The child and the curriculum*. Chicago: University of Chicago Press.

——— (1916). *Democracy and education*. New York: Macmillan Co.

——— (September 1923). The schools as a means of developing a social consciousness and social ideals in children. *Journal of Social Forces* I. *1*(5), 513–517.

District Institutes of Education and Training (2008). Eleventh five year plan activities. Retrieved November 12, 2009 from http://dietuthamacholapuram.org/activity.htm.

Eisler, R. T. & Miller, R. (Eds.) (2004). Educating for a culture of peace. Portsmouth, NH: Heinemann.

Freire, P. (1998). *Pedagogy of freedom. Ethics, democracy, and civic courage*. Translated by P. Clarke. New York: Rowman & Littlefield.

Galtung, J. (2004). *Transcend and transform. An introduction to conflict work*. Boulder: Paradigm Press.

Harris, I. M. & Morrison, M. L. (2003). *Peace education*. Jefferson, NC: McFarland.

Howlett, C. (2008). John Dewey and peace education. *Encyclopedia of peace education*. Retrieved November 12, 2009 from www.tc.edu/centers/epe/htm%20articles/Howlett_ch3_22feb08.doc.

Kosmanova, T. S. (2009). Peacemaking in Ukrainian teacher education classes through peer meditation. *Journal of Stellar Peacemaking 4*(2). Retrieved November 12, 2009 from http://74.127.11.121/peacejournal/volume_index/11/v4n2a01.html.

Ministry of Human Resource Development (June 6, 2005). National curriculum framework for school education—2005 backgrounder. *Press Information Bureau of India*. Retrieved November 12, 2009 from http://pib.nic.in/release/release.asp?relid=9606.

Mukhopadhyay, M. (2005). *Peace education framework for teacher education*. New Delhi: United Nations Educational, Scientific and Cultural Organization.

National Council of Educational Research and Training (2005). *Education for peace*. Retrieved November 12, 2009 from http://www.ncert.nic.in/html/education_peace.htm.

Ndura-Quédraogo, E. & Amster, R. (Eds.) (2009). *Building cultures of peace: Transidisciplinary voices of hope and action*. Newcastle upon Tyne, UK: Cambridge Scholars.

Salomon, G. & Nevo, B. (Eds.) (2002). *Peace education. The concept, principles, and practices around the world*. Mahwah, NJ: Lawrence Erlbaum.

State level Consolidation Report of the Peace Education Training Programme, DIET, Perundurai, & DTERT, Chennai.

United Nations Educational, Scientific and Cultural Organization (2001). Learning the way of peace. A teachers' guide to peace education. *United Nations Educational, Scientific and Cultural Organization, New Delhi*. Retrieved November 12, 2009 from http://unesdoc.unesco.org/images/0012/001252/125228eo.pdf.

Vygotsky, L. S. (1978). *Mind in society: The development of higher psychological processes*. Cambridge, MA: Harvard University Press.

Wenden, A. L. (Ed.) (2004). Education for a culture of social and ecological peace. Albany: State University of New York.

PART 3

Program Applications

Program development for peace is the manifestation of a vision. An important element of the human pursuit of peace has been the envisioning of a better situation, which is the catalyst for its advancement. Bringing about the desired situation is typically a creative initiative that considers and uses various approaches to fulfilling evident needs. When each approach has a transparent philosophical foundation, it becomes easier to attract support for and engagement with them. Mission statements help clarify programs' goals and beliefs.

Peace movements that respond effectively to structural conflicts have transparent ideology. Their philosophical roots can range from the simple to the complex, as long as their participants carry a vision of a better situation and can describe the beliefs that motivate their actions. Governments recognize collective action and have positively responded to it when either the politicians see the desired changes as worthwhile or the growing movement for change cannot be stopped without violence. In popular government and program operations one can see evidence of the belief that harm can be avoided in regular functions, as well as during the response to conflict.

This part of the book describes program initiatives that have used formal or informal education to end or avoid harm. The programs discussed put ideology into action and engaged in creative efforts to develop and sustain peace. They are a sample of many other existing and possible initiatives throughout the world, and together they are pieces of the peace puzzle, which when completely assembled, illustrates a collective vision of a better world and humanity's manifestation of it.

CHAPTER SEVEN

Restorative Practices for Reconstruction

CANDICE C. CARTER

Until all humans develop peace-oriented conflict-response abilities, there will continue to be opportunities for restoration from harm. When harm from inappropriate responses to conflict results in indirect and direct violence, there is a need for restoration. Whether the damage is widespread or contained, across world regions or in the mind where violent thoughts occur, the need for change with reconstruction exists. This need has been increasingly recognized and responded to in recent years by people throughout the world who are in professions in which they have identified some of the ways harm can be avoided or repaired. This chapter focuses on two fields wherein the need for such accomplishments has been addressed. Professionals in education and law have been proactively changing interactions in response to conflict. After describing the theories and aspirations that underlie their accomplishments, this chapter briefly presents the ways in which restorative practices have become evident in those two fields. However, the limited scope of the chapter is not intended to undervalue the restoration that people have been doing throughout human history and across professions. Rather, the chapter represents my direct experience with and research on restoration in the two fields described herein. Before I had many theoretical tools at my disposal as a new teacher in schools, I experimented with restorative practices in order to address the high levels of violence my students and other school members experienced. My subsequent learning about philosophy enhanced my call for peace education, and it shaped the methods I created for restorative education.

Theoretical Framework

The theoretical underpinnings of restorative practices include conceptions of humans as agents of change based on their abilities to care about, and for, others and to construct what is missing in the fulfillment of recognized needs. In some settings, human involvement in restoration has been facilitated by notions of spirituality and an overall sense of "connection" to others, including spirits. The goal of unification is common in restoration. People often need each other for the healing of harm and the reconstruction of damaged contexts. In reference to restorative practices with youth, Bazemore points out that beyond repairing harm, members of a community "make new connections with each other and enhance their own skills as parents and citizens, while increasing community capacity [for peace]" (Bazemore, 2009, p. 53). With post-conflict peace building as an identified goal, the facilitation of restorative practices continues throughout world (McGlynn, Zemblas, Bekerman & Gallgher, 2009). The reasoning evidenced by restorative practices was present long ago in the establishment of religions as well as in thoughts about the conditions of life and the human capacity for repairing and healing during it (Wilkinson, 1997).

Humans as a species are distinguished by their ability to love and care for themselves and all other life forms. In his analysis of Darwin's (1871) writings about humans, Loye (2004) explains that Darwin emphasized many times our moral sensitivity and love. With the capacity to care, humans reconstruct relationships with an "ethic of care" that supports peace (Noddings, 1992). Social reconstructionism holds valuable the development of a more peaceful society, especially through formal and informal education (Brameld, 1956; Counts, 1932; Illich, 1970). Humanism provides a view of holistic learning in which people mindfully cultivate capacities for caring, as well as computation for assessment of needs. Frederick Edwords points out that "Humanism is...an open-ended approach that allows for the testing of new alternatives [in problem-solving]" (Edwords, 2009). In the humanistic perspective, people are capable of co-creating the relationship that responds in the present to injustice and other types of violence. Not anticipating divine intervention in the afterlife, humanists react in the present. They focus on human efforts to make needed change. Apart from humanistic philosophy, the notion of repair exists in creeds of religion and other spiritual engagements.

In spiritual traditions and religions there is a common notion of restoration (Bouta, Kadayifci-Orellana & Abu-Nimer, 2005; Hadley, 2001). Ravindra Kumar reminds us that "every religious community emphatically calls upon the human beings for universal peace" (Kumar, 2006, p. 109). In their article "Spiritual But Not Religious," the Network of Spiritual Progressives explains that "we are building a movement in which we can talk about love and caring for each other..." (2009). This spiritual movement aims to restore "love, kindness, generosity, peace, non-violence, social justice, awe and wonder at the grandeur of creation, thanksgiving, humility and joy at the center of our lives" (The Network of Spiritual Progressives, 2009). Prescriptions for the restoration of peace include individual and collective acts (Diamond, 2000; Galtung, 2004; Ndura-Quédraogo & Anster, 2009). The restoration of the spirit has an important role in the well-being of a community. In some indigenous cultures, the restoration of the community has focused on restoring the good in the individual. Recognition of the individual as a good human being who has performed an incorrect act enables the repair of self-concept and of relations in the community (Mirsky, 2009). For example, intensive affirmations by members of the community for the individual who did a wrong action facilitate the needed restoration. Recent models of community involvement resonate with Maori practices of restoration that others have adapted for their own use. Four current models of restorative conferencing involve the community in decisions about the repair of harm done (Bazemore & Umbreit, 2001). Repair is an aspect of improvement.

Improvement Aspirations

Core in restoration ideology is recognition of the capacity of humans to improve themselves, their relationships, and their world. Eastern conceptions of education include the goal of self-improvement. One of several aspects of that accomplishment is developing the ability to forgive, something that children learn in religious rituals, if not in secular education. Kenneth Morgan recognizes that "participation in rituals from an early age is a powerful influence in setting the path to be followed throughout life" (Morgan, 1990, p. 94). He acknowledges that the participation may a response to social pressure or a means of manipulating for personal advantage. However, a selfish motivation for participation in a restorative practice does not preclude learning from it as a model of prosocial engagement. Modeling restorative practices provides tacit instruction and situates the interaction in the observer's or participant's schema, which is their psychological framework for future use. In *The Little Book of Restorative Discipline for Schools*, Amstutz and Mullet ask, "What are you modeling for your school?" before they explain the characteristics of modeling in peaceable schools (Amstutz & Mullet, 2005, p. 35). As antecedents of peace education, Amstutz and Mullet call for identification of the structures in schools that can include restorative practices. Structures that influence pedagogy include standards for peace education as well as school mission and policy statements (Carter, 2008). For example, the incorporation of dignity as an educational mission can bring attention to its role in teaching about peace through restoration (Morse, 2009).

Shirley Steinberg recommends a "pedagogy of human dignity" that incorporates spirituality into the curriculum (Steinberg, 1999, p. 170). In agreement with Purpel (1990), Steinberg calls for instruction that teaches about the misery in the world and the responsibility for alleviating it. Restoration of human dignity through education that instructs about and incorporates the diverse cultural ways in which people experience spirituality and connection is more than an ideal incorporated into peace education. It is a "practice" that can evidence improvement following careful attention to how the practice is done. Besides comparative religion in the curriculum, knowledge of spiritual notions and norms can be incorporated in several components of curriculum, including mindfulness lessons (Between Four Eyes, 2009). Maria Montessori recognized the need for and developed a pedagogy that fosters spiritual awareness and additional peace-building processes that others in secular education as well as in faith-based schools have been facilitating (Montessori, 1972; Weaver & Biesecker-Mast, 2003; Wolf, 1999). That spirituality has been used as a cornerstone for building peace can be seen in some of the ecologies evidencing restorative practices. In others, the promotion of partnership has built a foundation for restoration (Eisler, 2000; Gordon, 2004).

Building connections across cultural divides is another pursuit in schools and youth programs in which restorative practices construct intergroup bridges (Danesh, 2009). Crucial to the success of such practices are sustained and positive cross-cultural interactions (Hammack, 2009). Additionally, recognizing that reducing student conflicts in their classrooms maximizes instructional time has motivated educators' uses of restorative practices (Harrison, 2007). Construal of the practice as a "conflict resolution technique" (Sherman & Strang, 2007, p. 32) should be considered within a framework of conflict transformation in which structural improvements occur over time (Carter, 2010; Lederach, 2003). Examination of these realities reveals the different ecological characteristics of the restorative practices that are facets of peace education.

Education for Restoration

Learning and teaching about restoration contributes to peace development in the present and the future (Staub, 2009). The Alternatives to

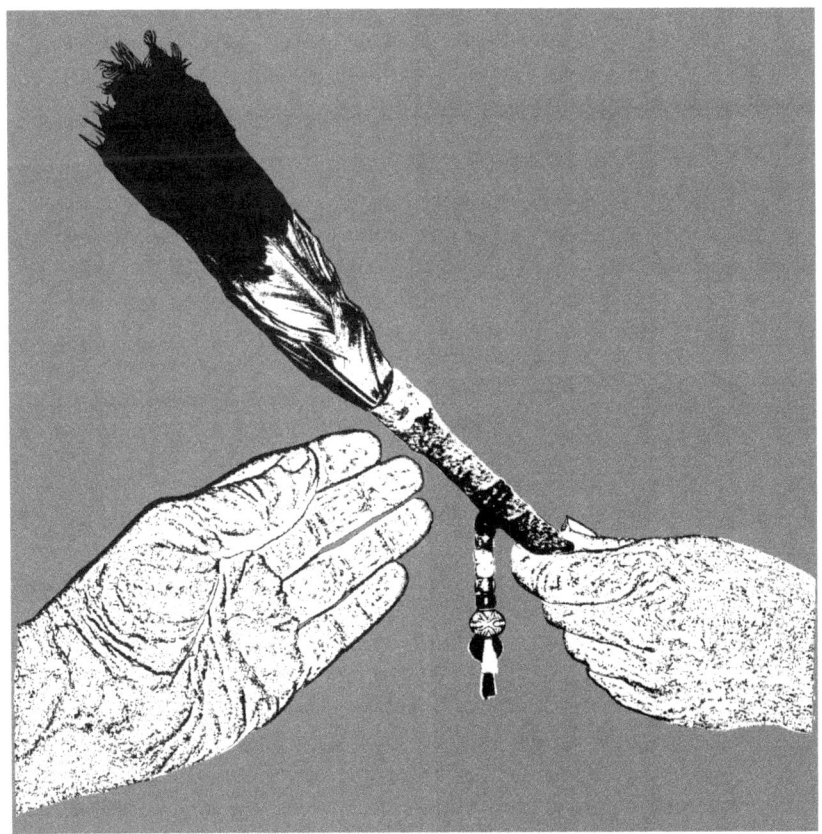

Figure 7.1 Passing a Talking Stick

Violence Organization points out "that it is easier to build a healthy child than to repair a broken adult" (Alternatives to Violence Organization, 2009). Knowledge about restorative practices used in the past by other cultures as well as within one's own identity group enhances the repertoire of possibilities for restoration. When I teach my students about traditions of the past, they subsequently consider adaptations of those traditions for use in present and future contexts of harm. For example, we have adapted the practice used in native cultures of passing of the talking stick in council circles for use in our circle time, during which everyone in the class has a turn to speak about an issue (Pranis, 2005). After my students learned to use a talking stick in a discussion circle, they requested opportunities repeat that activity to communicate about an emotive conflict. The stick-holding turn, in which only the stick holder is allowed to speak, enabled the uninterrupted expression of felt harm and of perceptions of its cause. Such expressions aid identification of viewpoints and needs. Although the same past approach to restoration may not be used, knowledge of it sometimes stimulates creativity through the adaptation of one or more past methods of restoration.

A foundation of peace is the fulfillment of needs. Restorative practices that enable the identification of unmet needs, which underlie harmful acts, contribute to the healing process—which aids prevention of subsequent damage as a response to that harm. With these two benefits of restoration, healing and prevention, a variety of approaches to peacemaking have been initiated in schools.

Applications

Recent practices in formal education hark back to some cultural traditions of restoratively responding to harm. These practices include affirmation and other forms of communication that promote the restoration of self-concept, which affects behaviors and relations. Reviewed here are examples of recent practices that schools have been facilitating, including bully intervention, conflict mediation, restorative discipline, and narrative counseling. These emerging efforts in schools intend restoration of various types.

Restorative responses to bullying include problem solving. Initial methods focused on how to stop this problem in schools, mainly through the enactment of discipline policy and the setting up of corresponding training programs for school personnel, but a narrow focus on the disruption of bullying and discipline responses overlooked the personal and contextual conditions that need attention (Barton, 2006; Sprung, Froschl & Hinitz, 2005). Broader than the restoration of orderly interactions in schools and on school buses is the need for the reconstruction of personal and group well-being (Chmelynski, 2005; Harrison, 2005). Recognizing this need, Kearns comments that "possible solutions may be found in moving away from neglectful, punitive and permissive practices by focusing on an approach that involves working with young people in a respectful, relational way (2006, p. 16). Isolation reduction and empathic involvement characterize effective bullying prevention in schools (Hazler & Carney, 2006). For example, affirmations by group members intended to build a positive self-concept do more than repair the self-worth of the subject person—both the bully and the bullied (Buckley & Maxwell, 2007). One such affirmation is "I am respectful and respectable." Self-respect and external respect empowers. Quite often a bully feels a need for power, as does the victim, due to previously experienced harmful interactions. The cohesion of a group that engages in the restorative process positively demonstrates their power. A bully "finds it very difficult to continue with the hurtful behavior in the light of the supportive strategies provided by the rest of the group" (Robinson & Maines, 2008, p. 43). A review of support methods (Table 7.1) reveals the importance of listening to students as they analyze and reconstruct hurtful interactions.

The purposeful selection of diverse group members who have different roles in the school and different perspectives provides a balance of experiences and identity representation that has been useful. Cornerstones of a support-group structure for bully prevention and

Table 7.1 The Support-Group Method

Step	Activity
1.	Talk with and listen to the person who is the target of the bullying.
2.	Convene a meeting with the people involved, including the bully.
3.	The facilitator explains the problem and describes the damage to the target, without blaming or inclusion of many details of the incident(s).
4.	Develop constructive mood and explain shared responsibility for problem solving.
5.	Ask the group members for their ideas about how to solve the problem.
6.	End the meeting after designating the group as the creator of the problem solution.
7.	Facilitator reconvenes the group to review their solution processes.

Source: Robinson & Maines, 2008.

intervention have been the facilitation of empathy and altruism as the foundation for problem solving with a bully. The support-group method has restored self-worth after sometimes stimulating shame for harmful acts. Crucial to the success of this method has been self versus external judgment, which happens in the process of recognizing the harm that one caused. Avoidance of judgment in understanding of problems between school members also occurs in the facilitation of conflict mediation.

Conflict mediation was brought to schools as an adaptation of disputeresolution interventions that have been used in the legal profession and by community boards. The goal of mediation is to empower individuals to resolve the conflicts they are experiencing. Whereas in a regional community or in court settings mediation occurs with the aid of professional mediators, schools allow trained students to assume that role. In a typical mediation setting, two "conflict managers" act as mediators for two or more student "disputants," who voluntarily choose or accept the assistance. With the aid of the mediators, students describe their problem and develop a resolution to the conflict it evidences. The culminating agreement they make in the intervention sometimes requires a follow-up step to ensure it has been useful in addressing the problem. The improvement in the school climate and the restoration of lost instructional time in teacher management of students' conflicts have been recognized as benefits of mediation by students (Community Boards, 2009). While the focus of this intervention is on conflict resolution versus conflict transformation that addresses the roots of the problems, it retains its value if students of all identities can be benefited in mediation sessions (Carter, 2002).

Restorative discipline involves students in repair after they have caused harm. The damage addressed includes harm to self, others, or the environment. Discipline is instructional. It teaches an individual responsibility for purposeful action that is undesirable due to its potentially harmful effect. With a goal of developing self-control, discipline signals inappropriate responses to conflicts. Discipline that restores not only provides a directional signal for behavioral changes but also responds to other needs of the disciplined whose inappropriate behavior evidence (Sakamoto, 2005). With an ethos of concern for everyone, restorative discipline includes recognition of everyone's needs—beyond a behavioral change of the harmer (Cavanagh, 2009; Redekop, 2007). Marshall Rosenberg points out the importance of identifying needs in *Life-Enriching Education* (2003). Belinda Hopkins (2004) identifies the following needs that student misbehaviors evidence: attention, belonging, friends, displacement of their felt hurt, power, control, and challenges. Humanistic responses to misbehavior by students recognize these needs and proactively respond to them as well as to the needs of the harmed.

Reconstruction of the identity of the harming student occurs along with relationships at school and in other contexts in which the unmet needs have manifested in misbehavior. For example, in primary and secondary schools, as well as in university classes, I have used both as a teacher and a colleague "put-ups" to repair the harm of a "put-down." The generator of the denigrating remark, which is a "put-down," has been required to produce or write (5–10), depending on skill level, a list of true "put-ups," or affirmations of the target. This includes the self as the target of the negative comment, such as "I am so stupid!" In the process of creating the list of affirming "put-ups," the harmer must verify the good qualities of the target. This transforms the outlook of the harmer and helps the target restore, or develop, a positive self-concept. The discipline of producing true statements can be construed as punishment for misbehavior. However, the restorative purpose is obvious and reluctance to doing the task has only been temporal. Producing the list takes time—to learn about and verify the positive aspects of a person. One approach to restorative discipline is to facilitate class meetings in which students talk about their concerns and the problems they have witnessed. These meetings focus on nonpunitive solutions to the problems the students analyze (Amstutz & Mullet, 2005; Nelson, Lott & Glenn, 2000). Counseling is another method of restoration that responds to the needs of a student.

Reconstructive counseling involves listening and observing, through body language, to description of one's life, especially the conflicts in it. Restorative counseling enables the reframing of one's life to see it in a different perspective. Drama counseling and narrative counseling are two methods that provide reconstruction opportunities. Drama counseling involves gathering information that illustrates a problem and a way it may be worked out before acting (Blatner, 2007). In a sculpting technique, the counselor moves the client from a physical stance and facial expression that shows the damage to a healed or at least more empowered stance. The creativity in dramatic counseling resonates with the use of creativity for problem solving in multiple contexts of conflict. Both storytelling and visual arts have been useful in restorative counseling.

Narrative counseling uses storytelling to situate a problem in its context. This broadening of the focus allows for recognition of conflict sources and development of counter stories in which students are empowered to see and respond to situations in their lives differently. In the re-authoring process counselors help students revise their stories, "and use self-descriptions through which they would prefer to live" (Winslade & Monk, 2007, p. 77). Narrative therapy or narrative transformational conversations create a shift in individual perspectives of relationships by changing language before changing behavior and perception. Problems are not obstacles to be overcome; rather they are opportunities for individuals to transform their view of themselves in relation to the problem. This transformation involves deconstructing the problem and shifting language from problem-saturated stories to more meaningful action-based stories that heal and empower (Wynn, Wilburn &West-Olatunji, 2010).

New narratives avoid deficit discourse due to the narrative's orientation towards pathology description instead of the competence and health that the intervention helps the student construct in self-concept. Deficit discourses are descriptions of what is not normal about a student, including the labels schools use to identify students' special needs. The goals of avoiding deficit descriptions of students include the elimination of resistance, self-enfeeblement, reliance on professionals, and devaluing of local knowledge that has an important role in reconstruction. This avoidance of deficit discourse allows for inclusion of culturally different methods of responding to conflict that a school does not normally facilitate. In a holistic approach to restoration, culturally relevant practices of students' families are understood.

A whole-school approach to restoration is a compilation of practices that intend recovery from and avoidance of harm. The cover of the book *Just Schools: A Whole School Approach to Restorative Justice* (Hopkins, 2004) depicts these practices as pieces of a puzzle. Each piece names one practice that contributes to restoration at school. The label on one of the puzzle pieces is just a large question mark, which indicates the openness of holistic education. In that approach there is room to accommodate cultural differences and educate the "whole child." The growing field of social-emotional literacy addresses that often-overlooked aspect of learning. Other initiatives, such as antiracist and social-justice education have as a goal the healing of harms that have occurred in societies and their schools (Howard, 2004). Hearing the experiences of those who have been maligned is crucial for restoration. A key piece of the whole-school approach is active listening. This involves body language that indicates receptivity to other perspectives and a caring response versus denial or dismissal of conflict. The latter happens when the response equates personal experience to the problem of or harm to another. In other words, the listener injects personal information about experience with the problem, which distracts from the focus on the speaker who described the conflict. Active listening refrains from comparison of experiences and pain associated with them. Sometimes, just the act of compassionate listening to one who feels harmed is enough to restore relations.

Facilitating compassionate education occurs across the school as well as in the classroom. There are "pockets of peace" in the daily interactions where compassion and listening can occur (Carter, 2004). Reminding us of the impact of those interactions, Assistant Superintendent Joe Nardo comments that "we remember most how we were treated in school rather than what we were required to learn (Nardo in Hart & Hodson, 2004, p. 2003). In the lesson-planning section of their book describing compassionate education, Hart and Hodson (2004) ask guiding questions including "To what extent is the study of human life connected to the community, to all other life forms, the biosphere, and the planet?" (p. 178). Within and across subjects, modeling an ethos of concern about and care for all life forms enables students' learning about restoration in a web of interdependent existence. When they learn about restorative practices across their community, students see how their school experiences are preparing them for restoration everywhere. In the past decade, documentation of restorative practices throughout the Near East and the Far East, in concert with applications in the West, evidence increasing interest in and results from the changes the practices evidence as informal education outside of schools as well as in them (Hayes, Maxwell & Morris, 2006; Keenapan, 2007; Maxwell, Wong & Wing Lo, 2006).

Education for restoration has had "dramatic results" for some schools (Adams, 2008; Mirsky & Wachtel, 2007; Riestenberg, 2007). Findings on restorative practices in schools reported by Lewis (2009) for the International Institute for Restorative Practices encourage the development and use of reconstructive education that has a humanistic foundation. Teachers and all school personnel need preparation for these comprehensive practices in their education programs. The peace-focused teacher education that De Paul describes is an important initiative supported by both policy and philosophy (Carter, 2007; Carter & Vandeyar, 2009). Policies for the provision of restoration interactions have brought government back from the brink of destruction through harmful punishment of students to reconstruction through caring actions with students that help them and others with whom they interact. Results of restorative education in prisons brought attention to the possibility of avoiding legal infractions and of dispute resolution (Alternatives to Violence Project, 2009). Evident in the legal field and in education is an aid-oriented ethos that enables reconstruction of individual identity, relationships and institutions.

Restoration in Legal Contexts

Reconstruction as a response to and for the prevention of crime has become evident globally through initiatives that focus on restoration. The organizations that support restorative projects and the schools that offer preparation for such work, created by nonprofit and commercial enterprises, have been expanding. These initiatives range from support for disputants who have not violated a law to victim-offender interventions that have at least one, if not all, possible participants such as the victim and family members. On a broader scale, forgiveness initiatives are other humanistic activities aimed at restoring peace where it has been lost to direct violence. Core to these practices is the belief that restoration is not only possible; it can also be a normal response to conflict in modern societies. The humanism evident in legal contexts has been supporting peace where it was formerly lacking in courts, detention facilities for youth, and prisons. Especially encouraging in the prevention of direct violence are innovations by attorneys that enable their clients to settle disputes outside the courts. In his discussion of Spirituality and Practicing Law As A Healing Profession, Floyd (2007, p. 473) explains the importance of listening in responding to the brokenness they encounter While these restorative practices reduce requirements for government agency, embodied in law-enforcement, law chambers, and courtrooms, they evidence the increasing prospects for peace through agents of civil society.

Comprehensive Law

Recently diversified are methods of responding to conflict that lawyers, certified mediators, and other professionals facilitate in legal contexts. Comprehensive law is an encompassing descriptor of these practices. As alternatives to contentious forms of dispute resolution, these approaches combine reconstructive techniques that have been commonly taught in the social sciences, not law school. Schools of law now offer courses about dispute resolution that avoids litigation. The goal of these methods is restoration of well-being in legal matters and relationships. Lawyers facilitate the restoration through consideration of beliefs, values, identified needs and goal development, resources, and relationships.

Methods included in this reconstructive approach to conflicts that can involve legal agreements include preventive law, therapeutic jurisprudence, procedural justice, holistic justice, restorative justice, transformative mediation and collaborative law (Diacoff, 2010). A brief description of each method illuminates its role in relational and societal reconstruction. Preventive law is the oldest method, and it intends the avoidance of lawsuits as responses to conflicts. Litigation became a widespread approach to conflict resolution. In recognition of this overuse of the legal system for problem solving between individuals and institutions, lawyers have been facilitating alternative responses. For example, subsequent to an assessment of the legal situation, a prevention lawyer may develop policy and corresponding procedures to proactively respond to a contentious situation, such as a compensation dispute between an employee and employer or a client and a service provider. Restoration of working relationships also results from therapeutic responses by the legal field.

Therapeutic jurisprudence is a very established form of legal restoration. It involves recognition of the relationship between disputants and of their psychological needs. After identifying those needs, the lawyer considers how to fulfill them in developing a course of action that will have optimal psychological, and possibly legal, outcomes. For example, a client may feel the need for an apology from an offender, which the lawyer would enable and document. Or, a client may evidence the need for rehabilitation from addiction, and an agreement is made to use that in a response to a deteriorated relationship. Legal rights are always maintained, as are options for exercising them, when the lawyer uses therapeutic techniques for identifying and responding to needs.

Procedural justice responds to a client's need to be heard and treated with dignity in the midst of a conflict. The use of respectful listening addresses a client's need more than litigation in a court, where the opportunity to communicate about the harm is very limited. Conversely, in a damages lawsuit, a client's communication with the judge is typically minimal and oriented to a quick assessment of damages for the defendant to pay. The litigant's perception of the judge, based on communication about the agreement in a procedural court, is important. Crucial in this method is the belief that the agreement about resolving the conflict is fair. In this approach, as well as others in comprehensive law, an apology by the defendant has been accepted for restoration. In the legal field, facilitation of restoration is most comprehensive when, as in other fields, it has a holistic framework.

Holistic justice explicitly advocates peace through the practice of law. On the website of the International Alliance of Holistic Lawyers (IAHL), the following acrostic poem is a creative expression of this goal:

> **P**romote peaceful advocacy and holistic legal principles.
> **E**ncourage compassion, reconciliation, forgiveness, and healing.
> **A**dvocate the need for a humane legal process.
> **C**ontribute to peace building at all levels.
> **E**njoy the practice of law.
>
> **L**isten intentionally and deeply in order to gain complete understanding.
> **A**cknowledge the opportunity in conflict.
> **W**holly honor and respect the dignity and integrity of each individual.
>
> (International Alliance of Holistic Lawyers, 2009)

"Authentic Lawyering: Practicing from the Heart" was the theme of the IAHL 2008 conference, and it highlights humanism in the legal field (International Alliance of Holistic Lawyers, 2008). The coalition of lawyers who hold membership in the IAHL use a variety of approaches to legal matters to identify the root problems and find ways to address them. Their holistic methods have included setting goals for the personal and spiritual development of their clients in order to continually transform, as well as immediately resolve, conflicts. An example of this that Diacoff (2010) offers is helping a client to recognize and manage his anger while he is making a decision about how to respond to a conflict that could have resulted in a lawsuit. The commitment to restoration is most obvious in the approach that explicitly expresses that goal.

Restorative justice involves the co-creation of responses to injustice. In *An Ancient View of a "New" Paradigm*, Breton and Lehman explain the philosophical background of restoration in response to injustice (2001, p. 32). In current practice, restorative justice typically involves victims and the offenders who harmed them in reconstructive-oriented communication, or "constructive conflict." John Braithwaite explains, "When hurt is communicated, shame acknowledged by the person or persons who caused it, respect shown for the victim's reasons for communicating the hurt, and respect reciprocated by the victim, constructive conflict has occurred between victim and offender" (2002, p. 80). Restoration in this approach has ranged from the condition of the victim to the offender and their community. In some cultural models of restorative justice, such as those used by First Nations, the community participates in sentencing of the offender through a "circle processes where perceptions and feelings can be shared by everyone, including those of the offender, the victim, their families, and friends. Within this communicative process, relationships have been built or strengthened on a foundation of forgiveness and understanding. One example is the development of the Tariq Kahmisa Foundation (2009) after a father forgave the teenage murderer of his son and then created an organization in partnership with the offender's father to teach other teenagers about how they can end a cycle of violence. Principles of needs-oriented peace building are flexibility and creativity (Sawatsky, 2008, p. 65).

Transformative mediation resembles facilitative mediation, in which disputants have an opportunity to both describe the problem and to agree on how they will respond to it. However, focussing on transformation through the intervention has two goals. The first is recognition of needs and the second is empowerment of the disputants in their co-creation of the solution. This transformation away from dependence on outside assistance for the creation of problem solutions empowers the former disputants.

Collaborative law facilitates communication between disputants and their attorneys to form an agreement that must resolve their dispute without litigation. The collaboration involves direct communication between all participants, attorneys and clients. A special characteristic of this method is the agreement of attorneys to withdraw from the case if their clients find that they require litigation to resolve their conflict. The incentive to help their clients without court hearings avoids societal dependence on government agency for conflict resolution. Collaborative law enacts the following:

The different types of techniques that have been used by law professionals as restorative practices evidence new lenses for observing the needs of people and creativity. Their restorative practices resonate with the use of peace dialogue in response to the systemic problems that are the root of many conflicts in schools and other institutions

(United Nations, 2005). When restoration from harm occurs, these practices restore the power of the participants and faith in law professionals as aides outside government facilities. While this recent trend fosters respect for the legal profession, eliminating dependence on the profession when responding to conflict remains a goal. The suggestion for development of a "nonjustice system" demonstrates dissatisfaction with use of a punitive-oriented justice system for responding to conflict. Kimmel provides the criteria for developing an "ideal Nonjustice System" for resolving life's conflicts.

- The ideal Nonjustice System would
- break the justice addiction, make forgiveness possible, and restore our happiness;
- instantly stop the pain of being wronged and make us feel united, loved, and happy again;
- assure us that we are not alone; and
- restore our self-esteem.

(Kimmel, 2005, p. 87)

Ideals, along with vision, are important as foundational ingredients for peace construction. The ideal of restoration and a vision of reconstructed relationships, along with flexibility and creativity in the processes used for them, have evidenced the human capacity for bringing about needed change. Connection through professional as well as personal concern and care has disrupted the cycles of violence that destructive responses to conflict perpetuate. When we have an ideal for and a commitment to reconstruction, we can identify what is missing when we observe and analyze for the needs that conflict evidences.

Conclusion

As professional fields where punishment has been a common response to conflict, recent changes that social reconstruction and humanism support in education and law demonstrate the possibilities that shared philosophy presents. While these two fields experience metamorphosis, other contexts for use of restorative practices have become evident—in personal and professional interactions. The accounts in this book that describe efforts to restore peace where it has been lost reveal more than the hope of humanity for a world in which all needs can be fulfilled. Reconstructed societies and the relations in them can enable human preservation of more than people. It has become evident that restoration of the biosphere is a requisite for the preservation of human and other life on this planet, and beyond it. Although that goal has become increasingly urgent, long-held ideas and recent ones about how and where to provide needed care belong in all aspects of existence. Sharing notions of care and how it has been, as well as how it might be, provided is at the forefront of the peace we are building.

Three engagements support normalization of care in contexts of conflict. First is the expansion of our knowledge base to include awareness of how both ancient and more recent groups incorporated restoration in their responses to conflict. Besides imparting knowledge, overcoming historical amnesia provides multiple perspectives that are helpful for recognizing possible solutions to problems. We must both learn and teach peace history in order to consider how strategies used in many places and time periods may be adapted now. We need to become aware of the ways in which harmful responses sustain conflict, normalize it, and thus motivate violent responses to it. Most immediately, we need knowledge of the personal and professional skills necessary for constructively responding to harm. These needs evidence the crucial role of education in all professions as well as in the preparation of children for a life of peaceful conflict management.

The second engagement involves professional as well as personal commitment. Analysis of the processes that are currently normalized in all professions, in addition to education and law, need critical examination for recognition of missed opportunities. For example, in her role as an attorney for a law firm, Daicoff recognized missed opportunities for personal and relational healing in response to clients' conflicts. She came to realize that instead of facilitating punishment-oriented legal actions, communication for and between clients might repair the damages they experienced and result in constructive legal agreements when those were needed. Through her commitment to reconstructive law, she changed the nature of her work in the field, advancing restorative opportunities for lawyers and their clients. Envisioning peace action in the practice of law, as well as committing to professional work for peace and development of knowledge about how peace has happened, enables transformation within and by that field.

The third component of restoration is vision. Envisioning care as a component of professional practice and restoration as a goal of the practice portends well for peace. Throughout history, visions have been the catalyst for needed change. With our special capacity for love and our creativity in the development of visions, we are capable of expanding the range of restorative practices across fields. Making a commitment to do that is a choice professionals have.

References

Adams, C. (2008). The talk-it-out solution. How can you promote safety? Try getting rid of metal detectors. *Scholastic Administrator, November/December,* 33–34.

Alternatives to Violence Organization (2009). Helping women and children become safe & self-sufficient. Retrieved December 1, 2009 from http://alternativestoviolence.org/.

Alternatives to Violence Project, International (2009). Retrieved December 1, 2009 from http://avpinternational.org/index.html.

American Humanist Association. (2003). Humanist Manifesto III. *About humanism.* Retrieved December 1, 2009 from http://www.americanhumanist.org/who_we_are/about_humanism/Humanist_Manifesto_III.

Amstutz, L. S. & Mullet, J. H. (2005). *The little book of restorative discipline for schools: Teaching responsibility; creating caring climates.* Intercourse, PA: Good Books.

Barton, E. (2006). *Bully prevention: Tips and strategies for school leaders and classroom teachers.* Thousand Oaks, CA: Corwin.

Bazemore, G. (2009). Getting and keeping it real: Less than perfect restorative justice intervention and the value of small connections. *The Journal for Peace and Justice Studies 18*(1 & 2), 31–61.

Bazemore, G. & Umbreit, M. (February 2001). A comparison of four restorative conferencing models. *Juvenile Justice Bulletin* NJC 184538. Rockville, MD: Juvenile Justice Clearinghouse.

Between Four Eyes (2009). *A collaborative for mindful awareness.* Retrieved November 14, 2009 from http://www.btwn4eyes.org/.

Blatner, A. (2007). Morenean approaches: Recognizing psychodrama's many facets. *Journal of Group Psychotherapy, Psychodrama and Sociometry 59*(4), 159–171.

Bouta, T., Kadayifci-Orellana, S. A., & Abu-Nimer, M. (2005). *Faith-based peace-building: Mapping and analysis of Christian, Muslim and multi-faith actors.* Washington, DC: Salam Institute for Peace and Justice. Retrieved December 1, 2009 from http://www.salaminstitute.org/FaithBasedActors.pdf.

Braithwaite, J. (2002). *Restorative justice and responsive regulation.* New York: Oxford University Press.

Brameld, T. (1956). *Toward a reconstructed philosophy of education.* New York: Dryden.

Breton, D. & Lehman, S. (2001). *The mystic heart of justice.* West Chester, PA: Chrysalis.

Buckley, S. & Maxwell, G. (2007). *Respectful schools: Restorative practices in education.* Wellington, NZ: Office of the Children's Commissioner and The Institute of Policy Studies, Victoria University.

Burns, R. J. & Aspeslagh, R. (1996). *Three decades of peace education around the world: An anthology.* New York: Garland Publishing.

Cameron, L. & Thorsborne, M. (2001). Restorative justice and school discipline: Mutually exclusive? In H. Strang & J. Braithwaite (Eds.), *Restorative justice and civil society*, 180–194. New York: Cambridge University Press.

Carter, C. C. (2002). Conflict resolution at school: Designed for construction of a compassionate community. *The Journal of Social Alternatives 21*(1), 49–55.

——— (2004). Whither social studies? In pockets of peace at school. *Journal of Peace Education 1*(1), 77–87.

——— (2007). Teacher preparation for peacebuilding in USA and Northern Ireland. In Z. Bekerman & C. McGlynn (Eds.), *Addressing ethnic conflict through peace education*, 245–258. New York: Palgrave Macmillan.

Carter, C. C (2008). Voluntary standards for peace education. *Journal of Peace Education 5*(2), 141–155.

——— (Ed.). (2010). *Conflict resolution and peace education: Transformations across disciplines*. New York: Palgrave Macmillan.

Carter, C. C. & Vandeyar, S. (2009). Teacher preparation for peace education in South Africa and USA: Constructing compassion and commitment. In C. McGlynn, M. Zemblas, Z. Bekerman, & A. Gallgher (Eds.), *Peace education and post-conflict societies: Comparative perspectives*, 373–396. New York: Palgrave Macmillan.

Cavanagh, T. (2009). Creating a new discourse of peace in schools: Restorative justice in education. *The Journal for Peace and Justice Studies 18*(1 & 2), 62–85.

Chmelynski, C. (2005). Restorative justice for discipline with respect. *Education Digest 71*(1), 17–20.

Community Boards (2009). Conflict manager program benefits. *Community boards conflict manager program*. Retrieved October 25, 2009 from http://www.communityboards.org/.

Counts, G.S. (1932). *Dare the schools build a new social order?* New York: John Day.

Daicoff, S. (2010). Comprehensive law: Transformative responses by the legal profession. In C. C. Carter (Ed.), *Conflict resolution and peace education: Transformations across disciplines*, 97–126. New York: Palgrave Macmillan.

Danesh, H. B. (2009). Unity-based peace education: Education for Peace Program in Bosnia and Herzegovina. In G. Salomon & E. Cairns (Eds.), *Handbook on peace education*, 253–269. Location: Psychology Press.

Darwin, C. (1871/1981). *The descent of man* (First edition). Princeton, NJ: Princeton University Press.

De Paul, S. V. (2010). Peace education in elementary teacher education of Tamilnadu. In C. C. Carter (Ed.), *Conflict resolution and peace education: Transformations across discipline*. New York: Palgrave Macmillan.

Dewey, J. (1916). *Democracy and education*. New York: Macmillan.

Diamond, L. (2000). *The courage for peace*. Berkeley, CA: Conari.

Edwords, F. (1989). *What is humanism? Changing the world, one mind at a time*. Retrieved December 1, 2009 from http://www.jcn.com/humanism.html.

Eisler, R. T. (2000). *Tomorrow's children: A blueprint for partnership education in the 21st century*. Boulder: Westview.

Floyd, T. W. (2007). Spirituality and practicing law as a healing profession: The importance of listening. In M. A. Silver (Ed.), *The affective assistance of counsel*, 473–492. Durham, NC: Carolina Academic Press.

Galtung, J. (2004). *Transcend and transform. An introduction to conflict work*. Boulder: Paradigm Press.

Gordon, T. (2004). Nonviolent partnership parenting and teaching: Leaving behind the old control model. In R. Eisler & R. Miller (Eds.), *Educating for a culture of peace*, 80–100. Portsmouth, NH: Heinemann.

Hadley, M. (Ed.) (2001). *The spiritual roots of restorative justice*. Albany: State University of New York Press.
Hammack P. L. (2009). The cultural psychology of American-based coexistence programs for Israeli and Palestinian Youth. In C. McGlynn, M. Zemblas, Z. Bekerman, & A. Gallgher (Eds.), *Peace education and post-conflict societies: Comparative perspectives*, 191–216. New York: Palgrave Macmillan.
Harrison, L. (2007). From authoritarian to restorative schools. *Reclaiming Children and Youth 16*(2), 17–20.
Harrison, M. M. (2005). Bully on the bus. *Teaching Tolerance 28*(Fall), 38–43.
Hart, S. & Hodson, V. K. (2004). *The compassionate classroom. Relationship based teaching and learning*. Encinitas, CA. PuddleDancer Press.
Hayes, H., Maxwell, G., & Morris, A. (2006). Conferencing and restorative justice. In D. Sullivan and L. Tifft (Eds.), *Handbook of restorative justice: A global perspective*, 91–104. New York: Routledge.
Hazler, R. J. & Carney, J. V. (2006). Critical characteristics of effective bullying prevention programs. In S. R. Jimerson & M. J. Furlong (Eds.), *Handbook of school violence and school safety: From research to practice*, 275–291. Mahwah, NJ: Lawrence Erlbaum.
Hopkins, B. (2004). *Just schools: A whole school approach to restorative justice*. London: Jessica Kingsley.
Howard, G. (2004). How we are white. *Teaching Tolerance 26*(Fall), 50–52.
Illich, I. (1970). *Deschooling society*. New York: Harper and Row.
International Alliance of Holistic Lawyers (2008). *The Whole Lawyer 17*(1). Retrieved November 20, 2009 from http://www.iahl.org/articles/newsletters/Winter2008/Winter2008Newsletter.html.
——— (2009). *About holistic law*. Retrieved December 1, 2009 from http://www.iahl.org/index.cfm/hurl/obj=AboutHolisticLaw/AboutHolisticLaw.cfm.
Lewis, S. (Ed.) (2009). *Improving school climate. Findings from schools implementing restorative practices*. Retrieved October 26, 2009, at http://www.iirp.org/books_n_videos.php#Improving-School-Climate.
Kearns, M. (2006). *Curriculum evaluation and restorative practice*. Christchurch, NZ: Canterbury Christ Church University.
Keenapan, N. (2007). Restorative justice. *Real Lives*. Bangkok, Thailand: United Nations International Children's Emergency Fund. Retrieved December 1, 2009 from http://www.unicef.org/thailand/reallives_7282.html.
Kimmel, J. P. (2005). *Suing for peace. A guide for resolving life's conflict (without lawyers, guns, or money)*. Charlottesville, VA: Hampton Roads.
Kumar, R. (2006). *Religion and world peace*. New Delhi: Gyan.
Lederach, J. P. (2003). *The little book of conflict transformation*. Intercourse, PA: Good Books.
Loye, D. (2004). Darwin's lost theory and the hidden crisis in western education. In R. Eisler and R. Miller (Eds.), *Educating for a culture of peace*, 42–56. Portsmouth, NH: Heinemann.
Maxwell, G., Wong, D., & Wing Lo, T. (2006). Diversion from youth courts in five Asia Pacific jurisdictions: Welfare or restorative solutions. *International Journal of Offender Therapy and Comparative Criminology 50*(1), 5–20.
McGlynn, C., Zemblas, M., Bekerman, Z., & Gallgher, A. (Eds.) (2009). *Peace education and post-conflict societies: Comparative perspectives*. New York: Palgrave Macmillan.
Mirsky, L. & Wachtel, T. (2007). *The worst school I've ever been to*: Empirical evaluations of a restorative school and treatment milieu. *Reclaiming Children and Youth 16*(2), 13–16.
Montessori, M. (1972). *Education and peace*. Translated by Helen R. Lane. Chicago: Regnery.

Morgan, K. W. (1990). *Reaching for the moon: On Asian religious paths.* Chambersburg, PA: Anima.

Morrison, B. (2001). The school system: Developing its capacity in the regulation of a civil society. In H. Strang & J. Braithwaite (Eds.), *Restorative justice and civil society,* 195–210. New York: Cambridge University Press.

Morse, J. (January 27, 2009). Efforts of ordinary people support human dignity: University of Minnesota program provides intense 10-week fellowship. *America.gov.* Retrieved November 14, 2009 from http://www.america.gov/st/hr-english/2009/January/20090123154720ajesrom0.241955.html#ixzz0Wx92M7i8.

Nelson, J., Lott, L., & Glenn, H. S. (2000). *Positive discipline in the classroom: Developing mutual respect* (Third edition). Roseville, CA: Prima.

Ndura-Quédraogo, E. & Amster, R. (2009). *Building cultures of peace: Transdisciplinary voices of hope and action.* Newcastle upon Tyne: Cambridge Scholars Publishing.

Noddings, N. (1992). *The challenge to care in schools: An alternative approach to education.* New York: Teachers College Press.

Pranis, K. (2005). *The little book of circle processes: A new/old approach to peacemaking.* Intercourse, PA: Good Books.

Purpel, D. E. (Ed.). (1999). *Moral outrage in education.* New York: Peter Lang.

Redekop, P. (2007). *Changing paradigms. Punishment and restorative discipline.* Scottsdale, PA: Herald.

Riestenberg, N. (2007). The restorative recovery school: Countering chemical dependency. *Reclaiming Children and Youth 16*(2), 21–23.

Robinson, G. & Maines, B. (2008). *Bullying. A complete guide to the support group method.* Los Angeles: Sage.

Rosenberg, M. (2003). *Life-enriching education.* Encinitas, CA: PuddleDancer Press.

Sakamoto, W. (2005). From angry kid to peace-prize winner. In J. Canfield, M. V. Hansen, C. C. Carter, S. Palomares, L. Williams, & B. Winch (Eds.), *Chicken soup for the soul: Stories for a better world,* 41–44. Deerfield Beach, FL: Health Communications.

Sawatsky, J. (2008). *Justpeace ethics: A guide to restorative justice and peacebuiding.* Eugene, OR: Cascade.

Sherman, L. W. & Strang, H. (2007). *Restorative justice: The evidence.* London: Smith Institute.

Sprung, B., Froschl, M., & Hinitz, B. (2005). *The anti-bullying and teasing book for preschool classrooms.* Gryphon House.

Staub, E. (2009). Healing in Rwanda. In G. Salomon & E. Cairns (Eds.), *Handbook on peace education,* 269–286. Location: Psychology Press.

Steinberg, S. (1999). Social justice, curriculum, and spirituality. In D. E. Purpel (Ed.), *Moral outrage in education,* 153–172. New York: Peter Lang.

Tariq Kahmisa Foundation. (2009). Program summary. *Ending the cycle of violence.* Retrieved December 1, 2009 from http://www.chariotvideos.com/education/cycle.shtml.

The Network of Spiritual Progressives. (February 25, 2009). Spiritual but not religious. Retrieved December 1, 2009 from http://www.spiritualprogressives.org/article.php?story=spiritual__butnot.

United Nations. (2005). *Peace dialogue in the social integration process: An alternative to violence and silence.* Retrieved December 1, 2009 from www.un.org/esa/socdev/sib/egm/pd-sip—ovrvw.pdf.

Weaver, J. D. & Biesecker-Mast, G. (Eds.) (2003). *Teaching peace: Nonviolence and the liberal arts.* New York: Rowan and Littlefield.

Wilkinson, R. A. (1997). A shifting paradigm: Modern restorative justice principles have their roots in ancient cultures. *Corrections Today*, December. Retrieved December 1, 2009 from http://www.drc.state.oh.us/web/Articles/article28.htm.

Winslade, J. M. & Monk, G. D. (2007). *Narrative counseling in schools: Powerful and brief* (Second edition). Thousand Oaks, CA: Corwin.

Wolf, A. D. (1999). *Nurturing the spirit in non-sectarian classrooms*. Holidaysburg, PA: Parent Child Press.

Wynn, R., Wilburn, S.T., & West-Olatunji, C. (2010). Multiculturalism, conflict transformation and peacebuilding: Practitioner and client working together. In C. C. Carter (Ed.), *Conflict resolution and peace education: Transformations across disciplines*, 7–32. New York: Palgrave Macmillan.

Zehr, H. (2009). The intersection of restorative justice with trauma healing, conflict transformation and peacebuilding. *The Journal for Peace and Justice Studies 18*(1 & 2), 20–30.

CHAPTER EIGHT

Cosmopolitanism as a Philosophical Foundation of Post-Yugoslav Peace Studies in Higher Education

ANDRIA K. WISLER

What are the concrete stakes of this situation today? Why must the important questions concerning philosophical teaching and research, why must the imperative of the right to philosophy be deployed in their international dimension today more than ever? Why are the responsibilities which need to be taken no longer, and even less today in the twenty-first century, simply national? What do "national," "cosmopolitan," "universal" mean here for, and with regard to, philosophy, philosophical research, philosophical education or training, or even for a philosophical question or practice that would not be essentially linked to research or education?

Jacques Derrida (2002, p. 332)

The final decade of the twentieth century and the inaugural years of the new millennium have left much of the region of the former Yugoslavia[1] in the Balkans[2] of southeastern Europe affected by the direct, structural, and psychological violence of war and the unwieldy processes of transition. While the demise of Communism in 1989 propelled much of Central and Eastern Europe into a turbulent but generally nonviolent period of economic, social, and political development, the former republics of the Yugoslav federation engaged in a decade of violent conflict and human rights abuses. Other post-socialist and post-communist countries began their transformations, however awkward, into democratic governance, capitalist economies, and permissible pluralism. With their nationhoods and state identities stabilizing, many of these countries have moved into the global community at a symbolically and materially recognizable level, namely, membership in the European Union (EU).

The former Yugoslav republics sought their independence not long after the pivotal European moment of the collapse of the Berlin Wall in 1989. Slovenia achieved sovereignty after a short ten-day war while Bosnia and Herzegovina (BiH)[3] and Croatia acquired independent statehood after five years of violent conflict with the Yugoslav army and central government. After 83 years of existence, the name Yugoslavia disappeared from the maps in 2003, to be replaced by a looser union called Serbia and Montenegro, for the two remaining republics of the former federation.[4] Consequently, the violent conflicts of the 1990s stymied the development of all sectors of these societies, and the original democratic, capitalist transition inspired in 1989 across central and Eastern Europe evolved into national identity building based on the mirage of ethnic purity and difference. Such divisive identities constructed through nationalistic political messages perpetuated discrimination, tension, and distrust, and have directed human energy and fiscal commitment toward warfare, rather than economic and social development (Dimitrijevic & Kovács, 2004).

Since the end of major direct violence,[5] numerous attempts have been made as part of the region's transition from a dominating war culture in the 1990s to one normalizing a future-oriented peace. This maturation process requires the acquisition of habits of respect for both established legal and the more abstract rights of others, as well as the advanced learning of the praxis of peaceful living and nonviolent conflict transformation. The sectors of education, media, religion, and law, among others, have responded with reforms and strategic measures within this process. Although reforms are often rooted in EU hopes and rhetoric, membership in the Union remains a contested target for some of the countries of focus, one that seems to be constantly moving and burdened with conditions, specifically those of governmental compliance with the extradition of war criminals to The Hague Tribunal in the Netherlands.

Educational reforms and amendments have blanketed the post-Yugoslav states in response to their transitions toward democratic societies and out of war. Numerous actors in transitional societies, from international donors to university officials to civic associations, emphasize education as a nonviolent means toward the achievement of personal, national, and international security (Nelles, 2003). These actors believe that education holds the potential to shift the balance in the region from a culture of violence focused on the past to a culture of peace that envisions the future. Yet, education can be exploited in post-conflict societies as a means to rekindle tensions and encourage continued resentment, hatred, and intolerance (Bryan & Vavrus, 2005). Thus, it is imperative that educational efforts designed to cultivate a culture of peace be researched in transitional societies, especially those having endured recent periods of violent conflict.

Beyond presenting research on their products and outcomes, it is the objective of this chapter to attend to the process and philosophical foundations of these peace initiatives, especially within higher education. The focus on the *what*, or the content of education, and the *how*, or the pedagogy of education, continues to grow, but unfortunately, so does an assumption that the *why*—the philosophical underpinnings of peace education content and pedagogy—has been already sufficiently answered. In this way, this chapter responds to Page's (2004) observation about this philosophical deficiency:

> One intriguing and lingering lacuna within the critical literature has been the failure to develop and expound systematically the philosophical foundations of peace education...other than perhaps a general deontological notion that peace education is something to which humanity ought to be committed. (p. 4)

Humans have in fact been "philosophizing" about peace and peace education for as long as parents have taught their children to get along with one another. Yet, a rightful critique exists about peace education's lack of a deliberate inquiry into its socially-oriented philosophical foundations, a task that would enlighten its sometimes contradicting views of knowledge and conflicting trends that range from universalism to relativism (Gur-Ze'ev, 2001). To this end, Page (2004) offers five possible philosophical foundations of peace education: virtue ethics, consequentialist ethics, aesthetic ethics, conservative political ethics, and the ethics of care. Moving beyond Page's (2004) initial template, this chapter offers a "glocal" version of cosmopolitanism in the post-Yugoslav higher education fieldscape[6] (Wisler, 2008) as it is philosophically applied and grounds the lived experience of peace in unique, local ways.

Thus, this chapter is not about "what works," a tendency that can superficially constrict the intellectual efforts of researchers in many fields in an attempt to reduce complex questions to straightforward solutions. Rather, through the energy and time devoted to this inquiry's process, I "live the questions," as Rilke (2000) advised his young disciple to do, and as such explore cosmopolitanism as a philosophical foundation of peace knowledge, a product of the contemporary human condition that continues to suffer (from) the tragedy of violent conflict in post-Yugoslav societies. Peace knowledge is understood as one part of a region's intangible, intellectual heritage that constitutes the ways of knowing and living necessary for its own creation and the sustainability of a culture of peace.[7] It was peace knowledge that I explored in the post-Yugoslav educational fieldscape of recent war, primarily through methods influenced by phenomenology: dialogue and shared, lived experiences with students and professors in higher education programs in the region related to peace studies, who share intellectual commitments to peace, human rights, justice, and democracy, as well as observations and interactions in their classes.

Both major academic fields informing this research, comparative education and philosophy, have sequestered questions of conflict and peace in the Balkans into the hands of political scientists and historians. Edin Hajdarpasic (2001) backs up this impression:

> Most observers appear to have found in "politics" the most appropriate unit of analysis for explaining what transpired. For instance, the very notion of "Bosnian history" itself is implicitly understood as "political" history in its narrow sense: who ruled the country and how, what institutions and social organizations were in place, what impact all this had on all other areas of life, and so on. While illuminating in great detail the issues surrounding the rise of nationalism, political parties/leaders, and associated phenomena, analysts following this general trend usually posited other topics (like "culture" and "religion") as categories derivative of and secondary to "the real stuff" of history—politics.

This chapter responds to Hajdarpasic's critique by focusing on cosmopolitanism as a philosophical foundation of peace knowledge in this region, as it has manifested itself there in higher education. Specifically, it engages with conceptualizations of the other, as perceived within the philosophy of cosmopolitanism and as observed as lived by participants in a qualitative research inquiry. The research was an attempt to "discover, map and understand" part of what Beck and Sznaider (2006) call the "cosmopolitan condition" as I experienced it in relation to the cultivation of peace knowledge in post-Yugoslav higher education (p. 3). A subsequent goal of this chapter is to show how philosophical inquiry makes a necessary contribution beyond politics to how this region, and other war-torn societies, can be interpreted and reinterpreted, "un-known" and known again by educational researchers, scholars of peace and conflict, and members of the global human community. Through illuminating philosophy as a way to understand peace at the epistemological level in the post-Yugoslav higher education, forms of peace education can bear even more significance as they work to normalize the possibility of peace over the reality of violence. Moreover, as the Balkan region's reputation for violence pervades the global public and political spheres, an attempt to share, learn, and teach this region's peace knowledge is an ethical response to its experiences of recent violence and its present fragile economic and social stability.

Cosmopolitanism as a Philosophical Foundation of Balkan Peace Knowledge

Cosmopolitanism is certainly not new nor is it only relevant to or in the countries that formerly made up the state of Yugoslavia. Its recent reprisal is an advent long deemed necessary, and it builds on a history that begins in antiquity with the Cynics and the Stoics and carries through to the Enlightenment. It stands for "a recognition of otherness, both external and internal to any society: in a cosmopolitan ordering of society, differences are neither ranged in a hierarchy nor dissolved into universality, but are accepted" (Beck, 2004, p. 438). A cosmopolitan outlook offers an affirmation of the other as both different and the same. As an ethic of responsibility, cosmopolitanism suggests that the individual has an allegiance to the wider world; similarly, as a form of political governance, it recognizes a transborder obligation of societies of peoples to others. Due to its recent upsurge in popularity, one oversimplistic tendency within which to view cosmopolitanism has been "as mobility, rootlessness, openness to different lifestyles and detachment from the nation-state" (Papastephanou, 2002, p. 547). Marianna Papastephanou (2002) calls this version "light-hearted," a "'tourist's conception" (p. 547). Cosmopolitanism is not only reentering the social sciences as an alternative exercise of political judgment but is also making a definitive mark on research methodology by forcing researchers to reorganize typical research patterns that focus on the nation state as the basic unit of a research study.

A standard feature of cosmopolitanism is the idea and ideal of global citizenship, that if one viewed the world as if it were her polis, then she would have "multiple, overlapping allegiances which are sustained across communities of language, ethnicity, religion and nationality" (Benhabib, 2004, quoted in Delanty, 2006, p. 30). She would be a "citizen of the cosmos," the original meaning of cosmopolitanism dating back to the Cynics of the fourth century BC (Appiah, 2006, p. xiv). Her concern for the world and its people beyond her self-created or politically defined borders would manifest itself in how she lived the obligations that she had to others, "strangers" with whom she shared no familial relation (p. xxi). It is easy to find fault in the strange, and such disapproval often is, at closer examination, the repercussion of one's ignorance rather than a substantiated assessment. Not knowing someone or some thing is too often, especially in the public sphere, confused with and equated to simply not liking that person or thing of concern.

A local form of cosmopolitanism, based on this concept of others as strangers beyond one's borders, is what I began to understand and to observe in peace studies in post-Yugoslav higher education. The research does not suppose that cosmopolitanism is a new postwar phenomenon in this region. Prior to 1991, Yugoslavs were often hailed as one of the most cosmopolitan peoples in the world, a description I was reminded of regularly. This is a notable characteristic, different from other nation states that shift into civil war, which typically divorce themselves from global interconnections as the threat of instability ensues. Yet, as Yugoslavia splintered into five (and now seven) states, those with a once-shared Yugoslav identity became others to one another, politicized through ethnic and/or religious affiliation—for example, Macedonian Slav (Orthodox) or Bosniak (Bosnian Muslim) or Croat (Catholic). It was neighbors, colleagues, and even family members who turned from being "another" to "other" overnight, with declarations of independence and the gradual destruction of the Yugoslav state and the construction of borders. In other words, the other was not and (is not) always "strange." The other looked like, sounded like, and lived like another, only now separated by borders. The universal Yugoslav was subsumed by a relativism based on different ethnic markers and later cemented in peace accords such as those signed in Dayton, Ohio, and Ohrid, Macedonia, that compounded the division through state-sponsored segregation. The former republics that had been a part of

Yugoslavia hastened their attempts to make meaning of and publicize their individual nationhoods, often through destructive messages that offered divisive comparisons to their former Yugoslav counterpart.

In a place such as Yugoslavia, or in the state of BiH[8] upon the dissolution Yugoslavia, where such boundaries have separated families and made former neighbors into enemies, I observed how cosmopolitan attitudes and practices have been the thread for the fragile peace and a force sustaining higher education. I observed in this fieldscape "an unintended and lived cosmopolitanism...the peculiarity exists in the fact that this 'cosmopolitanization' occurs as unintended and unseen side-effects of actions which are not intended as 'cosmopolitan' in the normative sense" (Beck & Sznaider, 2006, p. 7). Although the creation of ethnically homogenous states of Yugoslav's constituent peoples was anticosmopolitan and based on principles of territorial sovereignty, the side effect of cross-border educational exchange as a form of resistance to state policies has persisted among academics and students in the region. I even recorded manifestations of cosmopolitan relations on a bureaucratic level. As the credits rolled after the black comedy *Karaula* (Border Post), Milena,[9] a master's student in a program on human rights and democracy, and I simultaneously noted the irony that the Ministry of Education of every former republic of Yugoslavia collaborated on its production. "If only they could play together so nicely all of the time," we remarked in agreement. Similarly, I also observed a cross-border cosmopolitan collaboration at the Sarajevo Book Fair in BiH, which showcased thousands of titles from exhibiting publishers from throughout the Bosnian-Croatian-Serbian-speaking region, a notable difference from the politicized discourse on the changes in the three standards of the language, which had previously been subsumed under the name "Serbo-Croatian."

At an individual level, I turn to the example of a professor in Macedonia[10] who told me of her long-standing relationship (since before the war and dissolution of their shared state and nationality) with colleagues in Slovenia, "You would never know we now live in separate countries," she remarked, describing their ongoing intellectual relations. Similarly, at a conference in Sarajevo, BiH focused on issues of regional democracy and stability, another professor from Macedonia noted that she was happy to be with "old friends, usual suspects" all from "fragments of a broken mirror." She remarked on the significance of the event's theme but suggested that its more important purpose was "to bring together people from the region" who could not normally see one another due to visa, travel, and financial restrictions. She alluded to the absurd amount of time and money she had spent to get there. There were no direct flights from Skopje, Macedonia, to Sarajevo, so she had to fly far out of the way north, through Vienna. As she put it in a conversation with me: "I think we are different but then I come here [a conference in Sarajevo] and we have the same issues... civil society, economics. They like to say that we are unique, but it's the same. We are taught, fed to think there is a difference because that legitimizes the break-up and war."

One interdisciplinary postgraduate program (IP) at a university in BiH offers a noteworthy example for observing the living out of this cosmopolitan obligation beyond borders. Within Yugoslavia, it was typical for one to have been schooled in various republics. One of my language professors, for example, earned a B.A. in Sarajevo; a M.A. in Belgrade; and a Ph.D. in Zagreb before coming to the United States of America as a Fulbright scholar. Similar diversity was seen in the IP class, which consisted of students born in the various republics of the former Yugoslavia. One of the program's tutors, Stefan, said to me: "The best thing about it, this program is not that they [the students] change their perceptions about whole groups of people, but that, um, they know now—they change their perceptions about each other." In today's normalized circumstances of visas and segregation, the fact that they are allowed to and have a reason to come to Sarajevo is a major opportunity. Further, Stefan explained, the students all have internships "somewhere else" (in the southeastern European region, but not in their home country) for several weeks in the summer before re-meeting for thesis writing. As one student from Kosovo shared, "they even let me into Croatia!" I am not naïve to think that the students' academic choice of the IP rests only on living out a local form of cosmopolitanism, but I was reassured by one Serbian student's words that this engagement with the other was a factor: "Look at this big step I took." This was something that the students also joked about, knowing full well how "special" their program was now, but how typical its student constitution would have been twenty years ago. Making light of the idea of real and imagined borders between her country (BiH) and those of her IP classmates, Vedrana would regularly joke, "I just love talking to foreigners," in reference to the Croatians, Montenegrins, Serbians, and others sitting around her.

One of the most revealing voiced sentiments of the cross-border obligations that former Yugoslavs in the field of peace studies felt toward one another came from a Slovenian social scientist who taught in the IP. He related the following story to me in which he describes his teaching in the IP as his "responsibility," due to what it seems he sees as unjustified catastrophe that the city endured.

> Last time I was in [city of IP], I met somebody who was without this right foot and his right hand. And he was asking for money, so I gave him twenty Marks [Bosnian currency] and he thanked me and said now his family will eat bread the whole week. They will make it and bake it. And he looked at me, and asked "where are you from?" Slovenia, I said. And he looked at me and said, "oh yeh, we lived in Slovenia, in Ljubljana". And he told me the street, you know, everything, you know. His parents were here, you know, he was a child here [Slovenia]. His parents were working here in some building industry. And then he told me his story. When they returned and after the war, and they were starting to build a new house and they was digging the ground and he, you know, put his foot on a mine and it exploded and it took his, you know, foot and his hand. And you always hear such some stories. Even in my hometown—I am coming from [name of town]—and he was telling...I mean you know, we [Slovenia] are now an independent state but still you know we are connected, related and I am a very busy person, but when they called me to teach this course I should say, you know, no, I am too busy. But [Bosnian city] means a lot to me. I mean, we had so many contacts before this war. I had so many friends there, you know, who got killed or, you know, or who are in a terrible situation now in war. I feel this is...[pause] my responsibility, my debt. I don't have economic problems. It is not comparable to how my colleagues were treated during those terrible years in [Bosnian city] and they were reporting what was happening there and nobody intervened.

This story also offers evidence of the interrelatedness of the peoples in the region; the family of the disabled man begging near the university was from Slovenia, not from BiH. The professor's face, as he retold the story, expressed his understanding that his fate and the fate of this man were not only intimately tied together but could have just as easily been switched.

There was another ironic way that I encountered the fostering of an "unintended cosmopolitanism" and that manifested itself through intellectual cross-border exchange. Some universities did not want to publicize the scholarship of their professors whose work focused on peace, violence, human rights, or related topics of a normative tone. To illustrate this point, I depend on my notes of the account of a social scientist in Skopje, Macedonia, who also taught at the IP in BiH. He pointed a finger at the academic bureaucracy and the survival of "old" professors (who once taught socialism, now teach capitalism, and will "just teach space in the future," as he expressed it to me) on the rebuttal of his home institution to draw effectively on his scholarship for his country's development:

> We have the curse of the small country. For example, I've been here ten years and everyone knows that I do ethnic relations but never my university never invited me to speak in front of students, on multiculturalism, ethnic conflict, never. The Balkans, it is the same story. We are really trapped. You can go teach in Sarajevo, in London you can make a presentation, but here at the university, I can't teach it [ethnic relations]. New knowledge? It is difficult. It is slow.

Interestingly, from my perspective, a cosmopolitan sensibility did not seem to instigate or propel research participants' desires to emigrate or to leave what in reality was a bleak economic situation in BiH and other parts of the post-Yugoslav landscape. In fact, it seemed to create an opposite stimulus to stay in the region, regardless of what the future held for its proliferation of borders. Dragan, a Serbian businessman in the IP, was often publicly invoked by his classmates as someone who would leave his country for economic gain, an assumption that visibly upset him and pressured him into a defensive, nationalistic stance. Another time, Emir related to me that he wanted to work in development in a post-conflict country in another part of the world and to travel before returning home to BiH, continuing,

> A Bosnian future? I really don't care. I don't care if it will be three parts [a reference to the Bosniak, Croatian, and Serbian sections of the country] or if it completely disappears. As long as there is not a war, there are no problems.
>
> For me it [referring to the name "Bosnia"] can disappear, but as long as people will be in it and as long as no one bothers me, as long as...I don't care if it is Bosnia. Bosnia-Croatia. Bosnia-Serbia. Bosnia-Europe. Or called some other country. As long as I can be there.

Emir was a rare example of an individual who had a fervent love for his Balkan country, but who had molded that into a borderless, cosmopolitan perspective, rather than into a discourse of nationalism.

Although this chapter has thus far focused on the regional cosmopolitan relations, this is not to suggest that the cosmopolitan sensibility that I encountered only influenced obligations and commitments within southeastern Europe among post-Yugoslav students and academics. The assumption prevalent in Western-based peace studies (as well as in other fields) is that war-torn societies, especially those categorized as being Third World or developing countries, are unsophisticated in their capacities to see outside their own narrow borders and issues and, thus, to exhibit cosmopolitan concerns for others. The peace knowledge created within this region is certainly not only about this region. One professor who worked at a peace institute explained how this global cosmopolitanism has changed peace studies in the region since the early 1990s:

There were those in peace studies who were directly involved in the Balkan wars of the 1990s. Today is another kind of peace studies. It means an involvement in the world, with what is going on in Iraq, what is going on in Slovenia, [border issues], minorities, gender issues. You have to be well aware that things are really complicated in reality, that research skills you use in mainstream institutions are, in a way, not enough. You have to touch those things that do not get caught in quantified ways of study. You have to be prepared to listen to narratives. You have to be prepared in the very old ethnologist's way or anthropologist's way, as it is called today, to examine what is going on in your own life. You have to be prepared to go and live in situation and to be involved doesn't mean to be just somebody who is watching what is going on. And so on... You have to be in these experiences all the time if you want to be in shape for the business we are doing. You know. So that's why we have to be and that is a very important point because no one else is doing that in the research society as [name of institute] in Slovenia. You cannot be just the researcher. You have to be involved. You have to understand why in one community there are three NGOs who are fighting with each other. And you can't just be this wise guy coming in. You have to be involved with all of them all of these conflicting and different issues. And it is hard because you get too involved and so after a few years you have to change the subject. And those are the skills you have to develop and those skills are a way of life. So it's not easy but it's very interesting and it's very, I would say, self-fulfilling to do this kind of job. And I am sure everybody working here after three or four years needs a sabbatical because of that. It's a lifestyle.

The cosmopolitan necessity of a global awareness that this professor alluded to was echoed by one of the professors of the IP, who was working on the genocide studies elective at the Law Faculty. He told me that people in BiH, "and Sarajevo included," had a tendency to consider themselves unique. "There is something that is maybe true in that," he continued, but more important was the understanding and knowledge that other people also had similar experience and "what was important" was to show Bosnia's "genocide in comparative perspective":

> It is not unacceptable for someone in Bosnia to be just upset with genocide in Bosnia, forgetting that in Rwanda, just a few years ago it happened. If we are not interested in Rwanda, how can we say that we are interested in Bosnia? Comparative perspective helps people to understand their own experience. People used to say, "Who knows one, knows none."

These cosmopolitan behaviors did not mask, however, arguments between students (and between students and teachers) that easily dissolved into nationalistic discourse in the higher education classroom. It is necessary to attend to the limits of cosmopolitanism, or selective cosmopolitanism, in post-Yugoslav higher education. Despite these occurrences, however, there was overall a cosmopolitan collegiality and obligation to one another's cross-border learning. In fact, it was at times nationalism that brought people together; my journal details a specific moment in May 2006 when an Albanian Kosovar congratulated a Montenegrin woman on her country's successful referendum for independence and final succession from Serbia.

Selective Cosmopolitanism

Without invalidating cosmopolitanism as a philosophical foundation of peace knowledge in the post-Yugoslav context, it is necessary to address some of its limits based on experiences in this fieldscape. I name this phenomenon selective cosmopolitanism in order to recognize when nationalism, ethnic identity, or religious affiliation trump obligation to the other. In order to affect the region's culture of peace, students, especially in peace studies, carry responsibility for the way dialogue inside and outside the classroom continues to be lived. Sadly, but realistically, as Heikinen (n.d.) contends, the presence of a cosmopolitan subculture in the classroom does not necessarily translate outside the classroom. It is not automatic "that, naturally, such students would reject that world in favor of naming their own world" (para 3). This absence of translation was evident in events surrounding the World Cup 2006.

The end of the semester brought one of the telltale signs of the European spring, international soccer matches. My fieldwork overlapped with the World Cup, the global sporting competition that takes place every four years. An article in the local newspaper reported the spike in sales of television sets, linked to the number of fans who were eager to see the World Cup. Cafés in the city center were outfitted with large outdoor screens, and one could hear waves of applause from any point in the city whenever a popular game was being played. I was naïve enough to think that soccer enthusiasts, especially those in the IP as the end of their academic year loomed, might use this opportunity to display some of their growing cross-border tolerance.

What I quickly observed was that the cafés in Sarajevo, Belgrade, or Zagreb were filled with "anti-fans" when that country's neighbor was playing in the tournament. On one of the last days of the semester, I dropped by the IP's building in order to offer my support to the students who were sitting for the final oral examination. The café next door to the IP's little blue building erupted into cheers and I, lagging behind in my knowledge of the current World Cup standings, asked if BiH was playing. It turned out that BiH had already been eliminated but that Croatia was playing Brazil. On cue, Rafis walked in to report that Brazil had scored a goal against Croatia, who remained scoreless. He mumbled some thoughts in disgust at the viewers' enthusiasm against Croatia (not for Brazil), noting that their cheers showed poor sportsmanship. Meanwhile, other students high-fived each other to celebrate Croatia's impending defeat. What occurred later that evening in Mostar, a city in Herzegovina divided by the Neretva River, was that the behavior of the "anti-fans" had depicted the extent to which the celebration of Croatia's defeat could and did transpire into events that seriously affected the region's culture of peace and tolerance. Bosnian Muslims and Bosnian Croats clashed in their opposing celebrations in Mostar's town square, a front line during the war and the now invisible border between the two parts of the city. Newspaper headlines the following day reported that gunshots had been fired, dozens injured, and ethnic relations set back yet again in response to the outcome of the soccer match.

The Promise of Cosmopolitan Education

Although presented in a geopolitical context-specific manner in this chapter, cosmopolitanism has promise as a theoretical and conceptual backbone to peace education and peace building efforts in other regions (Setalvad, 2010; Yager, 2010). Intentional reflection on the philosophical foundations of peace education can provide a rationale and direction for understanding the ebbs and flows between the cultures of peace and violence that coexist in war-torn and post-conflict societies. I need no more philosophical impetus for writing this than a few minutes of casual page turning of the daily *New York Times*. The headlines remind me that the world is not becoming less conflictual, at least according to the newspaper's editors. This observation, however, is not the cause of my unease or what converts my intellectual anxiety into a book chapter. Rather, coupled with my globe-trotting, a daily intake of news from diversified sources points not only to a dogged perseverance of violence as a form of conflict resolution but also to a global pessimistic resignation to its normalization. This resignation supports a tragic three-tiered framework to which comparative education, philosophy, and peace studies can respond through research, practice, and teaching.

The first tier is the false synonymous equation of conflict with violence. A society within which there is direct violence due to a political struggle becomes a "conflict society" (i.e., Darfur). A society within which the direct violence has (purportedly) abated and for which peace accords have been signed is relegated to the rank of "post-conflict" society. This framework detrimentally assigns salience to direct violence and pushes manifestations of cultural and structural violence by the wayside because violence is relegated to overt action. Moreover, it camouflages a society in which there is no nationwide, systemic, direct violence (i.e., USA) as one in which there is no conflict. In this chapter, references to the post-Yugoslav region as "war-torn" are intentional, on the advice from one professor from Croatia who reminded me that this region is not "post anything just yet."

The second tier of the framework ingrains a fallacious notion of peace as a manufactured policy that ends violence (such as the Dayton

Peace Accords) and as a static position on a conflict/post-conflict trajectory, rather than as a living, dynamic process. Peace is human practice that exists in the relationships between and among individuals. Although its manifestation as practice changes, peace is underpinned by philosophical traditions that, when explicitly exposed, reveal the normative values of that society.

Finally, the third tier normalized by this tragic framework situates the post-conflict society as one in need of reconstruction. The international community has a commitment to objective reconstruction measures in a war-torn society, especially one devastated by external intervention or left unattended to as a result of the stature of sovereignty in international politics. Yet, what Balkan peace knowledge revealed to me is that reconstruction is not always re-creation, nor is it linear or predictable. Reconstruction does not always find its more favorable solutions in externally founded and funded ideals. In some war-torn or post-conflict places, reconstruction cannot or need not create instantaneous equilibrium. Throughout this inquiry, I was reminded daily to respect the fragility and volatility of human relationships, to be humble in my own understanding of global connectivity (the slightest change in one place can cause tremors elsewhere), and to remain faithful to the concept and promise of human agency. I came to understand how people in the post-Yugoslav region use conflict and reconstruction positively to engage in peace building.

Applying Cosmopolitan Philosophy for Peace

Together, peace knowledge and its philosophical foundations create ripe grounds for what was introduced to me as *tvorenje za mirot* (the constant creating of peace), a concept coined by a peace studies professor whom I was honored to meet in Macedonia. Re-reading my field notes on the explanation of her concept evoked David Hansen (2007) who writes: "what individual persons think and do can make a genuine difference in the course of events. Mind and imagination can transform the quality of life" (p. 1). *Tvorenje za mirot* implies the daily hard work in which one learns (thinks) and lives (does) peace. It implicates millions of people in this part of the world alone, not to kill their neighbor but to "tolerate tolerance." The term simultaneously connotes the envisioning of living out peace in the future, of creating processes and knowledge that may not yet exist, rather than merely maintaining that which is present.

In this way, this chapter hopefully contributes to theory building in the area of peace knowledge by approaching this concept from the vantage point of individuals in the war-torn societies of BiH, Croatia, FYROM, Serbia, Montenegro and Slovenia, who are engaged in postgraduate academic peace studies programs. Carolyn Nordstrom (2005) emphasizes that "when violence erupts, few people take notes and most people take sides" (p. 400). Although major direct violence has been quelled in the region, it was and is not too late to pick up a pencil and learn from ongoing transformations there. Events in this region were influenced by a unique set of factors, but the experiences and lessons acquired from here could be potentially relevant for future postwar societies, today's present conflict zones. These lessons need not be limited to evaluations of Balkan-based military or peacekeeping operations for postwar planning in Iraq and Afghanistan (Pantev, 2006). Rather, they can, if pursued, focus more consciously and comprehensively on the significance of local peace knowledge as intellectual heritage and on the domestic moral and ethical resources that promote social change.

There are no simple answers for anything, especially in a war-torn society, and moral ambiguity is often the most one can ask for from people who have suffered the realization that universal human rights guidelines did not protect them from the threat of genocide. Yet, ironically, moral ambiguity does not sit well with that part of human nature that creates a binary between someone being right and someone being wrong in any situation. The post-Yugoslav war-torn society does function on "the balancing point between stability and total mess" (Davies, 2004, p. 31). There is a bizarre sense of order that makes the post-Yugoslav context work. It is an acceptance that life, although out of balance, will continually correct itself. These times are filled with knowledge creation because there are simply so many problems to deal with on a regular basis. Philosophy is an undervalued frame of reference from which to view the contradictions and chaos that make up the daily normalcy of the war-torn society.

The unintended cosmopolitan actions of the students and professors of this research were a refusal to be constrained by the real borders between the now seven countries that were once a single nation state. They show that borders between countries cannot and do not break the interconnections among people that, as cosmopolitanism argues, create the grounds for humanity belonging to one morally bound community. Through continued cross-border relations and exchange, peace studies students and scholars in the region depict "the only morally acceptable way of living with a morally unacceptable truth" (Mamdani, 1998, quoted in Jolly, 2001, p. 699).

Inquiries into the peace knowledge and its philosophical foundations in other contexts has promising possibilities, especially in those regions that have traditions of tolerance and coexistence and are multiconfessional, such a context being as small as a classroom or as large as a region. Peace studies programs are just one venue for cultivating and learning such knowledge, and other contexts will provide additional sources for investigation.

Notes

1. Yugoslavia was comprised of six republics: Bosnia and Herzegovina, Croatia, Macedonia, Montenegro, Serbia, and Slovenia, and two autonomous regions, namely Vojvodina and Kosovo.
2. The geographical term "Balkans" actually refers to a mountain range in southeastern Europe. The geographical boundaries of the region often called "the Balkans" are contested by members of the international community as well as by those countries of this chapter's concern.
3. Despite BiH's status as an independent country, the highest political authority in the country is the High Representative, the chief executive officer representing the international civilian presence in the country. Although the sovereignty of BiH is internationally recognized, this abiding political structure imposed by the Dayton Accords has contributed to BiH not feeling like, or not being treated as, an independent state.
4. Macedonia broke away from Yugoslavia in 1991 and ten years later suffered a short civil war between Albanian forces and the country's military. Montenegro declared independence from Serbia in 2006 in a public referendum. Kosovo, an autonomous region within Serbia, declared its independence in March 2008, after tumultuous years of violence and external intervention.
5. Galtung (2002) identifies direct violence as physical, visible violence, as that which "refers to physical acts of violence such as a man beating his wife, children fighting in school, or soldiers going to war" (p. 17). The most extreme form of direct violence is war. He is accredited with expanding the definition of violence from only meaning direct violence to including what he calls structural violence: "the violence built into the very social, political and economic systems that govern societies, states and the world. It is the different allocation of goods, resources, opportunities, between different groups, classes, genders, nationalities, etc., because of the structure governing their relationship. Examples of structural violence are apartheid, patriarchy, slavery, colonialism, imperialism, the former state authoritarian regimes of eastern Europe, and today's global imperialism/capitalism" (p. 18). Cultural violence "can be taken to be those aspects of a culture that legitimize or make violence seem an acceptable means of responding to conflict" (p. 18).
6. Fieldscape is my own concept inspired by Appadurai (1996, 2000) and developed in Wisler (2008). Fieldscape embraces the "world of flows" beyond the typically geographical-delineated field site. The concept of fieldscape, in this case as the landscape of post-Yugoslav higher education related to peace studies, is more conducive to conceptualizing the flow of knowledge, people, and ideas across the borders of academic disciplines, universities, and countries.

7. I recognize Reardon's (1988) use of the term "peace knowledge" and intend to contribute to the theoretical and conceptual development of it.
8. The Dayton Accords confirmed BiH as a single, independent state, comprised of two highly autonomous entities: the predominantly Bosnian Muslim and Bosnian Croat Federation, and Republika Srpska, which is predominantly Bosnian Serb. The federation is further divided into ten cantons, five of which are majority Bosniak, three of which have a majority Bosnian Croat population and two of which are 'mixed.' Brčko, in the northeastern corner of the country, is another 'mixed' autonomous city. The boundaries add to an ethnic separation in the country.
9. All names in this chapter are pseudonyms.
10. The internationally-recognized name of the country is the Former Yugoslav Republic of Macedonia (FYROM) but for brevity's sake, I refer to the country as Macedonia in this chapter.

References

Appadurai, A. (1996). *Modernity at large: Cultural dimensions of globalization*. Minneapolis, MN: University of Minnesota.

―――― (2000). Grassroots globalization and the research imagination. *Public Culture, 12*(1), 1–19.

Appiah, K. (2006). *Cosmopolitanism: Ethics in a world of strangers*. New York: Norton, W. W. & Co.

Beck, U. (2004). The truth of others: A cosmopolitan approach. *Common Knowledge 4*(3), 430–449.

Beck, U. & Sznaider, N. (2006). Unpacking cosmopolitanism for the social sciences: A research agenda. *The British Journal of Sociology 57*(1), 1–23.

Davies, L. (2004). *Education and conflict: Complexity and chaos*. New York: Routledge Falmer.

Delanty, G. (2006). The cosmopolitan imagination: Critical cosmopolitanism and social theory. *The British Journal of Sociology 57*(1), 25–47.

Derrida, J. (2002). *Negotiations*. Stanford, CA: Stanford University.

Dimitrijevic, N. & Kovács, P. (2004). *Managing hatred and distrust: The prognosis for post-conflict settlement in multiethnic communities of the former Yugoslavia*. Budapest: Central European University.

Galtung, J. (2002). *Searching for peace: The road to Transcend*. London: Pluto.

Gur-Ze'ev, I. (2001). Philosophy of peace education in a postmodern era. *Educational Theory 51*(3), 315–336.

Hansen, D. (Ed.) (2007). *Ethical visions of education: Philosophy in practice*. New York: Teachers College.

Hajdarpasic, E. (2001). Book review of "Windows: Words and images." Balkan Academic Book Reviews. Last retrieved January 11, 2010, at http://groups.yahoo.com/group/balkans/message/1565.

Heikinen, D. (1998). *From Freire to Bakhtin: The role of carnival in the composition classroom*. Last retrieved January 11, 2010, at http://www.paulofreireinstitute.org/Documents/from_Freire_to_Bakhtin_by_Heikinen.html.

Jolly, R. J. (2001). Desiring good(s) in the face of marginalized subjects: South Africa's Truth and Reconciliation Commission in a global context. *South Atlantic Quarterly 100*(3), 693–715.

Nelles, W. (Ed.) (2003). *Comparative education, terrorism and human security: From critical pedagogy to peacebuilding?* New York: Palgrave Macmillan.

Nordstrom, C. (2005). (Gendered) war. *Studies in Conflict and Terrorism 28*, 399–411.
Page, J. S. (2004). Peace education: Exploring some philosophical foundations. *International Review of Education 50*(1), 3–15.
Pantev, P. (2006). Lessons of post-war rehabilitation in South East Europe and by South East Europeans. Retrieved January 11, 2010 from *Post-conflict rehabilitation: Lessons from South East Europe and Strategic Consequences for the Euro-Atlantic Community*, http://www.bmlv.gv.at/pdf_pool/publikationen/10_wg_pcr_10.pdf.
Papastephanou, M. (2002). Arrows not yet fired: Cultivating cosmopolitanism through education. *Journal of Philosophy of Education 36*(1), 69–83.
Reardon, B. (1988). *Comprehensive peace education*. New York: Teachers College.
Rilke, R. M. (2000). *Letters to a young poet*. Trans. J. Burnham. Novato, CA: New World Library.
Wisler, A. (2008). *Peace knowledge: An inquiry in post-Yugoslav higher education*. Ann Arbor, MI: Proquest/UMI Digital Dissertations, AAT 3317618.

CHAPTER NINE

Children Are Made to Love: Liberation Education in India

Michael R. Hubert

Vision: We strongly believe children are made to love. They are not merely a matter of a reproductive result.
Concept: *Shabnam* (the first refreshing rain after a dry spell)
Shabnam Resources, 2010

The Concept and Philosophy

The registered nonprofit charitable trust Shabnam Resources focuses on the welfare of children and senior women in rural and semi-urban areas in India, particularly on the fulfillment of their needs they are experiencing in destitution. It has practiced peacebuilding in many different spheres for years, modeling a philosophy that does not remain academic yet is practiced every day. The word "shabnam" means "the first rain after a dry spell." It is the rain that refreshes the earth's organisms and the minds of people; likewise, Shabnam restores by enacting aspects of love.

United Nations Convention on the Rights of the Child

International legislation evidences the philosophical foundation of caring for children as an aspect of world peace. Article 1 of the United Nations Convention on the Rights of the Child defines a child as any "human being below the age of eighteen," unless, it adds, "under the law applicable to the child, majority is attained earlier" (United Nations 1989). It is a standard principle of child welfare law and policy that the "best interests" of a child should be promoted. Article 3.1 of the Convention states that in all actions concerning children, whether undertaken by public or private social welfare institutions, courts of law, administrative authorities or legislative bodies, the best interests of the child shall be a primary consideration (United Nations, 1989).

Article 12.1 of the Convention goes on to say,

> States Parties shall assure to the child who is capable of forming his or her own views the right to express those views freely in all matters affecting the child, the views of the child being given due weight in accordance with the age and maturity of the child (United Nations, 1989).

Section 8 of the Convention discusses the child's right to be heard and establishes the

> "best-interest principle" (BIP). The principle has been given different explicit formulations. Indeed, it should be noted that the principle's possible definitions vary in at least two important dimensions: what is being given weight and how much weight it is being given. Thus, we may speak of a child's "best interests" or simply of a child's "interests" or "welfare." The former is the more familiar interpretation of the principle, and it is one used in this chapter. Welfare can also be seen as having to do with love; the concept might be better described by the Greek word *agape*. Child welfare needs have been increasing in India and throughout the world. Thus there is an urgency to applying peace philosophy for today's children and tomorrow's adults—who are all potential peace builders.

Prevalence of Violence

Child labor, among other forms of structural conflict that youth have been experiencing, is one form of prevalent violence for which philosophy provides a transformation platform (Lederach, 2003). Shabnam works to save children from child labor and child abuse, especially from rag picking and working in the hazardous brick industry, located primarily in the Tiruvallur district near Madras, India, where child labor and trafficking is rampant. Shabnam rescues and cares for these children, mostly orphans, while it provides an education that will give them a future.

An article in *The Hindu* (Kannan, 2005) newspaper describes the hazardous context of the brick labor and its damaging effects on children: missed education, chronic health problems, and injuries. For taking these risks,

> the children are paid pathetic sums as wages. Most times their wages are subsumed in the wages that are paid to a family. Of this, an amount is held back towards settling the advance amount borrowed by the workers. (Kannan, 2005)

Child laborers working in the brick-making industry often drown in the mud or suffer other serious physical injuries. Working in the oppressively hot weather of southern India can lead to cases of heat exhaustion. Just to survive, orphaned children expose themselves to these dangers every day—for slave wages. In rural India, public education is very ineffective, little more than babysitting, while most private schools are expensive and ultracompetitive.

The forms of child labor that need to be abolished fall into three categories: (1) the use of underage children, that is, children who are under the minimum age specified for a particular type of work as defined by national legislation, in accordance with accepted international standards; (2) hazardous work, that is, labor that jeopardizes the physical, mental, or moral well-being of a child, either because of its nature or the conditions in which it is carried out; and (3) slavery, that is, trafficking, debt bondage, forced recruitment of children for use in armed conflict, prostitution, and pornography, and other illicit activities.

Compounding the problem is the brokerage system, through bigbroker to small-broker arrangements, in a multiple-brokerage and distribution system, whereby the child, when in isolation, is more prone for anything like being traded or sold for hard labor, sadistic treatment, forced child prostitution and for child sacrifices. The exploitation of children in a brokering system that profits from their labor is not an act of love, even if they are given or sold to support their destitute families. Responding to all of this seems natural to those who operate with an ethic of care (Noddings, 1992). However, prevention and rescue efforts have transparent ideological foundations and operations. The missions of rescue efforts by organizations need clarity in their transformation goals.

Liberation Education

Liberation education is a transformation philosophy that maintains the value of learning for freedom from oppression. It is one ethical vision of education (Hansen, 2007). Another vision, articulated by Maria Montessori after World War II, is education for peace (Montessori, 1992). One purpose of education is transformation of structural violence through the preparation of students for empowerment. Power derives from a state of well-being sufficient for learning and applying skills with knowledge. The power of love comes from being loved. Resonating with Paolo Freire's liberatory education goals, teaching students how to analyze and respond to conflicts around them is possible with "pedagogy of the heart" (Freire, 1997). This is especially needed in rural places where state-provided education, when it is available to children, has not been sufficient preparation for a peaceful life in their society—resulting in their inability to fulfill their life-sustaining needs and that of others in their community. Foremost in liberation education is the notion of freedom from oppression and violence. Simultaneous cultivation of a care ethic through demonstration and application contributes to learning for peace through love. Liberation from violence, of any source, advances with holistic education (Shelton-Colangelo, Mancuso, & Duvall, 2007).

Shabnam's Programs

Liberation of children from direct and indirect violence, including neglect, can be done through education in a range of settings. Shabnam uses multiple contexts for its work with children, thereby combining holistic education with community-based learning. Learning about life in the local community and the world occurs in responsive and purposeful learning activities. The website of Shabnam continues to describe recent programs involving children and, occasionally, community elders (Shabnam, 2010). Cross-generational interactions have been liberating for participants on multiple points of the age continuum.

Shabnam's programs introduce children to important philosophical and logical principles in an engaging and intellectually safe environment. Students express themselves in guided philosophical discussions to positive effect, increasing their creative and logical-thinking abilities and, most importantly, their sense of wonder.

Shabnam features an alternative school and a migrant-education program, and it provides for the foster care of children. At the urban and semirural levels, broken family situations orphan children who then require foster care. The abuse of the child's mind, body, and soul prompts them to discreetly seek solace. Shabnam provides childcare and education, employing the "play way" methodology developed in India. Emphasis is given to environmental studies, communication, and values education. To promote health, the children receive nutritious meals daily. Their education is holistic, primarily mainstream schooling with concern and care, including foster or shelter care when needed. The children are taught to give back to society by having concern and care for others. Examples of their actions illustrate efforts for peace.

Table 9.1 Children's Community Activities

Goal	Activity
Cross-cultural acceptance	Children engaged in a "goodness in all" rally to counter growing hate factor.
Providing relief to tsunami survivors	Tsunami survivors joined Chennai children in meals and activities to build hope for their futures after loss of home and family.
"No Tobago" campaign	Children participated in a rally to change conditions of child-labor industry.
Value of giving	Children were oriented towards giving, versus getting, during national celebrations.
Value of caring	In a campaign of love, students made and delivered care packages to hospitalized children during the Festival of Lights.
Cross-generational care	Children learned during a camp program the need for kindness to elderly and animals.
Water safety	Children in poor neighborhoods were taught water purification.
Environmental preservation	Children participated in pollution control in a stop-burning campaign during the harvest festival and river restoration in a field trip.

Table 9.2 Advancing Liberation Education

1	Legislative Action Plan for the enforcement of the Child Labor Act and other labor laws to ensure that children are not used for hazardous labor, and for regulation and supervision of the working conditions in the places in which children are employed.
2	Educational Care Center for children rescued from slavery and other forms of abuse.
3	General Development Program that emphasizes the need for poverty alleviation and adult employment to advance family care of children.
4	Drop-out Mandate to provide education of children who drop out of school, who are typically marginalized, deprived, and socially rejected youth.
5	Alternative Education System, wherein the children least able to attend school can be educated in a shorter period at a minimum cost.

Recommendations

For advancement of liberation education and a concerted transformation for loving all children, additional developments could be helpful. Following in Table 9.2 are suggestions for further applications of the philosophical concepts this chapter illustrates.

Conclusion

This brief chapter provides a glimpse of liberation education based on the notion that children are made to love, and the giving nature of rain as a metaphor for needed relief. On the map of holistic education is a road to a better life for everyone, and our journey continues. We at Shabnam accept suggestions and support to continue on this path of loving children for many more years and educating them for peace.

References

Freire, P. (1997). *Pedagogy of the heart*. Translated by Donaldo Macedo and Alexandre Oliveira. New York: Continuum.
Hansen, D. T. (2007). *Ethical visions of education: Philosophies in practice*. New York: Teachers College Press.
Kannan, R. (May 11, 2005). 1 lakh children employed in brick kilns. *The Hindu*. Retrieved December 4, 2009 from http://www.hindu.com/2005/05/11/stories/2005051109730400.htm.
Lederach, J. P. (2003). *The little book of conflict transformation*. Intercourse, PA: Good Books.

Montessori, M. (1992). *Education and peace.* Translated by Helen R. Lane. Oxford: Clio Press.
Noddings, N. (1992). *The challenge to care in schools.* New York: Teachers College.
Shabnam Resources Trust (2010). Programs. Retrieved January 1, 2010 at, http://www.shabnamresources.com/programs.html.
Shelton-Colangelo, S., Mancuso, C., & Duvall, M. (Eds.). (2007). *Teaching with joy: Educational practices for the twenty-first century.* Lanham, MD: Rowman & Littlefield.
United Nations (1989) The convention on the rights of the child, reprinted in P. Alston, S. Parker, and J. Seymour (Eds.), *Children, Rights and the Law,* Oxford: Oxford University Press: 245–264; and in L. LeBlanc, *The Convention on the Rights of the Child. United Nations Lawmaking on Human Rights,* Lincoln: University of Nebraska Press, 293–316.

Conclusion

CANDICE C. CARTER

Philosophy is the love of wisdom, and restoration of peace optimally results from wise responses to conflict. Wisdom derives from contemplation and experience woven together. Reflection about problems and awareness of ideas about how to proactively respond to them are mental tools for weaving a shroud of peace that protects from, or restores after, harm. Reflection on and analysis of peace efforts enables the adaptation of existing ideas as well as the generation of new ones. Adjusting the peace shroud to fit the shape of a current conflict can result from these contemplative and analytical processes. Using shared wisdom in new circumstances leads to insights that can be helpful to others who grapple with how to develop peace for everyone where it is needed.

The contributors to this book describe this refitting approach to peace development. Informative for theoretical analysts as well as students and practitioners of peace are the insights gleaned from the applications of the philosophies this book describes. All three groups have important roles in current and future peace work with self, associates, and politicians who, with knowledge of peace wisdom, can make decisions and form policies that enable needed transformations.

Whereas there are many possible peace-focused applications for the philosophies described in this book and other theories, consideration of them is worthy beyond the context each chapter reviews. The ideas expressed in nonviolence, humanism, hermeneutics, pluralism, cosmopolitanism, pragmatism, social reconstruction, and liberation education have relevance in multiple aspects of life. It is worthwhile to contemplate them for the advancement of peace in the personal as well as professional and public realms of our lives. Envisioning how something would be different after an idea has been adopted is an important precursor of its application. In the vision, an idea, such as nonviolence, becomes realistic in pictures of peace action and its results. Picturing peace stimulates unseen as well as visible processes that enable achievement and maintenance of that condition. For example, obscure activities such as self-monitoring our inner voice for language and thought violence are very important applications of nonviolence philosophy. That initial "self-work" impacts relationships and visible interactions with "peace partners" in a conflict. Those interactions affect those surrounding us in the interdependent web of the global, as well as the local, community.

Table 10.1 will help you to in applying peace philosophy as peace action. For consideration of each philosophy, the table provides one row for a brief summary of inner action that occurs in the mind and another row for outer action that can be observed by others. This practical exercise in the use of existing wisdom for enactment

Table 10.1 Philosophical Applications for Peace

Philosophy	Inner Use	Outer Use
Nonviolence Example	Monitor inner voice and thoughts for violence.	Demonstrate harmless response to conflict.
Nonviolence		
Humanism		
Hermeneutics		
Pluralism		
Cosmopolitanism		
Pragmatism		
Social Reconstruction		
Liberation-Education		

CONCLUSION

of peace across dimensions concludes this book. It also evidences the aspirations of its contributors whose writing about peace work provides more than knowledge. It demonstrates the global initiative for change. As an aid for advancing that initiative, please consider the wisdom that this book describes, and many other knowledge bases, to contemplate and envision peace activities in multiple dimensions of your life. Thank you.

CONTRIBUTORS

Candice C. Carter is a professor at the University of North Florida, in Jacksonville, Florida, USA. Her research and scholarship topics include conflict transformation, peacebuilding, peace education, peace through arts, history/social-studies instruction, and teacher training. She serves in many international, national, and local peace, education, research, and policy organizations. Dr. Carter designs and facilitates peace education programs for all levels of education, including the interdisciplinary Conflict Transformation Program at the University of North Florida. Her publications in journals and books cover a multitude of topics related to human relations and social education. She is the editor of the *Journal of Stellar Peacemaking* and a member of the editorial board of the *Journal of Peace Education* as well as the journal *Global Peace*.

Savarimuthu Vincent De Paul is a senior lecturer and head in the Planning and Management Branch of the District Institute of Education and Training in Pudukkottai, Tamilnadu, India. He translated into Tamil from the original English the book by Ravindra Kumar titled *Non-Violence and its Philosophy*. Dr. S. Vincent De Paul was a member of the Tamilnadu state planning committee for teacher education during the Five-Year Plan for Teacher Education. He has published more than 20 articles about education appearing in various national and international journals. He is an editorial board member of the international journal *Global Peace* and one of the chief editors of the book *Quality Concerns in Elementary Education*, 2008.

Jacques Hersh is an emeritus professor at Aalborg University, Denmark, and the former head of the Research Center on Development and International Relations. In Danish literature, he has published articles on the Palestinian-Israeli question and the evolution of political

Zionism. Among his publications in English are *The USA and the Rise of East Asia Since 1945* (London: Macmillan Press Ltd. and New York: St. Martin's Press, Inc. 1993), *Soviet-Third World Relations in a Capitalist World,* with coauthor Ellen Brun (London: Macmillan Press Ltd., 1990) as well as various volumes on economic and political development in the Third World.

Michael R. Hubert is the marketing advisor for Shabnam Resources, a registered charitable non-profit trust in Chennai, India. He is a management graduate who has worked as a human-resources trainer for corporations and NGOs. He has written articles and initiated programs for peacebuilding with Indian youth and children through interreligious dialogue, harmony, and care as well as in health-related awareness programs. Among his other engagements are chairing an international conference on world peace and harmony held in Beruwala, Sri Lanka, presenting on child rights in Vancouver, Canada, on responding to child neglect by working parents' causes, effects and solutions at Penticton Canada, and on racism and "casteism" in a conference held in Penang Malaysia under auspices of Pax Romana.

Ravindra Kumar is an independent scholar, political scientist, peace-worker, and educationist whose more than 100 works analyze personalities of the Indian subcontinent, including Gautama Buddha, and Mahatma Gandhi, as well as social, religious, political, historical, educational, and cultural issues. As a renowned Indologist and former Vice Chancellor, Dr. Kumar has been associated in several countries with a number of national and international academic, cultural, educational, social, and peace institutions, delivering over 400 lectures on subjects related to Asian values, civilization, culture, history, cooperation, Gandhism, human rights, the Indian way of life, international understanding, and world peace. He is the editor of the international journal *Global Peace.* Besides being named Shan-i-Kaum, Ambassador of Peace; Shantidoot, Master of Wisdom; and other honors, the Padma Shri was awarded by the President of India to Dr. Kumar for his noteworthy service as a scholar and educator.

Kristofer J. Petersen-Overton is a doctoral student at the CUNY Graduate Center in New York. His research focuses on the (re)production of national identity and how this form of belonging interacts with issues of political responsibility. Prior to this, Kris worked as a human rights activist in the Gaza Strip.

Johannes D. Schmidt is an associate professor of Global Development Studies at Aalborg University, Denmark, where he teaches about development and international relations. His instructional and research interests include the fields of international political economy, as well as political and economic development, with special reference to Southeast Asia and the Middle East. He has published extensively on social change, the impact of neo-liberal globalization, welfare policies, and distributional issues.

Teesta Setalvad is a Mumbai-based journalist, educator and human rights' activist who has had to function under threat and intimidation, especially since her fearless intervention during and after the Gujarat genocide in 2002. A journalist in the Indian mainstream media until 1993, she has for the past 15 years been coeditor of the journal *Communalism Combat*, which has won international acclaim for its in-depth journalism on wide-ranging issues of diversity, nondiscrimination, and pluralism. In 1993, after the violence that ripped at Bombay following the demolition of the Babri Mosque, Setalvad pioneered KHOJ, Education for a Plural India Program. Ms. Setalvad has been a member of the Central Advisory Board of Education (CABE) and the CABE Committee on "Regulatory Mechanisms for Textbooks and Parallel Textbooks Taught in Schools outside the Government System." She received the Nuremberg International Human Rights Award in 2003 and the Padma Shri from the President of India in 2007.

Andria K. Wisler is a visiting assistant professor in the Program on Justice and Peace at Georgetown University, Washington, DC, USA. Her dissertation, completed at Columbia University in New York, was an inquiry into peace knowledge as intellectual heritage that focused on the development of peace studies in post-Yugoslav higher education. Andria's commitment to peace studies began during her undergraduate studies at the University of Notre Dame, Indiana, USA, and is a continuing thread running through her work for social change in various parts of the world, including Tanzania, Turkmenistan, and Israel, and as a middle-school teacher in New York City. She has publications in the journals *Peace Review, Intercultural Education,* and the *Journal of Peace Education.*

Kazuyo Yamane is a Japanese peace educator, researcher, and graduate of the University of Bradford, England (Ph.D. in Peace Studies). She has been a part-time lecturer in Peace Studies at Kochi University and Kochi Junior College, Japan. She is a member of the Advisory

Committee of the International Network of Museums for Peace and the editor of *Muse: Newsletter of Japanese Citizens* of the Network of Museums for Peace. She also holds memberships in the editorial boards of the *Journal of Peace Education*, *Journal of Peace & Conflict Review*, and *Global Peace*. Dr. Yamane's previous publications include "Hiroshima and Nagasaki: The Beginning of the Nuclear Age" and "Current Attitudes to the Atomic Bombings in Japan" in *Hiroshima and Nagasaki: Retrospect and Prospect*; and "Japanese Peace Museums" in *Peace Studies in the Chinese Century* (85–113).

Esther Yogev is an associate professor and the Dean of the School of Education at the Kibbutzim College of Education in Tel Aviv. She also lectures as an adjunct professor in the History Department at Tel-Aviv University. Dr. Yogev's research has examined the history of industrial work relations in the United States as well as the development of history education in Israel and the world. She currently examines theories and methods of teaching history in societies in the midst of war and conflict. In addition to various articles on her subjects, Dr. Yogev has published two books: *Histories, Towards a Dialogue with the Israeli Past* (2002); and *General Knowledge and Culture Infrastructure: Challenges and Objectives in Teacher Training and Higher Education* (2008).

INDEX

Aalborg, 218
Abe, Shinzo, 30
Acharya, 12
Acikgoz, 146
Act, the Armed Forces Special Powers, 14; the Black, 9; the Immigration, 9; the Pound Three Tax, 9; the State Protection, 14
Adumim, Ma'ale, 51
Afghanistan, 21, 29, 200; Taliban in, 29
Africa, 123; South, 7–9, 123, 179; Colonial Government of, 9; Satyagraha in, 7
African, 51
Ahimsa, 8, 16
Ahmedabad, 15
Akbar, the King, 109
Akota, 18
Albanian, Kosovar, 272
Algerian, 106; Soldiers, 106
Alkalai, Judah, 46
Allahabad, 18
Althaus, Martha, 35
Ambedkar, B. R., 111, 123
American, 8, 16, 52; Activist, 16; African, 8; Civil War, 123; Continent, 106; Indians, 106; North, 106; Soldiers, 24
Amstutz, 166
Andhra Pradesh, 11, 16
Angkor Wat, 131

Apartheid, African, 51
Al-Aqsa, 73
Arab, 47, 49, 54, 89, 130; Farmers, 49; Israeli, 45; Land, 49; Population, 47; Property, 48; Question, 54; Societies, 48; Tenants, 49; War Effort, 49
Arabs, 48, 94, 107; Society, 48; Students, 94
Arafat, Yassir, 50, 64
Arbil, in Northern Iraq, 31
Ariel, 51
Arulpragasam, K. D., 115–116
Aryan, 115; Indo Language, 120; Invasion, 120
Ashkelon, 59
Ashram, 12; Anandawana, 16; Banwasi Sewa, 16; Pawnar, 12
Ashramshalas, 16
Asia, 2, 39, 106–108, 121–122, 131–132, 134; East, 218–219; South, 106–108, 121, 131–132, 134, 219
Asian, Countries, 36; Peacemakers, 36; Region, 29; South, 107, 121–122
Asians, 9
Aśoka, Emperor, 22, the King, 109
Assamese, 112
Assembly, Provincial Legislative in Hyderabad, 18; Indian Constituent, 111
Association, Austrian Peace, 35–36
Australia, 146

Australian, 106; Culture, 106
Austria, 36; and Hungary, 36
Austrian, 36–37; and Jewish, 37
Azaan, 125
Azad, Abul Kalam, 129

Bagdad, 31
Bahujan, 111
Balkan, 185–186, 189, 195, 200; Countries, 195; Region, 189; War, 195
Balkans, 188, 194, 199
Banal, 132
Bangalore, 16
Bank, Sewa, 15; West, 44, 49–50, 53, 61; World, 60
Bapparawal, 136; Hindi Magazine, 136
Barak, Ehud, 43
Bar-On, 95–96
Bar-Tal, Daniel, 80
Barton, 82
Beck, 189; and Sznaider, 189
Beersheba, 59
Belgium, 113
Belgrade, 192, 197
Bengal, West, 13
Ben-Gurion, David, 47–48
Benvenisti, Meron, 81
Berlin, 92; Wall of, 92, 176
Bhakti, 120; and Sufi, 120
Bharati, Vidya, 114, 117–118, 136; Akhil Bharatiya Shiksha Sansthan, 136; Run by the RSS, 117
Bharatiya Janata Party, 136–137
Bhatt, Ela, 15
Bhave, Vinoba, 11–13
Bhoodan, Leader of, 13; Programme of, 12
Bihar, 13
Bill, the Indian Franchise, 9
Bodh Gaya, 115
Bombay, 127–128, 133; *see also* Mumbai
Borobodur, 131; and Prambanan, 131

Bosnia, 186, 194, 196; Croatia, 194; Europe, 194; Herzegovina, 176
Bosniak, 190, 194; or Bosnian Muslim, 190
Bosnian, 188, 193–194; City, 193; Croatian-Serbian, 197; Croats, History, 188; Currency, 193; Muslims and Croats, 197
Brahmanical, 115, 134
Brahmanism, 115
Brahmin, 110, 123, 134
Braithwaite, John, 176
Brazil, 197
Breton, 176
Britain, 31
British, 8, 24, 51, 95, 106, 111, 118, 126, 133; Broadcasting Corporation, 106; Colonial Rule, 8; 126; Conspiracy, 95; Hindu and Muslim, 118; Mandatory, 51; Quakers, 24; Rule in India, 126
Britishers, 126
B'Tselem, 51
Buddha, Gautama, 23, 115, 145, 218; Path of Virtue, 23; Wish of, 23
Buddhism, 23, 26, 108–110, 115; and Shaivism, 110; in Japan, 23; Sri Lankan, 115
Buddhist, 23, 114–115, 123, 126; Association in Japan, 23; Group, 23; Lions, 115; Monk, 115; Sangha, 115–116; Scholar, 23, 115; Sinhala, 114–115
Burma, or Myanmar, 14
Burmese, 14
Bush, George W., 54; U.S. President, 54

Cairns, 82
California, 16
Cambodia, 29
Canada, 23, 218
Caneri, Bartholomäus von, 36; Austrian Philosopher, 36
Carolina, North, 8

Index

Carter, Candice C., 3, 217
Catholic, Church, 113
Centre, Gandhi, at Coimbatore, 16
Chandigarh, 18
Chandrapur, 16
Chanu, Sharmila, 14–15
Charles de Gaulle, 106
Chennai, 152, 218
China, People's Republic of, 28, 30, 36, 123; and Western Colonialism, 36
Chinese, 35
Cholas, Dynasty, 131
Chomsky, 67
Christ, Jesus, 11, 145
Christian, 23, 80, 107, 110, 112–113, 118, 123, 129–130, 132, 136, 194; Agency, 80; Arab Speaking, 107; Catholic Church, 113; Children, 136; Goals, 136; Missionaries, 113, 136, 151; Socialism, 11; Socialists, 23
Christianity, 26, 119, 130–132; Colonial, 131
Chronicles, Sabhasad, 109
Civilization, Indian, 118
Clinton, Administration of, 8
Coast, Malabar, 132
Code, Indian Penal, 14
Coimbatore, 16
College of Education, Kibbutzim, Tel Aviv, 83, 94
Colonialism, British, 9
Colonial Rule of Britain, 8
Columbia, 8
Commission, Far Eastern, 27; Sri Lankan National Education, 115
Communalism, 134
Communism, 185
Communists, 11–12
Conference, Catholic Bishop, 116; the First Hague Peace, 35; Peace Studies Association of Japan, 32
Confucius, 22
Congress, Indian National, 129; U. S., 23–24

Constitution, Italian, 28, 113; of Cost Rica, 27–28; Japanese, 21–22, 26–28
Continent, North American, 106
Corporation, British Broadcasting, BBC, 106
Cosmopolitanism, 263
Costa Rica, 27–28; Constitution of, 27–28; Law of, 28
Council, National Educational and Research, India, 108, 113–114, 117, 134, 151; Teacher Education, 151, 153–154
Croat, 190; or Catholic, 190
Croatia, 176, 191–192, 197–200
Croatian, 191, 269; Bosnia, 194; Serbo, 191
Croatians, 192
Culture, Australian, 106; of the East, 33; and the West, 33
Cynics, 190; and the Stoics, 190

Dalit, 111–112, 123
Danang, 8
Dange, S. A., 109
Danin, Ezra, 48
Danish, Literature, 218
Darwin, 164
Dayton, 190; Accords, 190
Delhi, 12–13, 18, 134; New, 16, 152, 154; State Council of, 134
Democratic, Liberal Party, 32
Dengue, Fever, 18
Denmark, 218
Derrida, Jacques, 185
Dewey, John, 147–148, 153
Dhammapada, 23
Dharma, Sanatana, 8–9, 17
Diacoff, 176
Diaspora, 47
Die Wel, 35
Din-e-elahi, 109
Directorate, of Teacher Education, Research and Training, the DTERT, 211

District Institute, of Education and Training, the DIET, 151, 156; of Aduthurai, 155; Chennai, 155; Dharamapuri, 155; Erode, 154–155; G. Ariyur, 155; Kalaiyarkoil, 155; Kaliampoondi, 155; Kilapalur, 155; Kilpennathur; 155; Kothagiri, 155; Krishnagiri, 155; Kumulur, 155; Kurukathi, 155; Manangudi, 155; Manjur, 155; Mayanur, 155; Munanjipatti, 155; Namakkal, 155; Oddanchathram, 155; Palayampatti, 155; Perundurai, 154–156; Pudukkottai, 154–155, 217; Ranipet, 155; T. Kallupatti, 155; Therur, 155; Thirumoorthinagar, 155; Thiruvarur or Thirur, 155; Uthama Cholapuram, 155; Uthamapalayam, 155; Vadalur, 155; Vanaramutti, 155
Divine Revelation, 12
Dnyaneshwar, 108
Dudley, 146
Dunant, Henri, 36

Economist, the, 50
Edwords, Frederick, 164
Eelam, Tamil, 115–116
Eelamist, 116
Egypt, 89, 131; and Mesopotamia, 131
Egyptian, 51, 61
Einstein, Albert, 25
Ekal Vidyalayas, 136
Eklavya, 129; Bhil Tribal Boy, 129
Eknath, 108; and the Hind Turk Samvad, 108
Emir, 194–195
England, 219
English, 35, 111, 123, 125, 218
Epifanio de Los Santos Avenue (EDSA), 8
Erode, 154
Estate, Erez Industrial, 62
Etzion, Gush, 51

Europe, 8, 46, 49, 110, 185–186, 194–195; Central, 185; Eastern, 185–186; Southeastern, 195
European, 46, 49, 110, 115, 186; Countries, 36; History, 110; Jewry, 46; Orientalist, 115; Region, 192; Union, 186

Far-East, 131
Fascism, 136; and Nazism, 136
Finkelstein, Norman, 65
Florida, 217; North, 217
Floyd, 174
Foundation, Gandhi Peace, 16; M. C. Mehta Environmental, 16; Tariq Kahmisa, 176
France, 27, 30, 36, 106
French, 35, 106; Citizenship, 106; Nation, 106; Resistance, 106; Textbooks of, 106
Fried, Alfred, 37
FYROM, 200

Gadamer, Hans-Georg, 79, 83–88, 91
Gadamerian, 88, 92, 94, 98; Dialogue, 98; Hermeneutic-Humanism, 98
Galtung, Johan, 81
Gandhi, M. K., 7–13, 15–19, 21, 25, 120, 123, 142, 145, 218; Nonviolent Principle of, 197; Peace Philosophy of, 19
Gandhian, Ideas, 17; Organizations, 16; Philosophy, 8–10, 12, 14–19; Principle, 13; Satyagraha, 8–9, 14, 17–18; Techniques, 14
Gandhians, 19
Gandhigiri, 17–19
Gargi, 131
Gaulle, Charles de, 106
Gaza, Strip, 28, 44–45, 49–50, 53, 55–63, 66–67, 218
Gazan, 45, 58, 60–61; Egyptian, 61; Population, 62, 80, 86; Territory, 79
German, Peace Movement, 37

Germany, 8, 30, 36, 96, 121
Giri, 18
Global Peace, Journal, 217
Godse, Nathuram, 120
Golwalkar, M. S., 117, 121; Chief of RSS, 121
Gopal, 10
Gordon, 44, 51–52, 65
Government, Colonial in South Africa, 9
Gramdan, 12–13
Greco-Turkish, 47
Greek, 206
Gujarat, 9, 15–17, 134, 136, 219
Gujarati, 8, 11; Vaishnava Family, 8
Gulamgiri, 110; of Phule, 110
Gulf, Persian, 29
Gunawardana, R. A. L. H., 116
Guru Granth Sahib, 125
Gurukula, 149

Ha'am, Ahad, 46
Hague, the 35; First Peace Conference in, 35
Hajdarpasic, Edin, 188
Hamas, 62
Hansen, David, 199
Al-Haq, 57
Harel, Dan, 56
Harijans, 12
Hart, 173; and Hodson, 173
Hebrew, 47; Culture, 47
Hedgewar, K. B., 117
Heights, the Golan, 29, 50
Heikinen, 197
Heiwa, 37
Hersh, Jacques, 2, 217
Herzegovina, 176, 197; and Bosnia, 176
Herzl, Theodor, 35, 46
Hess, Moses, 46
Hill, Julia Butterfly, 16; American Activist, 16
Hind, 108, 117
Hindi, 125; Magazine, 136

Hindu, 48, 106, 110, 114, 117–121, 123, 125, 131, 134; Brahmanical Faith, 157; Child, 129; Fold, 111; India, 164; Mahasabha, 117, 120; Muslim and British, 118; and Muslim Population, 65, 146; Muslim Unity, 120; Nation, 106, 116; Philosophy, 131; Population, 48; Religious Icons, 129; Rightwing, 114; Scriptures, 134; Social Reform, 110; Social Reformers, 111; System, 110; the, 207; Vaishnavajana Bhajana, 125
Hinduism, 108, 129–132
Hindus, 110, 116, 126, 129, 133; Tamil Speaking, 116
Hindu-sthan, 131
Hiroshima, 21
History, Hindu-Muslim Communal, 119; of the World, 10; Maori, 106
Hitler, Adolf, 67, 117, 120
Hodson, 173; Hart and, 173
Hokkaido, 32; the Naganuma Lawsuit in, 32
Holocaust, 46, 92, 95; in World War Second, 123
Hopkins, Belinda, 170
Horio, Teruhisa, 26
Horizons, 93
Hubert, Michel R., 3, 218
Hue, 8
Hungary, 36; and Austria, 36
Hyderabad, 12; Central Prison of, 12; State, 11
Hyogo, 33

Ikezumi, Yoshinori, 32
Imam, 127
India, 2, 7–10, 12–16, 105–107, 110–112, 116–117, 119, 121, 130–131, 135, 151, 154, 205–207, 217–218; and, 114; Diversity of, 135; Pluralistic, 112; President of, 218; Project, 112, 132; Slavery in, 9; Union Health Minister of, 18; Western, 110–111

Indian, 9–10, 105, 107–108, 112, 114, 118–119, 120–121, 124, 129, 132, 135, 218–219; American, 106; Central, 129; Civilization, 118; Classroom, 105; Constitution, 111, 119; Christians, 130; Education, 134; Freedom from British Colonialism, 8; Government, 119; History, 108, 110, 122, 135; Immigrants in South Africa, 8; Institute of Technology, 132; Literature, 119, 130; Muslim, 129; Notion, 10, 111; Ocean, 29–30; Penal Code, 14; People, 10; States, 133; Subcontinent, 105, 114, 121, 129, 132, 218; Textbooks, 135; Way of Life, 218; Youth, 218
Indiana, 219
Indians, 9, 106, 179
Indo-Aryan, 120; Pakistan, 142
Indonesia, 29
Inoue, Hisashi, 33
Institute, Gandhian Studies at Wardha, 16; G. R. of Non-violence, 16; International Peace Research in Stockholm, 30
International, Alliance of Holistic Lawyers, 240; Court of Justice, 53–54; Minatory Fund, 61
Intifada, 87–88
Iraq, 21, 24, 29, 31–32, 34, 195, 200; Northern, 31; Southern, 31; War in, 21
Iraqi, 41, 43–44; Civilians, 24
Ireland, Northern, 81–82, 150
Islam, 119, 126, 130, 132–133, 136
Islami, Markazi Maktaba, 118
Islamization, 116
Israel, 2, 24, 43–45, 48–67, 81, 219–220; Aggression of, 31; Arab Conflict, 43, 45–46, 49; Greater, 44, 50–51; History of, 44, 55; Jewish Nature of, 50; Palestine, 24, 43, 61; Sate of, 89, 92; Zangwill, 47

Israeli, 28, 44–45, 49, 51–52, 54–55, 57–59, 61–67, 79, 81, 83, 89, 95–96; Arab, 45, 94; Citizens, 44, 50, 55, 57; Civilian, 44; Constitution, 37; Government, 28, 49; hegemony, 48; Historian, 89; History, 44, 55; Jewish, Leader, 43, 89; Minister, 50, 94; Occupation, 45; Officials, 51; Palestinian, 43, 54, 79, 81, 83, 94–96; People, 160; Policies, 44, 90; Ship, 57; Society, 89; State, 92
Israelis, 45
Italy, 8, 28

Jacksonville, 217
Jain, 123, 129; Faith, 129
Jainism, 9, 108
Jana Times (Weekly), 32
Japan, 2, 21–39, 123, 219–220; Constitution of, 21–22, 26–28, 33–34, 37–39; Cultural Affairs in, 23; Diet of, 29, 37–39; to Korea, 28; Militarism in, 33; Nonviolence in, 22; Nonviolent Ideas of, 21, 48; PEN Club of, 33; Self-Defence Force of, 29
Japanese, 21, 35–37, 220; Aggression, 27; Defense Agency, 30; Embassy, 36; Government, 27, 31; Ideas, 35; Intellectuals, 35; Language, 35; Pacifist, 25; Peacemakers, 37; People, 22, 27; Russo War, 36; Sino War, 36
Jayabala, 131
Jerusalem, 50, 53; East, 50, 53
Jesus, the Christ, 11
Jew, 94, 123; Students, 94
Jewish, 37, 45, 47, 65–66, 80, 89; and Palestinian, 80; Colonization, 54; Forces, 48–49; Immigrants from Europe, 49; Jewish, 89; Majority, 47, 49; National Fund's Land Department, 48; Palestinian Students, 90; People in Palestine, 45–46; Presence, 50; Settlement, 46, 48, 73; Settlers in Gaza, 55; State, 46, 89

Jewry, European, 46
Jews, 46–48, 50, 54, 94, 126; to Palestine, 95
Johnson, 146
Jordan, 123
Jordanian, 51
Junta, 14

Kabir, 108–109
Kagawa, Toyohiko, 25
Kalbhoj, Rawal, 136
Kalilavadamana, 131
Kalischer, Zvi Hirsch, 46
Kantarotai, 116
Karaula, 191
Karnataka, 13, 16
Karur, 18
Kashmir, and Jammu, 13
Kashyapnath, 136
Kato, Shuichi, 45
Katyusha, 59
Kearns, 169
Kerala, 13, 16, 129; Shores, 129
Keralite, 112
Kibbutzim, College of Education, 116, 130, 220
Kikuchi, Yumi, 38
Kimijima, Akihiko, 22, 26
Kimmel, 178
King, Martin Luther, Junior, 7; Moghul, 110
Kita Tama-gun, 32
Knesset, 55
Kobayashi, Takeshi, 32
Kochi, 25, 27, 34, 38; Constitution in, 27; Museum of, 38; Shinbunsha, 34
Korea, 21, 28; to Japan, 28
Korean, 28, 47; Language, 48; War, 28
Koshy, Renu, 128
Kosovar, Albanian, 196
Kosovo, 192
Kovel, Joel, 141
Kris, 218

Krishna, the Lord, 129; Gandhari's curse on, 129
Kumar, Ravindra, 165, 217–218
Kushans, 110
Kuwait, 31

Law, Order Maintenance, 23; Salt, 9
League, Muslim, 117, 120; of Nations, 37
Lehman, 176
Lele, Jayant, 109; and Singh, Rajendra, 109
Lewis, 174
Lincoln, Abraham, 123
Line, Green, 53–54
Livnat, Limor, 130
Ljubljana, 193
London, 18, 37, 106, 194
Loye, 164
LUNA, 16

MacArthur, Douglas, 26, 28–29; and Shidehara, 26
Macedonia, 190–194, 199
Madhya Pradesh, 118
Madras, 207
Mahabharata, 129
Maharaj, Shahu, 109
Maharashtra, 13, 18, 110, 136
Mahatma, the, 17–19
Mahavira, Vardhamana, 145
Mahmud of Ghaznavi, 136
Makino, Hiroyoshi, 27
Makovsky, 43
Malabar, Coast, 132
Malaysia, 218
Mandela, Nelson, 123
Manipur, 14
Maori, 106, 165; Practice, 165
Marks, Bosnian Currency, 193
Masalha, 50
Matthew, Saint, 23
McCully, 82
Mesopotamia, 131; and Egypt, 131

Mewar, Dynasty of, 136
Mexico, 8
Middle East, 43, 45, 60, 67, 83, 89
Miki, Mutsuko, 33
Miki, Takeo, 33
Mill, James, 118
Milner, Beryl, 24
Moghul Kings, 109; Rule, 110
Montenegrin, 196; Woman, 196
Montenegro, 176, 200; and Slovenia, 200; and Serbia, 176, 186
Montessori, Maria, 148, 208; after World War II, 208
Morgan, Kenneth, 165
Moses, 22, 46; Hess, 46
Mostar, a City in Herzegovina, 197
Movement, Boodan, 10–13; Civil Disobedience, 9, 17; Non-cooperation, 9; Quit India, 10
Mozambique, 29
Mukhopadhyay, Marmar, 149–150
Mullet, 166
Mumbai, 17, 122, 135, 142, 219; *see also* Bombay
Munnabhai, Lage Raho, 17
Museum, International Red Cross and Red Crescent, 22; Kyoto Museum for World Peace at Ritsumeikan University, 23
Muslim, 48, 109, 119–120, 123, 126, 129–130, 136; Azaan, 125; Community, 111, 122; Indian, 128; Language, 122; League, 117; Locality, 174; Minority, 127–128; Mosque, 127–129, 134; Nation, 117; Non, 109; Poor Children, 129; Prayer, 127; Young Girls, 127
Muslims, 107, 109, 128–129
Mysore, 109

Nadars, 132
Naganuma, 32
Nagasaki, 21
Nagoya, District Court of, 31; High Court of, 31–33

Namdeo, 108
Nation, the, 36
Navdanya, 15
Naveh, Eyal, 95
Nazis, 106
Nazism, 136; and Fascism, 136
Nepal, 29
Neretva, River, 197
Netanyahu, Benjamin, 52
Netherlands, the, 27, 186; the Hague Tribunal in, 186
Newman, Tony, 86
New York, 36, 198, 218–219; Times, 198
Niens, 82
Nirguna, 109
Nobel, Alfred, 35
Nonviolence and non-violent, 7–9, 16–18, 21–25, 35, 64–65, 142, 145, 213–214, 217; in Japan, 22; and its Philosophy, 217
Nonviolently, 66
Nordstrom, Carolyn, 200

Obama, Barack, 54; Administration of, 66
Ocean, Indian, 29–30
Oda, Makoto, 33
Oe, Kenzaburo, 33
Ohata, Yutaka, 26
Ohio, 190
Ohrid, 190
Okudaira, Yasuhiro, 33
Olmert, Ehud, 52, 58
Orissa, 13
Oslo, 52–53, 66; Accord, 64; Agreements, 53, 57; Post Period, 60
Ottoman, 51; and British Mandatory, 51

Pacora, Valley in Panama, 8
Pact, of Peris, 26; or the Kellogg-Briand, 26
Pakistan, 114, 116, 119, 121; and Indian History, 114; Islamization of the state in, 116

Pakistani, 126, 128, 142; Citizens, 142
Palestine, 2, 24, 43, 46–47, 95; and Israel, 24, 43; People of, 24
Palestinian, 24, 44, 46, 48, 51–54, 57, 59–60, 62, 64–66, 79–80, 83, 90, 94–96; Arabs, 48; Attacks, 59; Cause, 66; Fishermen, 59; Generation, 52; Government, 65; Human Rights' Organization, 58; Independence, 65; Institution, 53; Israeli, 43, 63, 65, 67, 79, 81, 83, 95; Land, 53; Leadership, 48, 52; Legitimacy, 67; Looters, 62; Militants, 57, 59; Movement, 64, 67; Narrative, 96; National Authority, 65, 90; People, 24; Population, 44–46, 49, 54–55, Public School, 90; Propaganda, 96; Question, 43; Refugees, 49; State, 44, 67; Strategy, 64; Strike, 64; Territory, 44, 64, 67, 92; Uprising, 60; Villages, 48, 55
Palestinians, 24, 46–47, 49–51, 54, 56–58, 60–61, 95–96; and Jews, 46
Pali, 115
Papastephanou, Marianna, 189
Parishad, Rajasthan Vanwasi Kalyan, 136; Vishwa Hindu, 136
Parmodharmah, 8
Parsee, 123, 125–126, 136; Kushti prayers, 123; or Zoroastrian, 136
Party, Liberal Democratic and Komei of Japan, 39
Patel, Sardar Vallabhbhai, 17, 121; Home Minister of India, 122
Patna, 18
Pawnar, 12
Pax, 218; Romania, 218
Penang, 219; Malaysia, 218
Peninsula, Liaodong in China, 36; Jaffna, 116
Penticton, 218
Persia, 131; King of, 131
Peru, 8
Petersen-Overton, Kristofer J., 2, 218
Philippines, 8

Phillips, Doug, 86
Phule, Jyotiba, 110–111, 123; Collected Works of, 110; and Low Caste Protests, 111
Phule, Savitri, 110
Pinellas, 8
Pluralism, 105, 110, 122, 186, 214
Pochampalli, 11–12
Poland, 8
Poonguntrnar, Kaniyan, 153; as Yathum Oore Yavarum Kelir, 152
Prakashan, Saraswati Shish Mandir, 118
Prambanan, 131; and Borobodur, 131
Prussia, 27
Pune, 18, 110; in Western India, 110
Putalibai, 9

Quakers, British, 24

Rabin, Yitzhak, 43, 45, 53
Rafah, 61
Rafis, 197
Rajasthan, 136
Rajkot, 16
Ramgarh, 129
Rashtriyashala, at Rajkot, 16; Rachnatmak Samiti, 16
Rawal, Bappa, 136; Bestowed on Rawal Kalbhoj, 136
Red Cross, International, 36
Reddy, C. Ramachandra, 12
Republic, Former Yugoslav, 186
Rice, Condoleezza, 61
Rilke, 188
Rolland, Romain, 25
Romania, 218; Pax, 218
Roosevelt, Franklin, 36
Rosenberg, Marshall, 170
Roy, Sara, 60, 66
Rule, British in India, 126; Colonial, 9–10
Ruskin, John, 11–12
Russell, Bertrand, 25
Russia, 30, 36; and Japan, 36

Russian, 36; Vessel, 36
Rwanda, 29, 196

Sabha, Andhra Mahila, 16
Sadhanadan, 12–13
Salomon, Gavriel, 81
Samaj, Gram Sewa, 16
Samarkand, 38
Samawah, in Southern Iraq, 31
Samiti, Saurashtra Rachnatmak, 16
Samvad, Hind-Turk, 108
Sanatana, 10
Sanchi, 115
Sangh, Jana, 121; Rashtriya Swayamsevak, the RSS, 114, 117, 119–121, 136
Sangha, Buddhist, 115–116
Sanskrit, 109
Sanskriti Jnan, 117–118
Sarajevo, 191–192, 194, 196–197
Saraswati Shishu Mandir Prakashan, 118; and Markazi Maktaba Islami, 118
Sarkar, 118
Sarvodaya, 10–11, 19; International Trust in Bangalore, 16, Mandal, 17; Parivar, 17
Satyagraha, 8–9, 14, 17–18
Savarkar, K. B., 117
Sawachi, Hisae, 33
Schmidt, Johannes D., 2, 219
Schools, Arab-Israeli, 90; Jewish, 90; Jewish Orthodox, 90
Sderot, Town of Israel, 59
Serbia, 176, 194, 196, 200; Croatia, 194; and Montenegro, 176
Serbian, 191–194; Businessman, 194
Serbians, 192
Serbo-Croatian, 191
Setalvadm, Teesta, 2, 115, 219
Shared Land, 112
Sharon, Ariel, 43, 53–56
Sharp, 66
Shertok, Moshe, 49
Shidehara, Kijūrō, 26–27

Shigaraki, Takamaro, 23
Shinbun, Asahi 30
Shinbun, Kochi, 32
Shiva, Vandana, 15
Shivaji, 109; the Maratha Ruler, 109
Shramdan, 12–13
Sikh, 125, 129
Sind, 129
Singh, Man Mohan, 142
Singh, Rajendra, 109; and Lele, Jayant, 109
Sinhala, 115–116, 120; Buddhist, 120; Ethnonationalists, 116; hegemony, 116; Language, 116
Sinhalization, of Sri Lankan Buddhism, 115
Skopje, 192–194
Slav, Macedonian, 190
Slovenia, 176, 191–193, 195, 200; and Montenegro, 200; Social Scientist, 192
Slovenians, 192
Socialism, Christian, 11
Socialists, Christian, 23
Society, of Ladies Friendship of Asia-Pacific, 33
Solferino, 35
Spain, 8
Sri Lanka, 25–26, 114, 154, 218
Sri Lankan, 114–115; Buddhism 115; Tamil, 120
Stockholm, International Peace Research Institute, 30
Sufi, 120, 178; and Bhakti, 120
Sunagawa, 32
Suttner, Bertha von, 35–37
Suu Kyi, Aung San, 14–15
Suzuki, Yasuzo, 27
Sweden, 82
Syed, Sir, 111
Sznaider, 189; and Beck, 189

Tagore, Rabindranath, 25
Taiwan, 123

Tamil, 114, 120, 153, 217; Buddhist, 120, 164; Elem, 116; of Jaffna Peninsula, 159; Kingdom, 116; in Sinhala Buddhist, 115; Speaking Hindus, 159; State of Elem, 115; Tigers, 115
Tamilnadu, 2, 13, 16, 141, 152, 154, 217
Tanzania, 219
Telangana, 11–12
Tel Aviv, 43, 83, 220
Thapar, Romila, 109, 118
Thiruvarur, 155
Thiruvellar, 108
Thomas, Aquinas, 131
Thucydides, 67
Timor, East, 29
Tipu Sultan, 109, 132
Tiruvalla, 132
Tiruvallur, 207
Tokyo, 32; Sunagawa case in, 32
Tradition, Nirguna, 109
Treaty, Portsmouth, 51; USA-Japan Security, 32
Tribal, 112; Non, 112
Tribunal, Hague in the Netherlands, 186
Trust, Shabnam Resources, 205–209; Sarvodaya International, 16
Tsurumi, Shunsuke, 33
Tukaram, 108
Turk, 108
Turkmenistan, 219

Ueki, Emori, 27
Umehara, Takeshi, 33
UNESCO, and World Heritage, 149, 152–154
UNICEF, 157
Union, European, 186
United Kingdom, 18, 30
United Nations, 21, 29, 39, 48, 63, 90, 205–206; Convention of, 205–206; Peacekeeping Operations Cooperation Bill, 29; Relief and Work Agency, 90; Security Council of, 53; Transitional Authority of, 29
United Provinces, or Uttar Pradesh, 9, 13
United States of America, 7, 18, 22–24, 27–31, 36, 38, 46, 54, 61, 66, 142, 192, 198, 217–220; Congress of, 23–24; Involvement in Vietnam War, 143; Japan Defense Cooperation, 29; Military base in Sunagawa, 32; President of, 36, 54; Soldiers of, 32
Universal, 185
University, Aalborg, 218–219; Aichi, 32; Aligrah Muslim, 111; Bradford, 219; Columbia, 219; for Educational Planning and Administration, 152; of Egypt, 131; Georgetown, 219; Kochi, 24, 219; Kyoto City, 33; North Florida, 217; Notre Dame, 219; Peradiniya, 116; Ritsumeikan, 30; Tel Aviv, 220; Tokyo, 33
Unto This Last, 11–12
Upanishads, 131
UP-ite, 112
Urdu, 121, 129; Poetry, 129
Ussishkin, Menahem, 46
Utilitarianism, 19
Utilitarians, 118–119
Uzbek, 38; Children, 38
Uzbekistan, 38

Vadod, 17
Vaishnavajana, Hindu Bhajana, 125
Vancouver, 218
Varkari, 109
Vedachhi, 17; Gandhi Vidyapeeth, 17; Pradesh Sewa Samiti, 17
Vedas, 108, 131
Vedrana, 192
Vichy, 106
Vidyalaya, Ekal, 136; Sampurna Kranti, 16
Vienna, 192

Vietnam, 8, 21, 33, 142; Anti-War Movement, 33; War of, 142
Vincent De Paul, S., 3, 173
Vishakhapatnam, 18
Vygotsky, 153

Wall, Berlin, 176
War, Cold, 29; First of Indian Independence, 111; First, World, 47; India-Pakistan, 142; Korean, 28; Russo-Japanese, 36; Second World, 21–22, 25, 27, 34, 46, 89, 106, 208; Sino-Japanese, 36; in Solferino, 35; Vietnam, 142
Wardha, 16
Warkaris, 109
Washington, 18, 219
Weisglass, Dov, 43
Weitz, Yosef, 48
Weizmann, Chaim, 47
West, Bank, 44, 49–50, 53–54, 84; Barrier, WBB, 44, 46, 53–54
West, the, 66
Western, Countries, 66; Goodwill towards Palestinian Legitimacy, 67; India, 110–111
White House, 74
Wisler, Andria, 3, 219
World, Bank, 60–62; Cup, 197; Food Program, 62; Third, 195, 218
World Food Program, 85; Religion, 126

Yadlin, Amos, 57
Yamamoto, Senji, 23
Yamane, Kazuyo, 2, 219
Yishuv, 48–49
Yitzhak, 53
Yoga; 157; Yogasana, 157
Yogev, Esther, 2, 220
Yomiuri, 40
Yubari-gun, 32
Yugoslav, 8, 185–189; Constituent People, 191; Counterpart, 191; Higher Education, 189; Identity, 190; Post, 189–190, 194–196, 199–200, 219; Republics, 176; Societies, 188; Universal, 190
Yugoslavia, 7, 185–186, 189–192
Yugoslavs, 190, 192
Yukio-Hatoyama, 39

Zagreb, 192, 197
Zamindar, 12
Zangwill, Israel, 47
Zapatist, Movement in Mexico, 8
Zionism, 35, 44–48, 50, 54, 57, 63, 218
Zionist, 44, 46–48, 50, 89; Project, 89; Thinker, 47

GPSR Compliance
The European Union's (EU) General Product Safety Regulation (GPSR) is a set of rules that requires consumer products to be safe and our obligations to ensure this.

If you have any concerns about our products, you can contact us on

ProductSafety@springernature.com

In case Publisher is established outside the EU, the EU authorized representative is:

Springer Nature Customer Service Center GmbH
Europaplatz 3
69115 Heidelberg, Germany

www.ingramcontent.com/pod-product-compliance
Lightning Source LLC
LaVergne TN
LVHW051913060526
838200LV00004B/121